Mastering

International trade

B 2

Palgrave Master Series

Accounting
Accounting Skills
Advanced English Language
Advanced English Literature
Advanced Pure Mathematics
Arabic
Basic Management
Biology
British Politics
Business Communication
Business Environment
C Programming
C++ Programming
Chemistry
COBOL Programming
Communication
Computing
Counselling Skills
Counselling Theory
Customer Relations
Database Design
Delphi Programming
Desktop Publishing
e-Business
Economic and Social History
Economics
Electrical Engineering
Electronics
Employee Development
English Grammar
English Language
English Literature
Fashion Buying and Merchandising
  Management
Fashion Styling
French
Geography
German

Global Information Systems
Human Resource Management
Information Technology
International Trade
Internet
Italian
Java
Management Skills
Marketing Management
Mathematics
Microsoft Office
Microsoft Windows, Novell
  NetWare and UNIX
Modern British History
Modern European History
Modern United States History
Modern World History
Networks
Novels of Jane Austen
Organisational Behaviour
Pascal and Delphi Programming
Philosophy
Physics
Practical Criticism
Psychology
Shakespeare
Social Welfare
Sociology
Spanish
Statistics
Strategic Management
Systems Analysis and Design
Team Leadership
Theology
Twentieth Century Russian
  History
Visual Basic
World Religions

www.palgravemasterseries.com

Palgrave Master Series
Series Standing Order ISBN 0–333–69343–4
(*outside North America only*)

You can receive future titles in this series as they are published by placing a standing order. Please contact your bookseller or, in case of difficulty, write to us at the address below with your name and address, the title of the series and the ISBN quoted above.

Customer Services Department, Macmillan Distribution Ltd.
Houndmills, Basingstoke, Hampshire RG21 6XS, England

Mastering
International trade

Chris Marshall, BA (Hons) MIEx (Grad)

Business Series Editor
Richard Pettinger

First published 2003 by
PALGRAVE MACMILLAN
Houndmills, Basingstoke, Hampshire RG21 6XS and
175 Fifth Avenue, New York, N.Y. 10010
Companies and representatives throughout the world

PALGRAVE MACMILLAN is the global academic imprint of the Palgrave
Macmillan division of St. Martin's Press, LLC and of Palgrave Macmillan Ltd.
Macmillan® is a registered trademark in the United States, United Kingdom
and other countries. Palgrave is a registered trademark in the European
Union and other countries.

ISBN 0–333–994612

This book is printed on paper suitable for recycling and made from fully
managed and sustained forest sources.

A catalogue record for this book is available from the British Library.

A catalog record for this book is available from the Library of Congress.

10   9   8   7   6   5   4   3   2   1
12 11 10 09 08 07 06 05 04 03

Printed and bound in Great Britain by
Creative Print and Design (Ebbw Vale), Wales

◪ Contents

Introduction – What is importing and exporting? – Why export? – Exporting to increase sales – Exporting to spread risks – Production-led exporting – Exporting to improve image – Exporting: the reality – Types of exporter – Why import? – The make or buy decision – International growth through acquisitions and mergers – Types of merger – Disadvantages of mergers – Developing economies and economic development – Globalisation – The international trade perspective – International companies/international strategies – The smaller company's perspective – First steps to export success – Choosing a market – Conclusions – Sources of information – Further reading – Questions for consideration

Introduction – What is marketing? – Market versus marketing research – Marketing planning – Market segmentation – The marketing mix – Promotion via the World Wide Web – Trade shows and exhibitions – Summary – Business planning – SMART – SWOT – The marketing plan – Conclusions – Sources of information – Further reading – Questions for consideration

Introduction – Market research – Market suitability – Product fit – Using economic indicators – Social questions – Political and legal considerations – Non-tariff barriers – Identifying competition – Summary of key market research aims – Data collection – The right person for the job – The market research ladder – Secondary data (sources, advantages and limitations) – Primary data (sources, advantages and limitations) – Analysing the data – Other

▼ List of figures and tables

Figures

Tables

Foreword

It does not matter if a company is just starting out or whether it has been established for 100 years or more; the prospect of becoming involved in some form of international trade is increasingly likely. There is, after all, a strong chance that the company's products, or at least the raw materials and components, have already been involved in some form of international movement. The globalisation of trade brings the likelihood of a company, which was originally set up to operate in the domestic market, doing a proportion of its business in foreign markets. The potential market for those already involved in selling abroad has also increased. Technological advances, particularly in terms of communication and the Internet, place products in front of a global audience. Anyone, from any part of the world, can make contact instantly and request a quotation. Indeed, many companies have been excited to receive an order from another country, only to have their excitement fade as it dawns on them that they have no idea how to price their goods for foreign markets or what the documentary requirements are. The globalisation of trade therefore means that all companies should have some form of international trade plan in place, regardless of whether or not they intend exporting. If exporting is conducted in a professional manner it can be both rewarding and lucrative. It should not be seen as an activity that will provide respite from a downturn in the domestic market, as it requires commitment and investment. Poorly prepared procedures, inadequately trained staff and an uncoordinated approach to foreign trade can be costly.

The Institute of Export is therefore pleased to write a foreword for *Mastering International Trade*, which goes a long way towards identifying and explaining the basic needs that every business should address in order to develop an effective export marketing plan.

It shows how companies must understand their potential for exporting, both in terms of export readiness and product fit, and demonstrates the importance of ensuring that the product meets the required standards and regulations of the importing country. However, this is just the tip of the iceberg. Companies also need to understand their motivation for trading overseas – is it for long-term expansion, to improve competitiveness, to exploit a niche in the market or to increase return on investment?

Mastering International Trade covers basic marketing concepts and tools, the importance of research to identify and evaluate potential markets, and strategies that can be adopted to assist companies in penetrating their target markets effectively. It also examines the principles of pricing, transport/logistics, currency, documentation and insurance, providing a comprehensive introduction to the core requirements of importing and exporting.

For a business to succeed internationally it is essential that those involved have a sound understanding of the subject and, ideally, are professionally trained. Exporting is not an activity that should be left to inexperienced staff, or sales managers failing to achieve results in the domestic market. The cost and time spent training staff can be recouped many times over through the development of an effective international marketing strategy that underpins the company's overseas business activities.

Mastering International Trade reflects this view and therefore provides a useful springboard for those who are either starting out in international trade or who simply wish to improve their all-round knowledge of the subject.

Hugh Allen
Chief Executive Officer (2000–2002)
The Institute of Export
www.export.org.uk

◼ ⩔ Acknowledgements

This book could not have been written without the assistance and expertise of the colleagues, clients and friends listed below. Grateful thanks to all these people for their time and encouragement, as well as to Suzannah Burywood at Palgrave Macmillan for her advice and patience. The author also wishes to thank the British Footwear Association for granting permission to reproduce statistics from their website for Table 4.2, HMSO for permission to print the tariff classifications in Figure 10.5 and HM Customs and Excise for permission to reproduce trade statistics in Table 2.1.

Mohammed Ahmed, MYCCI
Hugh Allen, The Institute of Export
Tim Ambrose and Daniel Anderson, Locum Destination Consulting
Esther Atkinson, Credit Suisse
Barry Bellenie, Partners In Export Ltd
Peter Bloom, MYCCI
Ann Bradley, Sutcliffe Play Ltd
Adam and Tracey Campbell, Jordan Clamps Ltd
Alyson Finney, MYCCI
Alan Greenwood, MYCCI
Steve Haynes, Classic Door Panels Ltd
Joanna Lavan, Univentures Ltd
Alan Raimes, ExportPro Ltd
Mark Rowbotham, Portcullis ISC
Iain Schofield, Black Rock Logistics Ltd

Thanks also to my family and especially my wife, Joanne, for her constant support and for helping in the final production, indexing and proofreading of this book.

■ ⌄ List of abbreviations

4Ps	Product, Price, Place, Promotion
ADG	Accord Dangereux Routiers
AFI	Airfreight Institute (FIATA)
APG	Advance Payment Guarantee
ASEAN	Association of South East Asian Nations
B/L	Bill of Lading
BCC	British Chambers of Commerce
BExA	British Exporters Association
BIFA	British International Freight Association
BOP	Balance of Payments
BSI	British Standards Institute
BWC	Biological Weapons Convention
BWTEC	British Wool Textile Export Corporation
CAD	Cash Against Documents
CAI	Customs Affairs Institute (FIATA)
CBI	Confederation of British Industry
CFR	Cost and Freight
CFSP	Customs Freight Simplified Procedures
CHIEF	Customs Handling of Import and Export Freight
CIF	Cost, Insurance and Freight
CIP	Carriage and Insurance Paid to
CISG	Convention on the Contracts for the International Sale of Goods
CISS	Comprehensive Import Supervision Scheme
CMR	Convention Internationale des Merchandises par Route
COTIF	Convention Relative aux Transports Internationaux Ferroviares
CPT	Carriage Paid To
CRF	Clean Report of Findings
CTM	Community Trade Mark
CWC	Chemical Weapons Convention
DAF	Delivered at Frontier
DDP	Delivered Duty Paid
DDU	Delivered Duty Unpaid
DEQ	Delivered Ex Quay
DES	Delivered Ex Ship
DGN	Dangerous Goods Note
DOA	Documents on Acceptance
DOP	Documents on Payment

DTI	Department of Trade and Industry
ECB	European Central Bank
ECGD	Export Credits Guarantee Department
ECO	Export Control Organisation
ECOSOC	Economic and Social Council
ECSI	Export Cargo Shipping Instructions
ECU	European Currency Unit
EDI	Electronic Data Interchange
EFTA	European Free Trade Association
EIC	Euro Info Centre
EMS	European Monetary System
EMU	Economic and Monetary Union
EU	European Union
EXW	Ex Works
FAK	Freight All Kinds
FAS	Free Alongside Ship
FCA	Free Carrier
FCL	Full Container Load
FCO	Foreign and Commonwealth Office
FIATA	International Federation of Freight Forwarders Associations
FOB	Free On Board
FTA	Free Trade Agreement
G8	The Group of Eight (council comprising representatives from Canada, France, Germany, Italy, Japan, Russia, United Kingdom and United States)
GDP	Gross Domestic Product
GNP	Gross National Product
GSP	Generalised System of Preferences
HMC&E	Her Majesty's Custom and Excise
ICAO	International Civil Aviation Organisation Technical Instructions
ICC	International Chamber of Commerce
ICD	Inland Clearance Depot
IMDG	International Maritime Dangerous Goods Code
IMF	International Monetary Fund
Incoterms	International Commercial Terms
INTRASTAT	Intra-European statistics (Customs document)
IOE	Institute of Export
IPR	Inward Processing Relief
IPR	Intellectual Property Rights
ISO	International Standards Organisation
ISP	Internet Service Provider
L/C	Letter of Credit
LCL	Less than Container Load
LNG	Liquid Natural Gas
MERCOSUR	South American common market between Brazil, Argentina, Paraguay and Uruguay, with Chile and Bolivia as associate members

MIA	Motorsport Industries Association
MIEx (Grad)	Graduate member of the Institute of Export
MNC	Multinational Corporation
MTI	Multimodal Transport Institute (FIATA)
NAFTA	North American Free Trade Agreement
NES	New Export System
NSG	Nuclear Suppliers Group
NVOCC	Non Vessel Owning Common Carrier
O/B/O	Ore/Bulk/Oil
O/O	Ore/Oil
OECD	Organisation for Economic Co-operation and Development
OGEL	Open General Export Licence
OGIL	Open General Import Licence
OIEL	Open Individual Export Licence
OPR	Outward Processing Relief
P&L	Profit and Loss account
PARTNERS	Products, After-sales service, Resources, Territory, Numbers, Experience, Reputation, Storage facilities
PESTLE	Political, Economic, Social, Technological, Legal and Environmental factors
PIRA	Research Association for the Paper and Board Printing and Packaging Industries
PSN	Proper Shipping Name
RHA	Road Haulage Association
RID	International Regulations Concerning the Carriage of Goods by Rail
ROCE	Return on Capital Employed
ROS	Return on Sales
SAD	Single Administrative Document
SEA	Single European Act
SESA	Support for Exhibitions and Seminars Abroad
SITPRO	Simplified Trade Procedures
SMART	Specific, Measurable, Agreed, Realistic, Time-bound
SME	Small to medium-sized enterprise
SSL	Special Security Label
SSN	Standard Shipping Note
SWIFT	Society for Worldwide Interbank Financial Transmissions
SWOT	Strengths, Weaknesses, Opportunities and Threats
T&Cs	Terms and Conditions
THE	Technical Help for Exporters
TIR	Transport Internationaux Routiers
TMR	Tailored Market Report
TPUK	Trade Partners UK
TRIPS	Trade-Related Aspects of Intellectual Property Rights
ULCC	Ultra Large Crude Carrier
ULD	Unit Load Device
UN	United Nations

UN/ECE	United Nations Economic Commission for Europe
UN/EDIFACT	United Nations rules for Electronic Data Interchange for Administration, Commerce and Transport
UN/ESCAP	United Nations Economic and Social Commission for Asia and the Pacific
UNCITRAL	United Nations Commission on International Trade Law
UNCTAD	United Nations Conference on Trade and Development
VAT	Value-Added Tax
VENTURE	Valuation, Equality, Neutrality, Trust, Understanding, Relationship, Exit strategy
VLCC	Very Large Crude Carrier
WIPO	World Intellectual Property Organisation
WTO	World Trade Organisation

■ ⚙ ▮ Introduction

International trade is, by nature, logical and systematic. Although in many respects it is similar to conventional, domestic trade, it does demand more from companies, from initial market research, through the different methods of distribution, to securing payment from customers on the other side of the world. It is often seen by the inexperienced business as a minefield of endless documentation designed to trip up the unwary and is influenced by practically everything from politics to personal relationships.

Mastering International Trade has been structured to reflect this. The book takes the reader from the decision to export and explains the procedures and considerations that need to be taken into account if the international venture is to be a success, that is, profitable and contributing to the company's overall business development and growth. There are many companies who fail to grasp some of the fundamental requirements of international trade and consequently find it to be a costly business. These are most likely the companies that view exporting simply as an extension of their domestic sales activity, failing to realise that the technical aspects such as shipping, payment, currency and documentation need to be managed effectively if the company is not to lose money. Equally, they may be the companies that have unexpectedly won orders from overseas through their website, perhaps not fully appreciating that their presence on the World Wide Web has turned them into latent exporters.

Exporting is not an activity that can be allocated to whoever in the sales department has a spare hour or two. It is a job for people who understand that different markets require different approaches, and the companies that are most successful globally tend to be the ones that demonstrate full commitment to their overseas development. This book is therefore intended as an introduction to the many factors influencing the sale, distribution and sourcing of products around the world. It also looks at the role that the Internet can play in international trade and the importance of global supply chain management, as well as providing the reader with some of the background knowledge required in order to put basic business finance and contract law into an international trade context.

International trade, whether in the form of exporting, importing or strategic global alliances, is only one part of the much bigger picture of international business, which is more concerned with global trade issues than with the mechanics of selling goods overseas or purchasing from foreign suppliers. Internationally active companies must therefore be aware of the global issues that can affect trade and should identify ways of ensuring that their overseas activities do take the wider forces of international business into account. This is certainly true in the first few years of the twenty-first century, as companies trading internationally face a variety of new challenges and opportunities, which in turn are accompanied by new responsibilities.

Not least of these challenges is globalisation, the phenomenon that has grown as a result of sustained trade growth, bringing great wealth to many nations whilst allegedly doing little to assist the world's least developed countries. The international business community tends to see globalisation as a natural capitalist development that goes beyond the purely commercial sphere, assisting in raising living standards in countries around the world. The anti-globalisation lobby, however, argues that it is an essentially undemocratic process that ignores the needs of undeveloped countries and peoples in order to secure material and economic gains for the multinational corporations seeking domination of the commercial world. Joint ventures, mergers and acquisitions in overseas markets are standard international trade practice and they do offer companies numerous possibilities for commercial success. However, with these strategies does come a moral obligation to consider the needs of poorer nations and the challenge to try and ensure that all trade is fair trade. Globalisation has become an increasingly contentious issue, as evidenced by the riots that marked the G8 summit in Genoa in 2001. There seem to be no easy solutions, and the debate looks set to continue for some time to come.

International trade must also meet its global environmental obligations. Following the Kyoto Agreement in 1997, whereby most of the world's industrialised nations signed up to a commitment to reduce greenhouse gas emissions, environmental policies have exerted further influence on the course of international trade. This is most evident in areas such as energy usage and transport, although packaging and production are also affected, and it does mean that companies need to be aware of any environmental restrictions imposed by countries they are trading with. For example, retailers in Germany are entitled to demand that their suppliers make arrangements to collect all the used packaging from their products for recycling.

Perhaps the biggest opportunity in the world of international trade is the opening of the Chinese market to foreign trade and investment. In autumn 2001, after 14 years of negotiating, China finally acceded to the World Trade Organisation, the international institution that administers the rules by which international trade is conducted between the majority of the world's nations. The opening of this huge market, and under established international trading standards, offers unrivalled potential for exporters and importers around the world. Companies that do not take steps to develop business with China now may find themselves losing out to their better-prepared competitors. One of the financial challenges, and opportunities, facing exporters and importers is the euro, the European Union's single currency. At midnight on 31 December 2001, the three-year transitional period came to an end and 12 European countries saw their traditional currencies cease to exist. It is now impossible to trade in Deutschmarks, francs, pesetas and so on, and pricing policies have become more transparent as the 'eurozone' has adopted the euro as its currency for both internal and international trade. Whatever exporters and importers feel about the single currency, it is here to stay and it does affect the way that companies approach the European market. As an introductory text, *Mastering International Trade* touches on these issues whilst following and explaining the core areas of the export/import process from market research to receipt of payment. Entire books have already been written on each of these topics, but the purpose of *Mastering International Trade* is to provide an overview of the subject from a practical perspective, fully supported by case studies, real-life examples and questions for consideration. It also refers the reader who wants to explore the subjects in greater depth to other appropriate texts, websites and sources of information.

The main focus of the text is actually importing and exporting from the manufacturer's perspective for the simple reason that issues such as distribution, insurance for goods in transit and documentation are more closely related to the physical movement of goods than they are for the international provision of services and consultancy. However, it is important to realise that the service sector is of immense importance to economies such the UK's. Although Britain imports and exports a phenomenal amount of goods, its global export of services such as management consultancy, retailing and marketing communications should not be overlooked. Several of the UK's largest retail outlets have established themselves overseas and, according to Trade Partners UK (the UK government department for export promotion) the United Kingdom has a 10 per cent share of the international public relations market, as well as being recognised for its marketing and advertising expertise. Again according to Trade Partners UK, the export of management consultancy and expertise in training and education is one of the UK's major exports, with growing demand for these services noticeable in Central and Eastern Europe, the Far East and Latin America.

The UK is also the leading centre for the provision of financial services and the British legal profession also has an excellent reputation around the world. Another industry sector that is often overlooked but in reality is one of the UK's more successful exports is the creative industry sector. This covers a wide range of disciplines, from art and antiquities to crafts, literature, design, software, music, broadcast media and the performing arts, contributing over five per cent of GDP, (£10.3 billion). (Statistics from the Trade Partners UK website, www.tradepartners.gov.uk.)

The fundamental requirements of importing and exporting for the service and creative sectors remain the same as for 'traditional' manufacturing industries. Companies must still market their goods or services effectively, must be satisfied that payment will be received for them and must have the capacity to deliver them in the target market. Peripheral issues such as financing, copyrights and currency must also be addressed. That said, *Mastering International Trade* does concentrate on the import and export of manufactured products. The international trade in goods is the lifeblood of modern economies. The so-called 'developed' nations have become used to being able to buy goods and components cost effectively from around the world and no matter how large or experienced a company is, the odds are that it will have to meet the demands of international trade sooner or later.

The book will provide support to those already involved in international trade, either as exporters, importers or as business advisers, as well as those keen to develop their knowledge of the subject. Although the main focus of the book is from the exporter's perspective, importing is also covered in some detail and the relationship between both disciplines is explained. Professionals aiming to put the principles of international trade into commercial practice for the benefit of their organisations will find this text to be a useful and informative guide, as will undergraduate and postgraduate students who wish to place the practical aspects of international trade into the wider perspective of international business. Above all, the book aims to remove the mystery and reveal the secrets of successful overseas trade.

Sources of information

European Union homepage – www.europa.eu.int
Information on globalisation – www.globalisationguide.org and www.globalize.org. The Organisation for Economic Co-operation and Development also discusses globalisation at www.oecd.org//ech/special.htm
International Chamber of Commerce – www.iccwbo.org
United Kingdom's Institute of Export – www.export.org
United Nations – www.un.org
World Trade Organisation – www.wto.org

■ ⅀ **2** Why trade overseas?

Introduction

Before looking at individual aspects of the international trade process, it is useful to first examine what makes a company decide to import or export. This chapter explores some of the reasons behind the decision, as well as highlighting some of the more common pitfalls. International trade is then put into the context of the growth of multinational corporations and globalisation. Although these issues are perhaps more appropriate for specialist texts on international business, they do have bearing on international trade and should be taken into account alongside the different types of importer and exporter.

The chapter concludes by describing the first steps to successful international trade development and identifying a target market, providing the reader with the foundations on which to build elements of the international strategy.

What is importing and exporting?

Quite simply, exporting is the process whereby a company or individual in one country sells a product or service to a client in a foreign market. Importing is the reverse side of this coin, being the process where products or services are sourced from suppliers in a different country and brought into the domestic market. What many companies often do not seem to fully appreciate is that both exporting and importing follow similar rules as for 'normal' sales and purchasing. Admittedly, international trade does make additional demands of companies in areas such as documentation, tariffs and duties, which may present difficulties for the uninitiated. Nevertheless there are in principle few reasons why companies that have experience of buying and selling in their home market cannot successfully employ the same skills and experience in trading overseas. This is certainly true of companies that recognise their limitations and are prepared to seek further advice from organisations such as Chambers of Commerce and other business support providers able to offer guidance in the development and implementation of international trade strategies.

Why export?

If a survey were to be carried out to identify why companies start exporting, it is likely that each respondent would offer a different reason. Some will have won their first international order by accident, perhaps as the result of an unexpected enquiry from overseas. Others will have recognised the potential of overseas markets and taken the time to think through an appropriate strategy designed to be of real value to their organisations. A small number will have started exporting simply from a desire to emulate their closest domestic competitors who happen to be achieving success internationally. The majority of the responses, however, will normally fall into one of four main categories.

Exporting to increase sales

Novice exporters often see export markets as an opportunity to increase the volume of the company's sales, and therefore profits, over a given period. One of the most common mistakes made by companies new to international trade is the assumption that a product, which has good profit margins in the domestic market will be able to maintain those margins, or increase them, in foreign markets. It may be that this is possible, although the additional costs of distribution, insurance, duties and other charges are more likely to see margins reduced unless prices are increased or production costs lowered.

Example: A UK-based manufacturer of orthopaedic equipment decided to export its product to Germany purely on the basis of the market having an ageing population. No further research was carried out and the company launched a vigorous promotional campaign that yielded several sales enquiries, two or three of which were quickly converted to orders. Only on shipping did the company realise that it had failed to take into account the cost of distribution, packaging, insurance and financing. Not only were the profit margins eliminated but in each case the company actually lost money on the sale of the goods to Germany.

Even so, the potential increase in sales in overseas markets is an attractive option to companies seeking to improve their sales turnover. Export markets offer a new, perhaps untapped, customer base and this opportunity to generate additional income often proves to be the main influence on the decision to export.

Exporting to spread risks

A company that depends on one or two markets for the majority of its business is potentially over-exposed to the risk that its trading position could be severely affected should one or more of the key clients suddenly cease trading with it. Under these conditions, the company might turn to overseas markets in order to spread the risk across a greater number of clients in the hope that any potential loss of business can be borne by the company through its other activities.

A wider client-base offers greater opportunity for sales and ultimately longer term security.

Equally, whilst the company experiences a downturn in certain markets or regions, it may be in a position to balance the scales with better performances in other markets. This approach is really a question of companies being keen to keep their options as open as the spread of markets they are active in will permit.

Production-led exporting

Production issues are often one of the key influences behind a company's decision to export. This is particularly true of companies that are actually able to reduce their costs by increasing production and consequently have surplus stock that they are unable to sell in the domestic market. Whilst it is not unusual for companies to deliberately increase their output with the aim of selling the excess into overseas markets, exporting should not be seen as a 'last resort' option for businesses looking to sell off unwanted stock. As later chapters will show, goods should be exported to meet an identified need and not just because the company wants to sell its products overseas. In other cases, companies may take the decision to look at exporting in order to find new markets for a product that has reached maturity in the domestic market. Products that have been available for some time and are well established are likely to reach the point where the maximum sales volume in their existing market has been achieved and there are few opportunities to increase sales without turning to new markets. Exporting can therefore be a means of extending the lifecycle of a company's products.

It can also be used to reduce the dependency of companies on seasonal variations in domestic demand. Companies may choose to manufacture their product throughout the year in order to try and meet demand in other parts of the world that either have different seasonal patterns or that have a need for the product all year round. An example of this might be a British company supplying thermal clothing to consumers. In the home market, the bulk of sales activity is likely to take place with the onset of autumn and winter. Whilst the company prepares for the seasonal demand, additional sales might be secured by exporting clothing to countries that have colder climates all year round.

Activity: Prepare a list of products and services that may be subject to seasonal demand and identify potential opportunities for the companies to reduce the impact of seasonality.

Exporting to improve image

As the experience gained in trading internationally can be useful in improving skills and abilities domestically, many companies look on exporting as a means of enhancing competitiveness. The knowledge gained through exporting can be used to improve domestic promotional activity, product design and packaging, as well as other aspects of the marketing strategy, not least profile. With the additional experience and skills that international trade develops in the exporting company comes a certain amount of prestige. Companies that can advertise themselves as successful exporters to a number of markets are able to demonstrate that they are capable of adapting to the needs of different markets. This, ultimately, should improve the company's image and reputation as well as impress existing and potential clients alike. Although it is rare for companies to start exporting solely for the enhanced reputation that overseas trade may bring, this is certainly an added benefit, which provides further encouragement for companies weighing up the advantages and disadvantages of international sales.

Exporting: the reality

It is not enough to take the decision to export on the strength of one of these four key reasons. Whilst overseas markets may offer opportunities to help a company with excess production, spreading risk or improving sales, they are likely to generate a new set of issues and problems for the business to contend with.

As Chapter 4 will show, market research is therefore an absolute necessity in order to identify any competition, restrictions, tariffs, legislation and unfamiliar business practices that could create difficulties or unexpected expenses for the company. Unfortunately, the more markets a company is active in, the more likely it is that it will encounter problems unless the markets and their requirements have been fully researched in advance. Figure 2.1 lists the typical problems likely to be encountered.

Types of exporter

There are four principle types of exporting company. They can be classified by the level of internationalisation of their business, ranging from the non-exporter

• Language barriers	• Cultural issues	• Legislative problems
• Insurance requirements	• Documentation	• Business practice
• Promotion and sales	• Not getting paid	• Managing agents
• Environmental issues	• Customs duties	• Increased competition

Figure 2.1 Typical problems likely to be encountered by novice exporters.

Figure 2.2   Different approaches to exporting.

with no history of overseas sales to the committed exporter that has built a business on international trade and values all sales equally, regardless of geographic origin.

- Passive/non-exporter: a company with no previous experience of exporting, maybe considering taking the first steps towards selling overseas.
- Reactive: businesses that receive sporadic enquiries from overseas companies. Reactive exporters respond to foreign clients rather than undertaking promotional work overseas and are generally less certain of how to secure and fulfil export orders.
- Proactive: companies with some experience of exporting and a growing commitment to developing business overseas. Proactive exporters are likely to feel more confident about international trade and how to achieve export success.
- Committed: the experienced company that sees exporting as a major driver of the business, responsible for the majority of the firm's turnover as well as its long-term growth and job creation.

Non-exporters and reactive exporters do not have a defined international trade strategy. Any growth achieved through export sales is generally unplanned and will be seen by the companies as a bonus. Proactive and committed exporters, on the other hand, make the effort to understand their markets and to identify sales opportunities. For these types of company, business growth through exporting is planned, and normally follows extensive market research, visits and the implementation of an appropriate entry strategy, which in turn facilitates sales and growth in the target market. The different approaches are illustrated in Figure 2.2.

Why import?

Companies purchase goods from foreign suppliers either for resale at a profit in the domestic market or as a means of sourcing cheaper components and raw materials for their finished products.

Companies that import goods for resale rather than for manufacturing purposes may do so by acting as independent buyers or as distributors for foreign suppliers, assuming that the supplier does not already have an established distributorship in the buyer's home market. Distributors, as will be explained in Chapter 6, contract with a supplier with the aim of purchasing goods and selling them on at a profit in the domestic market. Independent buyers fulfil a similar role but are not contractually bound to a preferred supplier.

Question: Why is importing often seen by governments as a necessary evil that is tolerated but not actively encouraged?

The make or buy decision

For most companies, including those in the service sector, there comes a point where management has to ask itself whether it is more cost effective to outsource manufacturing of certain components or delivery of services to a third party. Components manufactured in house offer several advantages: the company will be reassured of their quality and ready availability, may be able to promote their finished product as wholly made by the business and may be able to utilise excess production capacity in their manufacture. However, purchasing components from UK or overseas suppliers also has its advantages, particularly for companies that operate a 'just in time' management system. Purchasing as components are required can help companies to reduce their labour and machinery costs through not manufacturing in house. This can then have the result of improving efficiencies, permitting more cost effective and competitive production of the finished goods.

Each scenario raises a number of questions, which the company should address before committing itself either to manufacturing or outsourcing. Figure 2.3 lists some of the main situations in which a company might wish to make or buy components.

If the decision is taken to purchase components or products for resale, a suitable supplier must be identified either in the domestic market or overseas.

When to make	When to buy
• when the company has spare capacity	• when the company has no spare capacity
• when no appropriate suppliers can be found	• when only limited quantities are needed
• when the company does not want to rely on third parties	• when buying is cheaper than making
• when there are no evident financial benefits, such as import duty relief and so on	• when the company can take advantage of financial benefits from importing components
• when the company wishes to preserve confidentiality	• when the workforce would need to be increased
• when in-house manufacturing is part of the company's tradition	• when specialist skills are required
• when components require regular modification or alteration	• when the company wishes to concentrate on core areas of production

Figure 2.3 Examples of factors influencing the make or buy decision.

The supplier must be able to demonstrate that it can meet the company's specifications in terms of quality, delivery, packaging, cost and warranties or insurance. The buyer should therefore research all potential suppliers carefully in order to ensure that the most appropriate company is appointed. If an overseas supplier is identified, the buyer must also be aware of all the international trade issues that the importing process might raise, particularly payment terms, shipping and import duties.

In some cases, the company will be able to purchase from the foreign supplier's agent or distributor based in the buyer's market. Alternatively, the buyer may have to deal directly with the supplier without the benefit of a local representative.

International growth through acquisitions and mergers

Acquisitions and mergers are being increasingly used by companies of all sizes to fuel international business growth. Although we tend to hear most about mergers between large corporations, such as that in 2000 between America Online and Time Warner, smaller companies are also joining forces with one another to benefit from the advantages that mergers can bring. Mergers are often considered as a means of increasing sales and profits whilst reducing costs or diversifying production. They can reduce competition and therefore consolidate market position both at home and in overseas markets.

There are several reasons why companies consider acquiring or merging with other organisations. Firstly, companies experiencing a decline in their market share or noticing that the macro-market is slowing down may find themselves with excess production capacity and personnel. By merging with a competitor or supplier, these overheads can be reduced and the resulting company is likely to be stronger and more resilient to market forces.

Overproduction as a result of increasing efficiencies may mean that companies are able to supply more goods than the world market demands. Again, a merger or acquisition will enable the combined company to reduce overheads and staffing levels and so cut back on total production capacity whilst still being able to meet the needs of the market.

Many organisations and industries foresee a future in which a limited number of multinational corporations (MNCs) dominate their sector. As companies continue to increase their assets around the world through mergers or take-overs, so they become more powerful and are able to use their position to influence international regulations, pricing and potentially trade policies. There is no doubt that the quest for increased power is one of the key influences behind many a large corporation's decision to merge.

Whereas large organisations can influence global trade issues, similar benefits also accrue on a lesser scale to smaller companies who, by merging, can take more control of their market segment or industry sector in particular markets.

The main attraction of mergers and acquisitions from the international trade perspective is the improved access to overseas markets that can be achieved. Businesses that are successful in different markets may merge with each other in order to gain the opportunity to trade in the other company's territories. Thus mergers can bring market knowledge, experience and contacts that otherwise might have taken much longer to acquire.

Types of merger

A merger joins together two or more companies with the assets of each partner being consolidated to create a single corporation. Mergers have different purposes, depending on the ambitions and objectives of the companies involved, and will typically fall into one of four types.

Perhaps the simplest of these is the 'vertical' merger, which is driven primarily by supply-chain issues. For example, a company that relies heavily on a particular supplier may choose to merge with, or acquire, the supplier in order to ensure a regular and exclusive supply of components.

A 'horizontal' merger occurs when related businesses active in the same geographic and product areas combine in an attempt to build a monopoly of market share, for example as in the Exxon/Mobil merger of 1999. Horizontal mergers are often the result of competitors joining together to rationalise their product portfolio and so reach a larger combined market. The same result can be achieved by 'hostile take-over', where an organisation forcibly acquires a competitor or related business against their will.

Vertical and horizontal mergers are illustrated in Figure 2.4.

Finally, an 'extensional merger' may take place to assist two or more businesses to enter the same new market. This approach can often be the most cost-effective method to develop new markets and is equally useful for companies in the same industry as well as those working together in a supply chain. Extensional mergers permit the combined organisation to reduce research and development costs, as well as other expenses incurred in opening up a new market.

Each type of merger has its advantages for the organisations concerned and can be a useful means of utilising shared knowledge and experience for diversification into new markets around the world.

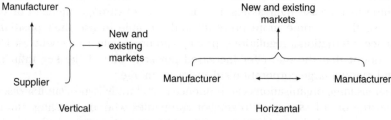

Figure 2.4 Vertical and horizontal integration.

Disadvantages of mergers

Mergers do, however, bring certain disadvantages. As explained above, one of the primary reasons companies consider mergers is to increase their market share in whatever part of the world they are targeting. The likely consequence of this approach is the development of an even larger organisation, reduced competition and less choice for consumers. In many cases, mergers also result in substantial job losses as companies streamline or rationalise their administrative, production and management functions. Smaller, community-based companies find it increasingly difficult to compete with the monolithic infrastructures of MNCs and may, too, have to contemplate redundancies or closure.

Market share in new or existing markets may well have increased, but at what cost? This is yet another example of a situation where internationally active companies have an obligation to consider the effects that their policies have in all markets, no matter how far removed from the boardroom those markets may be.

Developing economies and economic development

Looking beyond the 'developed' industrialised nations of Western Europe, the USA and others, the majority of the world's countries are often categorised as less-developed nations, emerging markets and third-world countries. The majority of these poorer countries are slowly moving away from traditional, rural economies towards more industrialised output, with greater emphasis on the growth of important sectors such as power generation, infrastructure, steel and petrochemicals. These are often considered to be the driving forces behind successful economic growth and it is therefore not surprising to find that these sectors are regularly cited as the priority industries for investment and development. Improvements to power generation and infrastructure will ultimately improve domestic manufacturing output, thereby generating more money for the economy, which leads to higher wages, increased investment into public services and so on. The free market conditions so familiar to industrialised nations are seen as the foundation for improving quality of life and economic performance in the developing world. In this sense, development is really being judged by the level and standard of education, health, living and housing in the market, as well as the availability of consumer goods. This in turn depends on trade to maintain progress and development. Trade alone, however, cannot assist emerging economies to develop. In the past, government initiatives, international aid agency donations and loans have been used to fund projects designed to help countries develop effective capital industries. This approach, led by governments and not their peoples, has been criticised for its imposition of development strategies without securing the 'buy in' of the country's inhabitants in the first place. By the same token, local trade initiatives aimed at stimulating sustainable, organic growth through education, experience and encouragement are increasingly favoured over large-scale government-led schemes as they do seek to secure the support and input of the population.

Globalisation

This leads quite naturally to the much-disputed issue of globalisation, which has come about as a result of a rapid increase in the flow of capital around the world and the sustained growth of international trade since the early 1990s. Although countless smaller and medium-sized businesses have proven themselves in trading internationally, the real growth in global trade has been driven by MNCs casting their nets further and further overseas. Companies with adequate resources and capital can quickly improve and develop their market presence and share through setting up satellite offices, branches or manufacturing facilities, which in turn impacts on the global supply chain.

Globalisation is not a speedy process, despite the rapid increases in global capital and trade flows, but it does result in permanent changes in the markets affected. It brings huge opportunities for economic expansion that must be seized and developed responsibly, something which to date has not always been successfully accomplished. Two schools of thought have been developed and propounded as businesses increasingly integrate their production and promotional strategies across national boundaries. On one side, the anti-globalisation lobby, which includes such organisations as Friends of the Earth, Greenpeace and countless pressure groups, sees the spread of globalisation as an inherently destructive force that exploits under-developed nations and peoples.

Although globalisation is driven by economic factors that, in theory, promote trade and investment in poorer nations, many see the global corporations as polluters and environmentally irresponsible entities that consider themselves above national regulation and control. The same pressure groups argue that globalisation leads to lower wages and working conditions, and that MNCs choose to invest in poorer nations simply because they can make greater profits from paying lower wages. The exposure of so-called third-world sweatshops producing training shoes, clothing and other branded goods on behalf of major international companies is often cited as evidence of the destructive and morally unacceptable face of international expansion.

This attitude towards globalisation also argues that the very organisations set up to govern and improve global trade development share the blame for the current world order. The WTO, IMF and the United Nations are all involved in the course of international trade and have rightly or wrongly become targets for the anti-globalisation movement.

The international trade perspective

Whilst this argument is finding increasing support around the world, culminating in the G8 demonstrations in Seattle (2000) and Genoa (2001) and leading to the G8 meeting in Canada in 2002 being held at a remote location in the Rocky Mountains, not to mention numerous anti-capitalist rallies across the world's developed nations, there is a very strong counter-argument.

The liberalisation of world trade, reductions in tariff and non-tariff barriers and the opening of markets to international trade continues to benefit more people than ever, including those in poorer nations. The majority of the world's organisations that represent the interests of business argue that, far from lowering living standards, globalisation does much to improve conditions and economic growth. Indeed, it is noticeable that the countries most regularly held up as victims of the destructive effect of globalisation are actually those least open to trade, for example many African and Asian states. International trade is therefore seen by bodies such as the UN, WTO, the World Bank and International Chamber of Commerce as a creative force that encourages sustainable economic development.

These organisations also argue that globalisation of trade is a much more effective and longer term solution to poverty than conventional aid programmes that offer short-term relief. Trade tackles the causes of poverty by developing stable and sustainable economies that do encourage local buy in, but there is an obligation on the 'all powerful' MNCs and smaller businesses alike to ensure that their international trade practices promote fair trade and are not to the detriment of less-developed nations.

Above all, it is useful to bear in mind that the term 'globalisation' implies that, regardless of geographic origin, wealth or belief, we all share one planet and as such have a responsibility to ensure that the benefits of fair trade are also shared.

It is not the role of this textbook to discuss globalisation in detail, as the subject is more properly suited to international business texts. However, it is important to bear the spread of globalisation in mind as it does form part of the backdrop to the current international trade climate, with exporters and importers being made increasingly aware of moral, social and ethical trade issues.

International companies/international strategies

A company may describe itself as international for any number of reasons. It may be a committed exporter with turnover largely attributable to overseas trading activities or a multinational corporation that has a presence in countless overseas markets. A truly international business, however, can demonstrate both commitment to overseas development and the existence of an international trade strategy.

In practice, what this means for the average exporter as well as the MNC is that the company has adopted a tailored approach to individual markets within the framework of its overall international expansion. For example, a German exporter targeting the NAFTA countries, European Union and Central Europe will have developed separate strategies for each country in the respective regions and will not expect the same marketing approach to be effective in several culturally diverse markets. For MNCs in particular, this approach effectively amounts to the development of regional corporate strategies that can operate autonomously within the framework of the corporation as a whole. Regional offices will be set up to develop and support business in different markets, continents or trading blocs and each regional office will have a strong management team responsible for growing the company within the territory. Apart from the scale and geographic spread of the operation, MNCs with several regional offices are little different to a national chain of retail outlets or solicitors' offices and so on: each has a defined remit and territory with locally engaged management that ultimately report back to head office.

Every internationally focused business will manage its international strategy differently, depending on the nature, values and aspirations of the company. What they all will have in common is a commitment to overseas development and a belief that this can only be achieved through the implementation of an effective corporate plan that takes international trade into account.

The smaller company's perspective

Small and medium-sized enterprises (SMEs) face additional challenges to those faced by larger businesses, not least in terms of financial and human resources. Where larger companies can absorb the costs of research, market visits and product modification into their larger infrastructures, smaller companies do not have this luxury. Consequently, many SMEs see exporting as an expensive gamble and tend to be more cautious and methodical in their approach to international trade. It cannot be denied that there are financial risks involved in exporting and importing, just as there are in domestic trade, but subsequent chapters will show how these risks can be minimised.

Business support organisations have long recognised that SMEs require more assistance and encouragement than larger companies. Nowadays there is a great deal of advice and guidance available to help companies of all sizes expand their trade horizons, much of which has been developed from the SME's perspective. There are therefore few, if any, reasons why even the smallest of companies cannot trade overseas successfully.

Activity: Define what constitutes a large, medium and small company and examine the restrictions each faces in trading internationally.

First steps to export success

It is all very well for a company to take the decision to start exporting its products but the real challenge lies in turning that decision into reality and in knowing where to begin. Having asked 'should we export', the company also needs to question what and when to start exporting, what resources are going to be needed and which market or markets to target, not to mention what support is available and how this is all going to be financed (see Figure 2.5).

These are the initial issues that need to be resolved if the company's first foray into the world of international trade is to be successful. Each has a bearing on the company's marketing strategy and should be taken into account individually

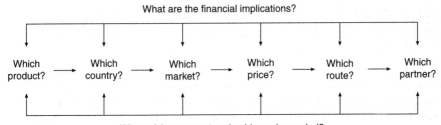

Figure 2.5 Key issues for new exporters.

and as part of the overall approach to export development. Once these questions have been addressed, the company can then begin to understand how the documentary, financial and distribution issues impact on the strategy. There is clearly much to take account of before the first export quotation is even written.

Fortunately, companies are able to access a wide range of support and advice at every stage of the import/export process. For example, managers new to international trade should speak with export development advisors in organisations such as Chambers of Commerce or Business Link to ensure that they are fully aware of what steps they must take to implement an effective international strategy. Such organisations have a duty of care to their clients and will always avoid leading new exporters into inappropriate markets. They will ensure that the decision to export is well founded, not simply a knee-jerk reaction to a sudden overseas enquiry, and they will also endeavour to assist the company in managing the transition from domestic to international trader. How companies might choose their first export markets is discussed below, whilst the other key considerations are explained in detail in the following chapters.

Choosing a market

The decision to target a particular country should only be made once research has confirmed that there is potential for the company to trade successfully in that market. The key market research issues and procedures are explained in Chapter 4, but before the research can be undertaken the company must first select the markets in which it is potentially interested.

In Europe, the majority of first-time exporters will choose to sell to clients in neighbouring countries. Ease of distribution, geographic location and familiar, 'Western' business practices and values make the European Union a logical first destination for companies new to international trade. Taking into account travel and accommodation costs, the EU is also a comparatively inexpensive market to develop business in. From the point of view of the British exporter, Europe is even more attractive as a target market as the English language is spoken widely and is often seen as the language of business. The ability to communicate effectively is essential in any sales situation and, although the use of English should never be taken for granted, it may be the decisive factor in determining which market to approach first.

Exporters are also advised to seek markets that are not too dissimilar to their existing or domestic markets, as this reduces the likelihood that their products will require modification or adaptation in order to meet the needs of the target market. Companies that know their products and core markets well will often be able to list their potential markets from instinct or knowledge of a competitor's overseas activities. However, further research will be necessary to confirm the choice of market (see Figure 2.6).

One of the simplest means of prioritising the potential export markets is by comparing the import/export statistics for the company's products overseas. For example, in the UK, the National Statistics Office can provide companies with details of the volume of goods imported by individual countries, broken down by product code (see Table 2.1).

Question: What conclusions can be reached from Table 2.1?

• Ease of access	• Language	• Business culture
• Cost	• Competitor analysis	• Trade statistics
• Few requirements for product modification	• Instinct	• Availability of support

Figure 2.6   Considerations for market selection.

Table 2.1   UK trade statistics showing the import and export of commodity code 95 to countries in Western Europe outside the EU (January to March 2002)

Commodity code 95: Toys, games and sports requisites, parts and accessories thereof.

	2002 Mar Pounds sterling	
	Total imports	Total exports
Andorra	—	5 373
Switzerland	319 982	1 812 148
Faroe Islands	—	3 985
Gibraltar	—	24 544
Iceland	21 740	138 744
Leichtenstein	—	—
Malta	8 771	89 607
Norway	348 154	2 679 465
San Marino	31 570	278 736
Turkey	26 274	454 659
Vatican City	—	—
Total	756 491	5 487 261

Source: HM Customs and Excise, www.hmce.gov.uk

These figures can be used to identify which markets are net suppliers or buyers of the company's products, and therefore which are likely to provide a market for the exporter. Using these basic criteria as a guideline, would-be exporters can draw up a list of overseas markets that may be appropriate for further research and development prior to implementing a strategy to achieve international sales.

Conclusions

This chapter has examined some of the common reasons why companies become involved with international trade and has identified the different types of importer and exporter. It has shown that, whilst internationalisation can yield increased sales and an ability to withstand falling trade in some markets by developing new trading opportunities with others, it is not an easy option. Companies new to exporting must be aware of the added requirements of overseas trade.

The growth of multinational corporations, and their role in the increasingly contentious issue of globalisation, has also been discussed, albeit briefly. For a greater understanding of both sides of the globalisation argument, readers are encouraged to refer to some of the international business texts and websites listed below.

Finally, the chapter has highlighted the first steps that companies should take towards becoming internationally active. The identification of potential target markets, as well as the products to export to them, forms the basis for the further development of the international trade strategy, key elements of which will be outlined in the following chapters.

Sources of information

British Chambers of Commerce – www.britishchambers.org.uk/exportzone
Friends of the Earth – www.foe.org
Greenpeace – www.greenpeace.org
Information on globalisation – www.globalisationguide.org and
    www.globalize.org
Institute of Export – www.export.org
International Forum on Globalisation – www.ifg.org
International Monetary Fund – www.imf.org
National Statistics Office trade data and information – www.uktradeinfo.com
Oxfam – www.oxfam.org
Pro-Act Global (UK company promoting fair trade with African nations) –
    www.pro-actglobal.co.uk
Trade Partners UK (UK government advice and support for exporters) –
    www.tradepartners.gov.uk
United Nations – www.un.org
World Bank – www.worldbank.org
World Trade Organisation – www.wto.org

Further reading

Bennett R, *Getting Started in Export* (2nd ed) (Kogan Page, 1998).

Daniels J, *International Business* (9th ed) (Addison Wesley, 2000).

Ellwood W, *The No Nonsense Guide to Globalisation* (Verso, 2001).

Nelson C A, *Import Export* (3rd ed) (McGraw-Hill, 2000).

Rugman A M and Hodgetts R M, *International Business* (2nd ed) (FT Prentice Hall, 2000).

Streeten P P and Streeten P, *Globalisation, Threat or Opportunity?* (Copenhagen Business School Press, 2001).

Tuller L W, *Exporting, Importing and Beyond* (Adams Media Corporation, 1997).

Wilson J R, *Getting Started in Importing* (2nd ed) (Kogan Page, 1998).

QUESTIONS FOR CONSIDERATION

1 Why might a company consider exporting or importing as a means of generating business growth?

2 How might a reactive exporter become proactive or committed to international trade development?

3 What are the benefits and drawbacks of international business growth through acquisition and merger?

4 What steps can an internationally active company take to ensure that it pursues a policy of fair trade in every overseas market it trades with?

5 How might an SME with no previous international trade experience identify potential export markets?

■ ⊻ **3** Marketing

Introduction

The purpose of this chapter is to give the reader an introduction to some of the more important aspects of the marketing process. It will also examine some of the tools that can be employed in the development of the marketing plan and will show how marketing is an essential part of international business planning. By the end of the chapter, the reader will understand and be able to use several marketing and planning methods in an international trade context.

What is marketing?

A great deal has been written about marketing, and from a number of perspectives. Some definitions suggest that it is a company-driven function concerned only with getting the goods to the consumer at the most advantageous price for the producer. Others show marketing to be driven by the needs of the customer, and that its main aim is to satisfy consumers by giving them the products they want, when they want them and for the price they are willing to pay. It is this approach which really does get to the core of the concept. It stresses that marketing is an important part of a company's business strategy, as it is the process that researches customer needs and assists the company in ensuring that it produces goods and/or services to meet those needs. Marketing is now rarely seen as the means by which a company attempts to sell the products it has already manufactured, regardless of whether or not there is an apparent need. Product-led companies are unlikely to be as successful as those that are market-led.

Marketing is therefore much more than just the promotional and sales aspect of the business. It also influences, but does not control, production, finance, distribution and management, which are the main drivers of business development and growth for both UK-focused and internationally active companies. Marketing is, above all, a strategic process that identifies competitive advantages and potential threats, and effective marketing planning is an essential part of any business strategy. International marketing shares many of the same disciplines and requirements as domestic marketing, and the processes outlined in this chapter should be followed no matter which market the company is targeting.

Market versus marketing research

Market research and marketing research are two very different concepts. Market research, which is covered in the next chapter, is focused on evaluating particular markets for the introduction of the company's products. It is used by companies to identify opportunities for their goods and services in the domestic market or overseas, as well as obstacles that may prevent those opportunities from being maximised. Marketing research is carried out in order to understand every component of the marketing strategy, including the product itself, pricing policy, distribution, promotional activity and internal factors such as the company's strengths and weaknesses. Marketing research therefore forms the basis for the entire marketing planning process.

Marketing planning

There are four distinct areas, outlined in Figure 3.1, which should be reviewed as part of the marketing planning activity if the exercise is to have any real meaning for the company. These are as valid for the export marketing strategy as they are for marketing in the home country. They are also as essential for providers of services as they are for manufacturers of physical products.

Firstly, the company should carry out an internal assessment in order to identify succinctly the nature of its business and core products/services as well as the main reasons behind the success of the company to date. This assessment should also set out the company's objectives, the product's strengths and

---

Internal audit
- What is the company's business?
- What are the core products/services?
- What makes the company successful?
- What are the product's strengths and weaknesses?
- Which aspects are profitable and which are unprofitable?

Customer profile
- Who are the customers?
- When, where, why and how often do they purchase the company's goods?
- How important is price to the customer?
- Why do customers buy from the competition?
- What are the main trends in the market?

Competitor analysis
- Who are the competitors?
- Are they internationally active?
- What makes them different?
- How do the company's prices compare with those of the competition?
- How well does the company compete with the competition and why?
- Does the competition pose a serious threat?

Business support
- Which organisations does the company use to access business support?
- Is support required in other areas?
- Do the company's suppliers provide any additional support?
- Are there any existing sources of support, which are relevant to overseas markets?

Figure 3.1   Examples of key marketing research issues.

weaknesses, and should highlight areas of the business that are particularly profitable or those that generate losses.

Secondly, an assessment of the competition will complement the internal review by evaluating how rival businesses are performing, how they have priced their products or services and precisely how much of a threat they represent. By taking time to examine its competitors, the company should be in a position to understand what makes them successful.

The next step is for the company to profile its customers in order to understand who they are, why they purchase the company's product, as well as when, where and how often they purchase it. This assessment may also show how important a factor pricing is for the customer and what it is about the product that creates customer loyalty. Once the customer base has been profiled, this should also provide valuable information relating to the size of the market and what the current market trends are.

Finally, the company should identify what support it currently receives from organisations such as Chambers of Commerce, banks, freight forwarders, suppliers and other business agencies and whether there is scope to make further use of these sources of expertise and experience, either in the UK or in overseas markets. The purpose of this assessment is to take a snapshot of the company's current position with a view to identifying and building on those aspects of the business that are effective.

> **Question**: How will the customer profile differ for companies specialising in the provision of architectural consultancy services, canning and bottling equipment and pre-packaged frozen meals?

Market segmentation

When a company sells its products into a particular market, it should do so with a relatively clear idea of how big the market is and how it is structured or segmented. Segmentation is the process by which the market is subdivided into the different categories (segments) of customer that the company would expect to see in the market as a whole. This is carried out in two defined stages. Firstly, the company will identify the overall market in which it seeks to operate, for instance by geographical boundary or product sector. The company might consider that its broad market is the provision of seating to consumers, which may be further refined to include a territorial focus such as the market for seating in Germany. Equally, a provider of education services may identify a broad market as the provision of training and education services in Malaysia, covering recruitment of students to study in the UK, distance learning and e-learning, not to mention a range of subject-specific areas (languages, engineering and so on). Having classified the total market population, the smaller segments within it can then be identified. Using seating type as the key variable, the segmentation exercise may show that there are six separate segments; as illustrated in Figure 3.2.

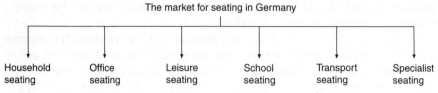

The market for seating in Germany

| Household seating | Office seating | Leisure seating | School seating | Transport seating | Specialist seating |

Figure 3.2 Example of market segmentation.

If desired, it should also be possible to further segment these submarkets by applying an even more sophisticated set of segmentation variables to identify different, focused categories of customer in each. For example, the leisure industry submarket may include seating purchased by hotels, football stadia, cinemas, and so on. The company must then decide which segments of the total market are most attractive for it to target and a strategy can then be built around specific objectives such as 'to sell fold-up plastic seating to sporting stadia in Germany'. Once the target market has been defined, the company can begin to design a targeted marketing mix, which lies at the heart of every effective marketing strategy.

The marketing mix

Understanding the marketing mix is one of the fundamental requirements of the marketing plan, and is as important for international trade as for domestic business. Traditionally labelled 'the four Ps', the marketing mix takes into account four areas of the company's marketing strategy (see Figure 3.3). Each of the four areas influences, and is influenced by, the other three. Consequently, it is not possible to alter one aspect without considering the impact on the others. The four areas are outlined below.

Product. This is not limited to the features, functions and core benefits of the product, but also encompasses the wider levels of the total product concept, including quality and safety issues, as well as added value services such as after-sales support. The key features, advantages and benefits that the product offers

Figure 3.3 The marketing mix.

to the customer are readily identifiable, but should be examined alongside basic issues such as reliability and purpose, as well as an evaluation of how that product fits within the company's existing product range. The actual design of the product is not enough to guarantee export success. The way the product is presented, branded or packaged must also take into account the needs of an international strategy.

If possible, the lifecycle of the product should also be identified. This is particularly important for a product that has been in existence for some time and may be classed as 'mature', as there may be little scope for further sales development. However, if a mature product has not yet been introduced into a potentially new target market and the evidence suggests that there is little or no competition, then the chances are that the launch of that product into the new market will be a success. This is often a very lucrative strategy for exporting companies, as their years of experience in producing the product is likely to have resulted in efficient production methods, economies of scale, consistency of quality and so on. Market development is consequently one of the lower risk options for an experienced company wanting to grow its business.

Price. The company should include information on what influences pricing policy and what the standard trading terms and conditions are. An indication of the company's attitude towards discounting and credit facilities should also be included to give a fuller picture of the pricing issue. Two of the main factors that will determine how the product is priced will be how the competition prices its goods and whether the company expects to compete on quality (which pushes the price up) or on price (which may bring it down).

For international trade, there are a number of other additional considerations, which can affect the cost of a product, from exchange rates to transport charges. These are described in subsequent chapters, and pricing is covered in more detail in Chapter 8.

Place. This aspect of the marketing mix is given over to understanding the channels of distribution, or how the product gets to market, and making sure that the goods are made available to the customer in the desired location and quantities. For example, is the product sold direct into the market, or through an agent or distributor? Are sales restricted to a number of outlets or is the product sold on a blanket coverage basis? How customers perceive a product or service will depend on the way it has been placed in the market, and this ultimately will depend on how the company approaches delivery and distribution.

Promotion. How a company advertises and promotes its products and services is the key to successful business development. The product, price and channels of distribution may well be clearly understood and identifiable, but if the promotional strategy is not correctly implemented, customers will not be aware of the product in the first place.

There are a number of traditional methods that a company can employ to promote its products and services. The method or combination of methods chosen will depend on the nature of the product to be promoted. Companies that aim to sell direct to the consumer may use display advertising in the local or national press and relevant journals, and may also consider advertising through radio and television. Companies that aim to sell to other companies (machinery sales, for instance) will make use of promotion through trade press, but are unlikely to utilise mass media advertising as a) it is expensive and b) the target audience is inappropriate.

When taking the decision to purchase advertising space in journals and magazines, the company must be aware of what it seeks to achieve through the advertising, who it aims to reach and when the advertising should take place. Additionally, a clear advertising budget must be agreed in advance of any decision. All potential advertising media will publish 'media packs' containing full rates and circulation details, as well as an editorial calendar showing forthcoming features and topics to assist advertisers to plan their budgets and scheduling. Many will also break their readership down into demographics, geographic region, industry sector, and so on, and the company should use this to make sure that their advertising will reach an appropriate audience. Advertising for international trade is as important as it is for the home market, and as much care needs to be taken with selecting an appropriate advertising vehicle overseas as would be taken domestically. In many cases, international journals and other publications may not be familiar to the exporter and in these situations further research will be necessary to ensure that the chosen publications do meet the company's requirements.

Publicity can also be achieved more cost effectively by improving public relations. For example, free editorial and media coverage may be gained by well-written press releases that draw attention to the company. The launch of a new product is certainly worthy of a press release, as is a company's first foray into a new export market. Anything that can be done to raise the profile of the company is of benefit and the power of the press both in the home market and abroad can be utilised to the company's advantage.

Other types of promotion take the form of sales presentations to potential clients, whilst some initiatives aim to stimulate sales through use of free gifts, seasonal price reductions and so on. Few companies will have the same promotional strategy, as each will have different requirements and will adopt different approaches. What all companies should have in common is that their strategies have been sensibly developed on the back of comprehensive research.

Promotion via the World Wide Web

The Internet is now established as an important promotional tool in its own right. When radio was first introduced, it took approximately 30 years to reach 50 million listeners. To reach the same number of regular viewers, television took about 14 years. It has taken the Internet just four years to reach these levels, and the number of people who have access to the World Wide Web is growing on a daily basis. Increasing amounts of money are being spent online as the world's consumers become more familiar with buying in cyberspace and, for companies employing well-designed and thought out strategies, the potential for business growth through the Internet cannot be underestimated.

Whilst some companies – the infamous 'dot coms' – have struggled to build business based solely on their web presence, other companies have successfully harnessed the Internet as an advertising medium that complements their existing strategy. Unless businesses set out to be web-based and build a business plan around this approach, the Internet should really be used as an extension of the promotional activity already employed by the company.

> **Activity**: Use the Internet to find three companies producing centrifugals for the sugar industry. Compare their websites and examine the relative merits of each, paying particular attention to how the products are promoted. Repeat the exercise for three environmental consultancy businesses and show how the two types of business differ in their approach to promotion on the World Wide Web and what they also have in common.

A successful website depends on many factors, not least careful planning and clear definition of purpose. Unless the company has the resources and skills to build an effective web-presence in-house, experts should be brought in to assist in the design and development of the website. Once the decision to develop a company website has been taken, a series of core questions needs to be asked:

- How will a website complement and support the company's objectives?
- How does the company expect the customer to benefit from the website?
- What are the company's immediate goals and expectations from a website?
- What are the longer term expectations – for example, will the site need expanding to include new products and stock monitoring facilities?
- Is an online payment facility required?
- What will the website look like? What content will it have? How much information will be made available to visitors to the site?
- How will the website be maintained and updated internally?
- How will the company expect to measure the success of the website?
- Has the target customer-base been consulted to determine their requirements from the website?
- How are the company's competitors using the Internet, and what do their websites look like?
- Will the website add value to customer service? For example, special offers for existing customers promoted through part of the website, which only current clients can access.

Once the initial objectives and parameters have been determined, a suitable 'host' (the organisation that provides web space and facilitates Internet traffic to the site) must also be found. Again, the company should be aware of its requirements and seek professional advice before entering into agreement with an Internet Service Provider (ISP).

There is therefore a substantial research and decision-making process, which has to be undertaken before progress can be made on the physical development of the website. Construction of the site is generally one of the last activities to be undertaken during the project, as building a website is an ongoing process that constantly reviews objectives and purpose.

Whatever approach to the Internet the company adopts, promotion via the World Wide Web should be seen as an essential part of the overall marketing strategy.

Trade shows and exhibitions

It seems that nowadays there is an exhibition or trade fair for every conceivable product, service and industry sector and, as is the case for most things, some are better than others. This type of event is a particularly useful opportunity for the company to meet potential clients, size up the competition and to keep up to date with what is happening in the industry. Trade shows can also prove useful for market research if visitors to the company's stand are asked for their opinions on the products exhibited, and so on. Participation in trade fairs is the best opportunity a company has to demonstrate its products to hundreds, even thousands, of potential customers during the course of the exhibition.

Participation in such events is, however, expensive. The benefits of the increased exposure have to be weighed against the cost of resources and the physical cost of erecting the company's stand. The costs increase if the company is attending an overseas exhibition as the stand, products to be exhibited and peripheral equipment will need to be shipped, cleared through customs and delivered to the venue. Yet again the company must undertake research to ensure that the selected show is appropriate in terms of size, target audience and other exhibitors. As most trade fairs publish catalogues of each year's exhibitors, and will often break down the total number of visitors by industry sector or job title and so on, there should be few problems in eliminating inappropriate shows.

For exporters appearing at international exhibitions it is worthwhile bearing in mind that financial support from their national government may be available as part of the country's commitment to increasing the international success of its companies. For example, the UK government's international trade development arm, Trade Partners UK, operates the SESA (Support for Exhibitions and Seminars Abroad) scheme to assist exporters in exhibiting overseas. A full list of the exhibitions supported by SESA can be found at www.tradepartners.gov.uk/sesa/ but these represent just some of the numerous trade fairs that take place globally each year.

Summary

It should now be apparent how the individual components of the marketing mix are so interdependent that changes made to one will affect the others. How a product is perceived by the target customer-base will be affected by the price, placing and promotional strategies adopted. For example, lowering the retail cost of the product may cause the consumer to feel that the product is cheap and of poorer quality. Equally, promoting goods as quality, niche items is hardly feasible if prices are low and the product is widely available in the market.

Product	Price
Develop new products	Alterations to price structure
Improve or modify existing products	Changes to terms and conditions
Alter the product's image in the market	Sales and promotions
Expand the product range	Use of credit facilities
Place	**Promotion**
New geographic markets	Improve advertising strategy
Change distribution methods	More effective public relations activity
Improve customer access to product	Changes to sales strategy

Figure 3.4   Examples of diversification within the marketing mix.

It is therefore important for the company to understand that modifications made to a product to suit the needs of the target market, or changes to the distribution policy, may have an adverse effect on issues such as price and perception. Any diversification needs to be considered carefully, and within the framework of the entire marketing mix (see Figure 3.4). The marketing mix is not just important in planning for the domestic market. It also needs to be rigorously examined and modified to meet the needs of international markets. Research into the target market will highlight a new set of issues, from cultural demands to logistical difficulties, that can impact on the success of the marketing plan and these need to be resolved before the strategy is implemented.

Business planning

The business plan covers a broader range of considerations than the marketing plan. It does not just look at the factors affecting the marketing function within the company, but also assesses all the opportunities for growth available to the company. As such, business planning takes a longer term view and includes an appreciation of all the resources and functions of the company, from staff skills through to capital equipment and procedures. Business planning is not an activity undertaken solely by large organisations, but is something that should be carried out by all companies, regardless of size. Companies engaging in international trade, especially for the first time, should certainly develop a comprehensive business plan, as different overseas markets will each have their own idiosyncrasies and will require different strategies, which will in turn place new demands on the company.

Production of the business plan can be assisted by using two diagnostic 'tools' to examine the company's objectives, its strengths and weaknesses, and the external factors that affect it.

SMART

The first of these tools is SMART, which breaks the company's main objectives down into those that are Specific, Measurable, Agreed, Realistic and

Time-bound. The purpose of SMART is to provide the company with a short checklist of issues to take into account:

1. Are the objectives set out by the company specific and clearly defined?
2. Are the aims quantifiable – will the company be in a position to measure the success of the business plan against the original objectives?
3. Have the objectives been agreed by all directors, and does the company have the full commitment of its staff to implement a strategy to realise these aims?
4. Are the objectives realistic, or are the company's expectations too high? Equally, will the defined objectives provide a challenge for the company, or are they easily achievable?
5. Has a timeframe for the attainment of the objectives been determined? Has the company agreed deadlines by which stages of the business plan should be completed?

The objectives set out by the company are likely to be based on existing activity and the possible expansion or diversification of that activity. Every aspect of the company therefore needs to be reviewed if the business plan is to have any value, and if the corporate objectives are to be met. As such, each department should be responsible for defining its own objectives and implementing a business plan. Individual departmental plans can then be appraised and incorporated into the overall strategy, complementing and supporting other elements of the business plan.

SWOT

The SWOT analysis covers the Strengths, Weaknesses, Opportunities and Threats, which affect the company's success (see Figure 3.5). The strengths and weaknesses are the internal factors that the company can control. Important issues for assessment include:

- The skills and knowledge-base of the company
- Current suppliers
- Current production methods/service delivery methods

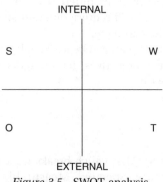

Figure 3.5 SWOT analysis.

- Quality of product or service
- Customer care/after-sales service
- Existing markets
- The company's financial position
- Condition of capital equipment
- Information systems and management controls

although any area which the company classes as essential to its progress ought to be included in the analysis. Staff knowledge and abilities are particularly important to identify. As with any business activity, the company must ensure that it has the resources and skills necessary to develop and implement a marketing strategy. If the marketing mix is to be effective, the company cannot rely on one or two experienced staff who understand marketing, but must be able to call on the skills of personnel involved in every aspect of the company, from production through to administration and promotion.

There is little point in identifying the need to diversify the company's product range if the production department is unable to fulfil that need, unless the company is prepared to invest in training and developing its staff to cope with the new objectives. Likewise, the successful use of the Internet as promotional tool will be restricted if the company does not have suitably experienced people in house who can maintain and update the website.

In each case, as much information as possible should be obtained in order for the company to have a clear understanding of where its strengths and weaknesses lie. For example, an initial examination might show them to be as follows:

Strengths	Weaknesses
Skilled and knowledgeable staff	High production costs
Solid UK experience	Poor quality control
Established customer base	Dependent on seasonal business
Financially sound	No experience of international trade

It is in the company's best interests to be honest in the evaluation of the strengths and weaknesses as they will be instrumental in how the other half of the SWOT analysis, the opportunities and threats faced by the company, will be dealt with. These tend to be the external factors that the company has little or no control over, for example consumer spending power, new production methods and technology, or the availability of European or government development grants. Generally, opportunities can be maximised by building on the company's strengths, whilst perceived threats will be exacerbated by its weaknesses.

Activity: Compile a comprehensive list of all the factors that companies should review when evaluating their strengths and weaknesses, explaining why each is a strength or a weakness.

The opportunities and threats can be reviewed using a third diagnostic method: PESTLE, which represents the political, economic, social, technological, legal and environmental factors that can influence the business plan. Sudden technological advances, which the company is unprepared for, could result in a loss of business and the company therefore needs to be aware of how it would react in these circumstances.

By the same token, if the company depends on a particular demographic structure, moving into a new market with a different structure is likely to require a substantial review of the marketing mix.

In some cases it is possible for external factors to be both an opportunity and a potential threat. For example, new environmental legislation may be seen as a threat due to stringent requirements for the company to install costly equipment to reduce emissions and pollution levels. Even though this may lead to increases in the cost of the goods to the customer, it could also be turned into an opportunity if the company chooses to promote itself as an environmentally conscious organisation committed to reducing harmful emissions. This slight change in promotional tactic may prove popular with consumers that are prepared to pay slightly more for environmentally friendly goods.

Note: It is useful to apply the SWOT analysis to target market selection. Whilst the strengths and weaknesses may identify competitive advantage and demonstrate synergy with the requirements of a target export market, the opportunities and threats can also be used to discount inappropriate markets. For instance, a UK media company specialising in post-production for the film industry may see itself as a market-leading expert in the UK (strength) but with an over-reliance on the UK market (weakness). The company may evaluate opportunities to enter into co-production agreements with partners in India, where the sheer size of the film industry is a clear opportunity to engage successfully with local filmmakers. By the same token, the company may discount the possibility of securing co-production work in Malaysia where the film industry is smaller and also subject to rigorous censorship laws that UK companies find hard to work with. Thus the company's review of its own strengths, weaknesses, opportunities and threats may be instrumental in identifying initial target markets, subject to further research and investigation.

The marketing plan

Once the issues described in this chapter have been addressed and a full analysis of the company's current position, attitudes and the risks likely to be encountered in implementing a new strategy has been conducted, a detailed marketing plan can be developed. This will normally cover six separate sections:

1. Company aims and objectives. Ideally the marketing plan should clearly demonstrate how it fits in with the company's overall business strategy and what it aims to achieve in relation to business development and growth. The

objectives should be concise summaries of aims such as 'within 12 months the company will have increased its customer base in Malaysia by 45%' or 'by February the company will have developed a new, high-quality product designed to meet the needs of the Spanish market'.

2. Marketing evaluation. This aspect of the marketing plan shows the research undertaken by the company on competition, markets and support (see Figure 3.1), and will list the main findings made by the research.

3. Marketing aims and objectives. Using the SMART tool described above, the company can list its main marketing objectives and can demonstrate that the decisions taken were based on sound research.

4. Marketing strategy. The core of the marketing plan is the strategy itself as it shows how the marketing mix will be adapted and implemented to meet the needs of the company and its business aims and objectives.

5. Action required. Quite simply, this section of the marketing plan lists the steps the company needs to take to fulfil the requirements of each aspect of the marketing plan. It should also show how the marketing plan will be monitored and its success evaluated.

6. Budget. No marketing proposal is complete without all the cost implications being highlighted and a budget for the exercise being approved by the company. This should ideally also take into account the cost in terms of manpower and other resources required in implementing and delivering the marketing plan.

The marketing plan should be seen as a continuous process, rather than a one-off exercise. Ongoing evaluation and monitoring of the marketing plan is essential in assisting the company to identify the strategy's strengths and weaknesses, enabling changes to be made to the marketing mix if necessary. Once the marketing plan has been developed in the framework of the overall business plan, the company is ready to take the next steps in researching new markets and preparing entry strategies for them.

Conclusions

This chapter has given the reader an overview of the basic disciplines of the marketing and business planning functions. It has shown how the marketing mix must be constantly reviewed and modified if the company's marketing strategy is to be effective, and it has shown how promotion through a variety of media is an important part of the planning process. The chapter has also demonstrated how tools such as SMART, SWOT and PESTLE can be used to evaluate the company's current position and provide a basis for recommendations for future action.

The reader should now be in position to understand and implement the principles of the marketing process in overseas markets as well as domestically.

Sources of information

Chartered Institute of Marketing – www.cim.co.uk
Communications, Advertising and Marketing Foundation –
  www.camfoundation.com
Marketing Council – www.marketingcouncil.org
Regional International Trade Website (Yorkshire and the Humber) –
  www.tradeportalyh.co.uk
Trade Partners UK (UK government advice and support for exporters) –
  www.tradepartners.gov.uk

Further reading

Brassington F and Pettitt S, *Principles of Marketing* (2nd ed) (Prentice Hall, 2000).
Cartwright R I, *Mastering Marketing Management* (Palgrave Macmillan, 2002).
Doole I and Lowe R, *International Marketing Strategy* (2nd ed), (International Thomson Business Press, 1999).
Eyre E C and Pettinger R, *Mastering Basic Management* (3rd ed) (Macmillan, 1999).
Groves L W J, *Principle of International Marketing Research* (Blackwell, 1994).
Jain S C, *Marketing Planning and Strategy* (4th ed) (South Western, 1993).
Kottler P et al., *Principles of Marketing* (3rd ed) (Prentice Hall, 2001).
McCarthy E J and Perreault Jr W D, *Basic Marketing* (11th ed) (Irwin, 1993).

QUESTIONS FOR CONSIDERATION

1 How is market research different from marketing research?
2 How does market segmentation affect the marketing mix?
3 Summarise the main promotional tools available to exporters and identify the advantages and limitations of each.
4 Explain how SMART, SWOT, PESTLE and the 'four Ps' relate to each other in the preparation of a business plan.
5 List the opportunities and threats that a technology company might face in the current economic climate.

Case study: Jordan Clamps Ltd

Background

Jordan Clamps Ltd manufactures a range of safety clamps with application in several industries. To date, the company's products have found most success in the construction industry, which is the market that they were originally designed for. Falls from scaffolding account for more than half of all fatal accidents in the construction industry and the company recognised the need for a safe anchor point above head height to provide a fail-safe security point for workers as soon as they leave ground level. The safety clamp is currently sold to scaffolding erectors and to distributors of health and safety equipment in the UK, although the company has also had success in selling to the major players in the offshore oil and gas sector. This case study examines Jordan Clamps' current marketing strategy, the thinking behind the decision to sell overseas and the company's preliminary thoughts on which export market to target first.

The decision to export

Jordan Clamps' innovative product quickly found favour with the UK Health and Safety Executive and the Construction Industries Training Board. UK and worldwide patents were applied for and granted and the company felt that it had the pedigree and reputation to begin looking at overseas markets. The decision to start exporting was based on the realisation that the products were becoming sufficiently well known in the UK so that it was only a matter of time before overseas companies recognised the potential and tried to get in on the act. Exporting was therefore seen both as an opportunity to generate profits from additional sales as well as preserving competitive advantage.

Market selection

One of the main advantages that Jordan Clamps felt they had for inter-national trade was the fact that their products could be used on all standard scaffolding structures, which construction companies in the majority of the world's developed countries were already using.

As a first export market, the company decided to investigate the potential of the construction industry in the Republic of Ireland. The company knew that there was a high volume of current and planned construction projects in Ireland and that the Irish housing and commercial building industry uses traditional construction methods that are very similar to those used in the UK. A newspaper report commented on the projected growth in the Irish construction industry and Jordan Clamps felt that this fact alone justified the selection of Ireland as a prime market for further research and consideration. This was supported by contacts in the industry that were able to pass on useful information on their experience in the market, as well as the added advantage of Ireland being a 'local', English-speaking market known to favour UK products and services.

Subsequent market research segmented the market into four main submarkets covering housing, commercial construction, civil works and industrial construction, and it quickly became evident that each individual segment offered substantial potential in itself. The research also identified the major construction companies, scaffolding companies and suppliers of health and safety equipment, which later would form the basis of the company's market entry strategy.

The marketing mix

Jordan Clamps has a policy of constantly reviewing all elements of the marketing mix in order to ensure that each is working to the best advantage of the company. At the time the decision to export was taken, the company's marketing mix and SWOT analysis looked as follows:

Marketing mix

Product
- Marketed as an innovative, quality product that saves lives
- Well researched and designed
- Quality assured and tested
- Exceeds current safety guidelines (therefore the safest product on the market)
- No other comparable product on the market
- High production capacity with the potential to subcontract to other manufacturers should demand exceed current capacity

Price
- Relatively low production cost per unit
- Relatively low overheads
- Price per unit is low compared to other fall arrest equipment on the market, but no comparable competing products to compare price with
- Excellent value for money – weigh up the cost of compensation against the low unit cost
- Current pricing offers room for discounts and credit terms
- Competing on quality and reliability of the product

Promotion
- Advertising in trade press
- Word of mouth
- Regular PR opportunities in local, national and trade press
- Participation in key exhibition
- Targeted mailings to potential buyers
- Promotional videos/CDs and demonstrations
- Direct sales

Place
- Targeting health and safety personnel in construction companies
- Also specifiers that can require subcontractors to utilise the product
- Sold direct rather than through distributors
- A 'must have' item for socially aware businesses committed to the well-being of their employees

SWOT analysis

Strengths
- Unique product
- Quality assured and patented

Weaknesses
- Young company with no international experience

- Simple, cost-effective device that saves lives
- HSE/CITB recognition

- Relatively weak financial position (which will improve as sales volume increases)

Opportunities
- Imminent rapid growth in UK due to promotional strategy and HSE/CITB support
- Further growth possible from overseas markets

Threats
- Growth of competition once reputation of product grows
- Reluctance of industry to adopt the product as not legally obliged to

The company's objective review of its current activities concluded that it was in a strong position to begin promoting itself internationally, particularly in terms of the product quality and production capacity. International trade would be a means of staying ahead of the competition, whilst increased sales would also demonstrate to domestic and international legislators, health and safety bodies and the like that the clamp has genuine value and should be an industry standard application.

Exhibitions

Jordan Clamps considered exhibiting at two major trade fairs in the UK during 2002. The first was a leading exhibition for the health and safety industry, which in previous years had attracted over 17 000 buyers of health and safety products from all over the world. The second exhibition was the UK's leading construction industry event, which also attracted thousands of international decision-makers. Both fairs were of interest to the company, but the marketing budget only had room for participation at one exhibition.

A full comparison of the two events, their visitor and exhibitor profiles and the promotional exposure that each could generate was undertaken. Ultimately, the decision was taken to exhibit at the health and safety exhibition. Jordan Clamps felt that this fair was more likely to attract greater numbers of buyers from their target sectors than the construction event, which included several sub-shows in unrelated sectors such as windows, bathrooms and lighting.

Having identified the most appropriate exhibition, the company then invested time and effort into designing an eye-catching stand and product literature, inviting potential clients (including representatives from the Irish market) to visit the stand, preparing press releases and so on.

As a direct result of the promotional work carried out, Jordan Clamps welcomed a steady stream of visitors to their stand, leading to numerous requests for quotations. The exhibition was also successful from the point of view of attracting interest from Irish buyers, two of who expressed interest in representing the company in Ireland.

Summary

This case study demonstrates that even a young company with limited international experience can begin to develop trade overseas. In the case of Jordan Clamps, the first steps taken to achieve sales in Ireland formed part of a measured approach that was fully supported by the company's own awareness of its strengths and weaknesses and how it was currently achieving success in the domestic market. Following extensive market research, the marketing plan implemented in the UK subsequently became a valuable template for the marketing plan adopted successfully for the Irish market.

■ ☑ **4** Market research

Introduction

This chapter will demonstrate the importance of market research in the preparation of an international marketing plan. It will explore reasons why research is necessary, and will identify key issues that must be addressed in order to reduce international trade risks. By the end of the chapter, the reader will be able to manage market research activity, assess markets using different research methods, collect data efficiently and analyse the data effectively.

Market research

It is not unusual for companies involved with international trade to choose their target markets through instinct or because they know that a competitor is also active in those markets. However, no matter how experienced a company is in international trade, market research is always necessary if the exporter is to dictate where and when to trade. The successful exporter cannot rely on instinct alone and should always carry out a full market assessment prior to market entry in order to evaluate opportunities overseas. This will not only assist in identifying the most appropriate entry strategy, but will also ensure that unattractive markets are avoided, and will help the exporter understand the key requirements for successful trade in the market. If it is done effectively, market research will determine the size and potential of the target market, barriers to entry (for example tariff or non-tariff barriers), distribution issues and the most appropriate means of approaching the market.

No internationally active company can afford to ignore market research. To do so risks exposure to financial, legal and commercial difficulties that can be avoided by taking the time to investigate the target market more thoroughly. Market research is an essential part of the export marketing process as it gathers together all the information a company will require to draw up a comprehensive strategy. It will highlight both the risks and the benefits of trading with the target market, should identify potential clients and competitors, and will give the exporting company an indication of how to overcome many of the obstacles to successful market entry.

Once the decision to export has been taken, and the potential target market identified there are a number of essential questions and considerations that need to be addressed and incorporated into the market research parameters.

Market suitability

One of the most important questions the company must ask is whether or not the chosen target market is appropriate for its products or services. In some cases, the answer will be obvious: there is not likely to be a large market for heavy woollen clothing in tropical areas or for snowmobiles in Egypt. Equally, it may be apparent that the country's infrastructure is not sufficiently developed to support the company's product. There would seem to be little point in trying to export niche products for use on aircraft to a market where the aerospace industry is under-developed or computer software to regions with limited access to information technology. However, in these circumstances, there may be an opportunity for management consultants to sell their expertise to assist in the development of the infrastructure.

The exporter is generally advised to seek markets that are similar to existing domestic or international markets as this reduces the likelihood of needing to modify products to suit the market. Demand for the company's product can then be ascertained through careful analysis of sales patterns in the target market. This analysis should take into account consumer and industry buying behaviour (how, where, when and why is the product bought, and so on?), as well as seeking to identify any regional and national patterns which may influence the approach to the market.

There are also several deeper issues that need to be resolved: does the target market readily import foreign goods, or are there restrictions in place to hinder foreign companies trading in the market? How well developed is the country's international trade activity? Fortunately, much of the background information required to answer these questions is readily available, especially through the Internet, although common sense also plays its part. For example, a simple analysis of how much a country imports and exports in comparison to its gross national product (a general indication of the state of the country's economy) can yield numerous conclusions:

- A high level of imports suggests that the target market is open to foreign suppliers and consequently will have a well-developed system able to cope with the demands of international trade. However, a high level of imports may also mean that there is more foreign competition and the company could find it harder to make inroads into the market as a result.
- A low level of imports suggests that the target market is able to meet its own requirements and has little need to source products from overseas. There may also be government restrictions or higher import duties in place to deter foreign suppliers.

Whatever the outcome of these initial enquiries, the exporter needs to believe that the market is right for the product as well as the product being right for the market before taking any further action.

Product fit

Having used the techniques demonstrated in Chapter 3 to understand how the marketing mix is composed and influences the company's behaviour, not to mention the size, structure, segmentation and suitability of the target market, the question of whether or not the company's product or service is appropriate for the market should always be asked. It cannot be assumed that a product will do well in other export markets simply because it sells well in the UK, France and Spain. Only very rarely will products be sold in several markets without any form of modification. Climatic conditions such as temperature or humidity, cultural idiosyncrasies, geographic location and the state of the local infrastructure can all affect the success of a product in the market, as well as potentially affecting the delivery of services.

Equally, the exporter may find that products require modification to suit a different power supply, to meet market-specific quality standards or simply to appeal more closely to customers' tastes. For example, many chocolate bars and drinks, although global brands, vary in taste from market to market. Religion can also affect product fit: pork products and derivatives will not succeed in Muslim countries, nor will bovine products (including bone china and hides) in Hindu cultures, where the cow is sacred. Another factor affecting a product's success if not taken into consideration is colour. In some cultures, white is the colour of mourning, and in others a particular shade of green has religious connotations. It is therefore easy to offend unintentionally through lack of proper appreciation of the market and its culture.

In each case there could well be a solution to the problem, such as different packaging, content, marketing or distribution methods, for example. The more information that can be collected to support these questions, the more likely it is that the company will find new ways of approaching the market rather than simply giving up. Some factors influencing product fit are listed in Figure 4.1.

If it can be ascertained that the target market is already using products similar to those that the company aims to export, then there is a good chance that the market will be receptive to the introduction of new competition. It is then a question of identifying how much the product needs to be modified in order to meet the needs of the customers. Further research can be carried out once the initial information gathering has been completed to assist in the development and modification of the product.

Climate	Official regulations	Standards
Location	Colour	Quality
Infrastructure	Religion	Health and safety
Cultural issues	Power supply	Size/Weight
Packaging	Taste	Raw material content

Figure 4.1 Examples of factors influencing product/market fit.

If initial research shows that there are no comparable products available in the market, this does not necessarily mean that there is no market for the product – it may be that nobody has thought of introducing that particular product and that there is a sizeable opportunity for the company to exploit. It may equally mean that there is no demand for the product. Again, further research will be needed to evaluate the potential more fully.

Using economic indicators

There are a number of economic indicators that can help to build an accurate picture of the target market's economy. Gross domestic product (GDP) and gross national product (GNP) are perhaps the most widely used expressions of an economy's growth or decline, and both can serve the researcher's needs. GDP reflects the average income of a country's citizens, and is the total value of completed goods and services produced in the country in a year. This is worked out as total consumer, investment and government spending plus value of exports *less* value of imports. However, GDP may not be an entirely accurate reflection of the country's wealth as the official population estimates may be inaccurate. Equally, it may take into account the income of its citizens living overseas, thereby distorting the domestic statistics.

GNP is a reflection of the country's total economic activity. It uses the same formula as GDP but includes income derived as a result of the country's investments overseas *less* income earned domestically which is due to foreign companies and countries investing in the market. It is important to bear in mind that GNP growth should always be compared with total GNP. A country with a total GNP of £4000 billion and 2.5 per cent growth (£100 billion growth) is more attractive than a market with 9 per cent growth on a total of £200 billion (£18 billion growth). Up-to-date figures for inflation, income distribution, unemployment, interest rates, manufacturing production and investment in the economy are also useful indicators of how a country is performing and can easily be obtained from a number of sources.

As well as taking into account the target market's general economic position the company must also understand the country's financial position. Currency fluctuations and exchange rate restrictions impact on international trade and a suitable pricing strategy may have to be developed (see Chapter 8). Research into the financial reliability of the target market should highlight whether or not the country has a reputation for non-payment of debts – clearly of concern to any organisation considering selling into the market.

Using the information in Table 4.1, what conclusions can be drawn about these four markets from the exporter's perspective?

Table 4.1 Examples of economic information

	Brazil	Germany	Malaysia	S. Africa
Population (2000)	172 860 370	82 797 408	21 793 293	43 421 021
0–14 yrs old	29%	16%	35%	32.46%
15–64 yrs old	66%	68%	61%	62.76%
65 + yrs old	5%	16%	4%	4.78%
GDP per capita ('99)	$6 150	$22 700	$10 700	$6 900
GDP growth	0.8%	1.5%	5%	0.6%
Inflation (1999)	5%	0.8%	2.8%	5.5%
Unemployment ('99)	7.5%	10.5%	3%	30%
Imports ($billion,'99)	$48.7	$587	$61.5	$26
Exports ($billion, '99)	$46.9	$610	$83.5	$28

Source: *CIA World Fact Book 2000* (www.odci.gov/cia/publications/factbook).

Social questions

To ensure that the product will be well received in the chosen market, research will be required to identify certain demographic trends. Population size is a good indicator of the number of potential consumers, but closer evaluation of the age distribution, employment rates, birth and death rates, income levels and proportion of the population living in rural or urban areas will help to segment the market further. Ultimately, this activity will serve to identify opportunities (or the lack of them) and will demonstrate market potential. For example, Mexico has a predominantly young population, which would suggest that suppliers of care equipment to the elderly currently have a limited market. Germany, on the other hand, has 16 per cent of its population over the age of 65, which paints a different picture for the same supplier.

The exporter must also take into account the language and social makeup of the target country, as both can affect the way companies in the market trade domestically and internationally. Further consideration will be given to cultural issues in Chapter 5. It is important to remember that, even when research yields no positive information and the company decides not to target that particular market as a result, the research can be seen as a success: at the very least it has prevented the company from investing heavily in a venture that will not succeed.

Political and legal considerations

The target market's political situation and legal requirements can also have a bearing on trade. Internationally active companies come to appreciate that, far from being esoteric and the preserve of politicians and lawyers, these factors shape the trading position and attitudes of every nation. Politics and law may not be seen as the most dynamic of subjects, but they certainly have much influence on the course of international trade between nations, and exporters are advised to obtain as much information on the country's current trading position and its political and legal background as possible. An obvious example is that unstable governments, or countries experiencing civil unrest, are likely to increase trade risks, whilst stable governments are more conducive to attracting both foreign investment and imported goods.

Note: Even war-torn countries or those experiencing other forms of unrest may be potential export markets for companies able to fulfil the needs of organisations in the country in question – for example, companies supplying goods to the humanitarian aid agencies, peace-keeping forces and so on. However, exporting goods to such markets, even as a second or third tier supplier, is likely to be closely controlled and permission to supply the markets may have to be sought (see Chapter 5, macro factors).

When looking at the political background, the exporter must be aware of the target market's relationships with other countries. This is particularly true of countries that have drawn up preferential trade agreements to stimulate and encourage bilateral trade. For example, free trade exists between the European Union's 15 member states since the Single European Act (1986) effectively abolished all barriers to trade within what was then called the European Community. This agreement extends to Iceland and Norway (the European Economic Area) and permits free movement of goods, people, capital and services across the EU, with little paperwork and no Customs controls to hinder trade. The EU offers a vast number of opportunities for practically every company. The harmonisation of technical standards across the EU allows companies in every member state to compete on an equal footing and there are a wide range of sources of expertise and advice to assist companies of all sizes to access opportunities within the EU.

Preferential trade agreements are also in place between the EU and a number of other independent countries across the world as a legacy of empire building and colonial activity. Many former colonies and dependencies have therefore been accorded the right to trade on a preferential basis with the EU. Generalised System of Preferences (GSP) agreements exist between Europe and the following countries:

- Iceland, Liechtenstein, Norway, Switzerland (EFTA)
- Bulgaria, Czech Republic, Hungary, Poland, Slovakia (Eastern Europe)
- Estonia, Latvia, Lithuania (Baltic States)
- The Faeroe Islands
- Bosnia-Herzegovina, Croatia, Former Yugoslav Republic of Macedonia, Slovenia
- Andorra
- Malta
- Cyprus
- Israel
- West Bank and Gaza Strip
- Egypt, Jordan, Lebanon, Syria (The Mashraq)

Current members	Accession countries
Austria	Bulgaria
Belgium	Cyprus
Denmark	Czech Republic
Finland	Estonia
France	Hungary
Germany	Latvia
Greece	Lithuania
Ireland	Malta
Italy	Poland
Luxembourg	Romania
Portugal	Slovakia
Spain	Slovenia
Sweden	Turkey
The Netherlands	
United Kingdom	

Figure 4.2 The current European Union and its planned expansion.

- Algeria, Morocco, Tunisia (The Maghreb)
- South Africa
- Mexico
- Ceuta and Melilla

The EU is currently preparing for further expansion as 13 countries are in various stages of application for full membership of the Union (see Figure 4.2). The majority of these countries are in Central and Eastern Europe (Bulgaria, Czech Republic, Estonia, Hungary, Latvia, Lithuania, Poland, Romania, Slovak Republic and Slovenia), with Turkey, Malta and Cyprus also in the 'accession' process. Some markets, such as Poland, may well become full members of the EU as early as 2004. Turkey is already a part of the EU Customs Union, but requires different export documentation to other EU markets (see Chapter 10).

This is the largest expansion that the European Union has undergone and it will lead to the creation of the world's largest free trade area, permitting free trade between 28 member states and preferential trade with countless countries world-wide.

Looking beyond Europe, the exporter should be aware of other free trade agreements, which will affect trading conditions in the target market. The USA, Canada and Mexico, for example, are members of the North American Free Trade Agreement (NAFTA), which will abolish all remaining trade tariffs between the member states by 2009. In 2000, Mexico also entered into a free trade agreement with Europe. Brazil, Argentina, Paraguay and Uruguay form the Mercosur common market, with Chile and Bolivia as associate members. In the Far East, 10 countries form the Association of South East Asian Nations (ASEAN), through which they co-operate politically, socially and economically.

Activity: Research and summarise the main provisions of the free trade agreement signed between Mexico and the EU in 2000.

In each case, the agreements set out preferential trading terms between the partner countries, and this may be to the detriment of companies trying to trade with the markets from outside the agreements.

The political situation of the target market will consequently bring about legal restrictions that must be complied with if trade with the market is to be successful. For example, tariffs on exports and imports are common, but vary from country to country (further information on tariffs can be found in Chapter 10). Many countries also demand that a minimum percentage of the product imported be manufactured or sourced locally. By stipulating that the exporter includes local components, the target market's government can ensure that its own economy benefits to a degree from importing foreign products. In some cases, legal requirements will also specify what packaging and labelling must be used, or what modifications must be made to the product. The EU in particular has a reputation for its imposition of regulations designed to protect the interests of its member states, not least in requiring that the EC symbol (the European Quality Standard) appears on goods intended for consumption in the market.

Where several demands of this nature are made of exporters before they can successfully trade with the market, the decision must be made as to whether it makes more sense financially to meet the target market's requirements or to look for other export markets. Companies cannot dictate the course of politics and law at an international level but they do need to be able to recognise their nature and to be prepared to tailor their export strategies accordingly.

Non-tariff barriers

Non-tariff barriers are similar to tariff barriers in that they are regulations affecting the import and export of goods. They are, however, more administrative in structure and are often imposed by governments seeking to protect the domestic market. The main types of non-tariff barrier are shown below and should be taken into account in the development of the export marketing plan. It is important to bear in mind that this sort of activity is often subtle in nature and may not be immediately recognised as the imposition of non-tariff barriers.

- Import quotas – restrictions on the maximum volume of a product that can be imported. Quotas can also affect price.
- National standards – countries may specify use of a particular national standard that is unfamiliar to exporters, placing them at a disadvantage.
- Voluntary export restraints – these are usually targeted at a specific country and prevent companies from exporting certain products to that market.
- Export subsidies – these raise the product's domestic price whilst higher tariffs lower imports and demand. Exports and production increase to the detriment of imports.

- Content-specific requirements of the importing market for a certain percentage of the product to include locally manufactured content.
- Dumping – when products or commodities are sold to foreign buyers cheaper than they are sold to buyers domestically. Dumping is not appreciated by the foreign country as cheap imports damage local productivity.
- Commodity agreements – control of commodities through international agreements restricts trade. Multilateral contracts can fix prices thereby creating an artificial trading environment for that product.

Identifying competition

The last major issue to be included in the market research brief is the identification of competition in the target market. This serves two useful purposes. Firstly, the exporter may expect to see the company's main competitors or market leaders already active in the target market – noting their presence there may be reassuring (unless the competition have made errors of judgement), whilst questions as to the suitability of the market may be raised by their absence.

Secondly, being able to identify all the competitors in a particular market will potentially generate new streams of information. A full analysis should yield information on how and where the competitors are trading and, through careful research, the competitors' trading terms, market share and promotional policies can be identified. Entry strategies and distribution patterns may be evident, and the research should also seek to identify the level of after-sales service offered by the competition. Examples of added value services could include advice on packaging, calibration, installation and maintenance, or may include complaint procedures, warranties or health and safety advice. The company may wish to include upgrades as part of the service, or a 24-hour help-line for emergency breakdowns. Being able to offer more added value through service and customer care in this way may be the competitive advantage the company needs to be successful in the market.

Even though there may be a high level of competition in the market, there could still be room for a company that provides a high quality product and has a unique competitive advantage. Comprehensive market research will identify these opportunities and will assist management to make the decision whether or not to trade with the target market.

Summary of key market research aims

- To identify potential target markets and their trends.
- To establish the level of demand for the product or service to be exported.
- To determine the level of modification to the product or service required.
- To seek markets that will be receptive to the product/service.
- To ensure that all information on tariffs and barriers to entry is collected.

- To be aware of any political or legal issues influencing trade.
- To collect information on competition in the market.

Note: Market research may well reveal that the country being targeted offers limited or no potential for the exporter. This does not mean that the market research has been a waste of time as, at the least, the exercise has prevented the company committing valuable time and resources to pursuing a market that will not deliver the return sought.

Data collection

Having identified the issues that the exporter needs to understand before approaching a market, consideration must be given to the physical collection of the information required before the export strategy can be fully developed.

Eager as many researchers are to collect information from a variety of sources, the first stage of any market research exercise should be a review of the knowledge, experience and information already held by the company. Details of market share, production costs, customers and historical sales activity can often form a basis for initial judgements and can be used as a starting point for further research. It is certainly useful to have a clear understanding of what the company may or may not have achieved in other overseas markets. Records of difficulties previously faced by the company can be analysed for recurrent problems and the solutions that were implemented. This information can then be used as a reference guide to help overcome obstacles identified in subsequent research.

The right person for the job

The choice of an appropriate person or team to carry out the research must be made carefully. The correct choice of researcher matches skills against research requirements and may be limited by the company's own in-house resources. Whilst larger companies may be able to put together small research teams, absorbing the costs of the research project into the larger organisation, smaller companies are unlikely to be able to do so. Allocating a full-time resource for market research has cost implications in terms of staff downtime and overall productivity of the company. In these situations, the market research brief tends to be handed to the sales or marketing department where it becomes a part-time activity. The timescale for completion of the research may increase, and the costs spread over a longer period of time, although the wealth of information available through the Internet has admittedly made the research process faster and more accessible.

The main advantage of using an internal resource to carry out the market research, regardless of how much time they can devote to the project, is that existing employees are already familiar with the company, its products and activities. Such researchers are more likely to understand what the company hopes to gain from the research, and their personal development as the project is undertaken will also add to the company's in-house capabilities. However, objectivity and an unbiased approach to the research must be ensured. This may not always be possible with in-house staff as internal politics and departmental agendas may influence the course of the research. If the company takes the decision not to use in-house staff, the remaining choice is to appoint an external company. There are a number of organisations that carry out market research, from Embassies in the target market, Chambers of Commerce and trade associations to specialist research agencies, and all offer similar core advantages.

External organisations are objective and retain an impartial view of the research brief. They have substantial experience of market research and can be recruited for a specified period of time. Where external researchers do fall short is in their knowledge and experience of the client company, its products and history. To redress this lack of knowledge, the company is advised to ensure that it appoints a member of staff to liaise with the market research agency and to manage or monitor the progress being made on the project. By doing so, the company can ensure that the research agency has access to internal information as required.

The market research ladder

Figure 4.3 shows a suggested approach to data collection through a systematic analysis of the information sources available to researchers, starting with in-house records and working up to personal contact with clients, competitors and potential agents.

Figure 4.3 The market research ladder.

Secondary data (sources, advantages and limitations)

Secondary data can be classed as material that is quite readily available in the form of statistics and information previously collated by other organisations (see Figure 4.4). These are generally accessible through libraries, the Internet, trade associations and from previously published market research reports which may also meet some of the company's needs.

The main advantage of this type of data collection is that the information already exists in an accessible format, saving the researcher time and effort. Secondary information, also called desk research, is a useful starting point for the main research project, but it does have its limitations. The very fact that this information is so readily available means that it has been in existence for some time. It is historical, and was collected to meet another organisation's needs. As a result, the researchers are using second-hand information and must ensure that the data gained still meets their needs without prejudicing objectivity and reliability.

Secondary data may not even be accurate or complete. The researcher has little choice but to trust the skills and capabilities of the people who originally collated the information, but should also try to verify the data's accuracy using other sources. For instance, what conclusions can be reached from the shown in Table 4.2 data gained through desk research? What might the advantages and limitations be?

• Small Business Service	• Academic libraries	• British embassies overseas
• Trade Partners UK	• Customs & Excise	• Banks
• Trade associations	• HM Treasury	• Online databases
• Business research organisations (for example Dun & Bradstreet)	• Chambers of Commerce	• British Standards Institute

Figure 4.4   Examples of secondary data sources (see also the list of other sources of market research information at the end of this chapter).

Table 4.2   British Footwear Market 1997–99

	pairs (million)			£m		
	1997	1998	1999	1997	1998	1999
Manufacturers' sales	88.9	82.8	62.9	1233	1067.5	1015.4
Exports	38.9	37.0	38.4	563	517.1	506.8
Imports	247.7	260.03	290.3	1768	1754.8	1923.4
Domestic supplies	297.8	305.8	314.7	2438	2305.3	2432.2
Import penetration	83%	85%	92%	72%	76.1%	79%

Source: British Footwear Association.

Primary data (sources, advantages and limitations)

Primary data can be classed as information or materials obtained solely for the purposes of the company's current market research project. It provides a greater depth of information and is often more qualitative in nature as it generally requires a third party's opinion on particular issues such as consumer attitudes, buyer behaviour and market values.

Primary data is collected during the latter stages of the market research project and serves to build on the information gained through secondary data collection. It is, however, a more expensive form of research as the information will generally be gained through interviews and questionnaires, often in the target market. Most of the sources of information listed under secondary data collection can be used for primary information, as can clients, suppliers and other existing contacts who may have experience of the market.

Research methods for primary data collection range in cost, time and limitations.

- Telephone interviews are relatively inexpensive, but take the shortest time to complete, risking incomplete answers and inadequate information.
- Mailshots are also inexpensive, but take longer and generally yield a poor response. They do not permit interviewers to seek further information.
- Personal interviews are the most costly, requiring a substantial investment in travel and time, but are the most effective in terms of the quantity and quality of data gained.

Test marketing or observation studies can also be used to collect primary data. Again, this activity is costly, but it can yield high quantities of useful information. To undertake a test marketing exercise, the company develops a sample of the product to be launched in the target market and distributes it to a small, pre-identified group of people who are asked to record their opinions of the product. The results are then collated and assumptions made about the market's likely reaction to the product on the strength of this representative group of consumers.

The researcher should also consider regular visits to the market as a means of undertaking research. Trade fairs, exhibitions and conferences or seminars can often provide competitor information, as well as information on product modification requirements and market forces.

Analysing the data

The most challenging part of the market research exercise is the analysis of the data collected and generating meaningful information from reams of statistics. This can only really be achieved with time, patience and an eye for spotting trends and patterns. Data analysis can be broken down into three main stages.

- Firstly, the accuracy and reliability of the data must be assessed, bearing in mind the limitations outlined above. The researcher should also take care to ensure that all the data collected will be converted into the same units of measurement to avoid confusion.

- Secondly, the data should be classified by information type and source. For example, research into the Australian market for sugar machinery might encompass information gleaned from trade journals, interview notes from meetings with potential clients at a relevant exhibition and the results of trials held at sugar refineries in the market.
- Finally, forecasts, trends and conclusions can be drawn from the information collected. Care must be taken to ensure that the conclusions can be justified and supported, and are based on accurately interpreted statistics.

Once these three stages have been completed and reviewed for accuracy, the information and conclusions can go forward for inclusion in the final market research report.

Other considerations

As well as the sources of information and research methods to be used, the researcher should be aware of other internal issues that need to be taken into consideration when compiling the report.

The cost of the market research will be offset as an opportunity cost against the potential benefits of trading with the target market. As described above, there is a cost implication in terms of staff time, but the company should also be aware of any peripheral costs likely to be incurred. For example, a budget will need to be set for the purchase of research information (databases, mailing lists, statistical reports, etc.), travel and specialist advice. It is therefore prudent to identify all the potential costs prior to commencing the research.

The researcher also needs to be aware of the level of sales, marketing and administrative support that the company can direct towards international development activity. Good communication between departments is essential if the export strategy is to be implemented successfully – as later chapters will show, exporting companies must demonstrate co-operation between departments if costly mistakes are to be avoided. Above all, the company must ensure that sufficient resources are in place to act on the report's findings. A report that recommends an immediate and aggressive sales strategy to maximise current opportunities in the target market will be meaningless if the company does not have the resources to act on the recommendations. Where the company is unable to meet the resource requirements for effective market entry, the report should highlight a realistic level of support that would be needed. It would also be useful to indicate a strategy that the company could employ as a means of entering the market with limited resources.

Compiling the report

The final report condenses weeks, even months, of research into a single, manageable document which management can then use to make informed decisions about the target market. As such, the report needs to be accurate, clear and concisely written. A comprehensive market research report should include the following entries:

1. Title page, including details of the person/organisation that undertook the research, as well as the date the report was completed.
2. Contents, showing headings of all sections of the report, including appendices.
3. Introduction explaining why the report was commissioned.
4. Aims and objectives of the report.
5. Rationale, explaining how the research was undertaken and why those research methods were used.
6. Executive summary of the report – ideally a one-page synopsis of the key findings.
7. Key findings. This section should include statistical, graphical and written analysis of the research undertaken and will form the main body of the report. It should make reference to all the market research issues covered by this chapter.
8. Conclusions drawn from the research.
9. Recommendations for action.
10. Appendices.
11. Copies of questionnaires and interview notes as appropriate.

If the research has been done professionally, the completed report will be instrumental in the development of the company's export strategy for the target market, and it will have laid the foundations for successful market entry. The following chapters will examine individual components of the international strategy and how their effective implementation depends on the information gained through market research.

Conclusions

This chapter has covered the main issues to consider when entering a new export market, and has detailed market research questions that must be addressed. The reader will now have a sound understanding of how market suitability and product fit can be influenced by a number of factors, such as political or legal forces, and will be able to identify potential barriers to entry and how to overcome them. The reader will also have an understanding of data collection procedures and the importance of compiling an effective, meaningful market research report.

Sources of information

A representative selection of the vast number of sources of advice and information available.

Assistance with sourcing goods internationally – www.thesourcinggroup.com
Association of British Market Research Companies, Templeton Lodge, 114 High
  Street, Hampton Hill, Middlesex, TW12 1NT

Brazilian Embassy in the UK – www.brazil.org.uk
British Chambers of Commerce Support for Export Marketing Research –
   www.britishchambers.org.uk/exportzone/emrs
British Footwear Association – www.britfoot.com
CIA World Factbook – www.odci.gov/cia/publications/factbook
Croner international trade advice – www.tradeinternational-centre.net
Dun & Bradstreet market research and information – www.dnb.com
Economist Information Unit – www.eiu.com
European Union homepage – www.europa.eu.int
German Bundesbank homepage – www.bundesbank.de
International tenders service – www.securetenders.com
International trade leads – www.worldbid.com
OECD directory of statistical sources – www.oecd.org/std/others1.htm
Online directory of embassies – www.embassyworld.com
Regional International Trade website (Yorkshire and the Humber) –
   www.tradeportalyh.co.uk
Technical Help for Exporters (advice on standards and legal requirements) –
   www.bsi-global.com
Trade Partners UK (UK government advice and support for exporters) –
   www.tradepartners.gov.uk
USA Office of Trade and Economic Analysis – www.ita.doc.gov/td/industry/otea
Online directory of international chambers of commerce –
   www.worldchambers.com
NATO homepage – www.nato.int
Links to trade associations – www.matex.co.uk/taf/lookup
Kompass Business Directory – www.kompass.com
Online UK business directory – www.kellysearch.co.uk

Further reading

Begg, Fischer and Dornbusch, *Economics* (3rd ed) (McGraw-Hill, 1991).
Eyre E C and Pettinger R, *Mastering Basic Management* (3rd ed) (Macmillan, 1999).
Groves L W J, *Principles of International Marketing Research* (Blackwell, 1994).
Jain S C, *Marketing Planning and Strategy* (4th ed) (South Western, 1993).
McCarthy E J and Perreault Jr W D, *Basic Marketing* (11th ed) (Irwin, 1993).
Wilson A, *Marketing Researcher's Checklist* (British Chambers of Commerce, Coventry).

QUESTIONS FOR CONSIDERATION

   1 How do non-tariff barriers differ from tariff barriers and how can exporting companies overcome them?
   2 How might the expansion of the EU affect trade with the USA?
   3 Why does market research have its limitations and what can be done to ensure that research is accurate and meaningful?

◼ ̌ **5** Macro factors

Introduction

As Chapter 4 has shown, there is a great deal more to market research than simply determining the potential for doing business in a foreign country. This chapter takes the fact-finding activity a stage further by examining some of the macro factors that can affect the course of international trade. These are the forces over which companies rarely have any sort of control, but which they must still contend with if the venture is to be a success.

This chapter therefore takes the reader through issues such as cultural and regulatory considerations that need to be addressed at an early stage. It also takes a brief look at the importance of protecting intellectual property rights in overseas markets. By the end of the chapter, the reader should have a clear picture of all the areas that need to be researched as part of the market research brief.

More barriers to entry

As if the exporter does not have enough to contend with when researching international markets, more obstacles are placed in the way of market entry over and above the geographic, political and non-tariff barriers previously discussed in Chapter 4. Exporters also need to understand the influence that factors, which they cannot control, have over their international marketing plans and entry strategies. These include more political issues, such as a government's protectionist attitude towards foreign imports and investment, or legal requirements, including legislation on pricing, mergers, acquisitions and competition. These 'macro factors' differ from market to market, depending on the economic and political situation of the country in question. In these circumstances, companies can do very little else but comply with the specific requirements set out by the government of the country in which they wish to trade. Such requirements must be taken into consideration as part of the international trade strategy and systems put in place to ensure that the exporter firstly understands the nature of the requirements and, secondly, can address the requirements effectively. There are, additionally, other macro factors that can impact on the export plan if not given due consideration.

Cultural issues

The first, and perhaps most obvious, of these is culture. Whilst politics and law are the instruments that support and bind societies, it is culture that gives each nation its own identity. Culture cannot be planned, developed and implemented in the same way that policies and legislation can, and neither can it be controlled. Yet it is culture that defines how people behave and respond in different situations, and making the effort to understand the cultural differences that exist between countries can ultimately make or break a contract. Stereotypes of the bowler-hatted British or humourless German businessman and the like are caricatures drawn on images that are ill-founded and bear little resemblance to the inhabitants of the nations portrayed. Even though stereotyping is far removed from reality, it nevertheless contributes to our perceptions of other races and nations, and it is therefore essential that the exporter make the effort to understand the cultural values and behaviour of the target market. Building an export strategy around inaccurate perceptions of the target customer's cultural attitudes is more likely to offend, or at best amuse, than be effective.

Communicating in the target market

Unless a company is prepared to limit the markets it is active in to those, which speak the same language, communicating with buyers, suppliers and partners has the potential to be a major stumbling block (see Figure 5.1). Conversations, negotiations and sales presentations may require the services of an interpreter, whilst written correspondence may need translating, assuming that there are no adequate language skills in-house. If the decision is taken not to communicate in the buyer's native language, the exporter must take further steps to ensure that any discussion or written communication is clearly understandable and is not likely to cause confusion. It is particularly important to refrain from using colloquialisms and slang, which may be misunderstood, and to avoid attempts at humour at all costs. Jokes and anecdotes rarely translate well and may cause embarrassment rather than levity.

• Written conventions (dates , titles and so on)	• Weights, measures and currencies	• Religious beliefs and practices
• Mealtimes and dietary considerations	• 'Personal space' and 'comfortzones'	• Attitudes to work/personal life
• Attitudes to family/friends	• Customs and traditions	• Use of leisure time
• Greetings and leave-taking	• Small talk	• Public holidays
• Giving and receiving gifts	• Telephone protocols	• Hours of work
• Attitude to punctuality	• Gestures	• Body language
• Advertising practices	• Use of images	• Dress/clothing
• 'Face' (esp. Far East)	• Gender roles	• Use of colour

Figure 5.1 Examples of cultural issues affecting communication and understanding.

Note: It is also important to be aware of the target market's criminal code in order to avoid unwittingly contravening local laws. For example, in Singapore, chewing gum is banned and even suppliers of gum designed to help smokers stop smoking are unable to sell their products in this market. Dropping litter in Singapore is also a crime, punishable by the birch.

There are many other areas capable of causing misunderstanding through a lack of appreciation of another culture's attitudes, values and beliefs. The exporter should always aim to communicate in the buyer's native language out of courtesy and respect and to demonstrate that the exporter is committed to developing business with the market. Although this has a cost implication if translators and interpreters are to be used, the enhanced, professional image and sales potential gained as a result could be the decisive advantage a company has over its competition.

It is, however, advisable to ensure that all translation work carried out is accurate, as inaccurate work will not create a good impression with the buyer. Translation agencies normally have a policy of only using native speakers to translate works, which immediately ensures a high level of language ability. Companies should spend time researching translation agencies in advance of appointing them to meet their language needs and should ensure that the translators not only have native language ability, but also have relevant industry knowledge and experience. This is particularly important for technical and legal translations. Again, the cost of having marketing literature and correspondence translated accurately is money well spent and should be allocated within the marketing budget.

Activity: Using information from www.tradepartners.gov.uk, review and compare the cultural requirements of doing business in a Latin American, Middle Eastern and Asian country.

In many respects, effective communication in a foreign country relies on little more than common sense, politeness and the exporting company's willingness to accept that it is the foreigner, not the client. Additional research into the business and social conventions in the target market should also be carried out alongside the main market research project in order to identify any cultural requirements that might impact on aspects of the export plan and promotional strategy.

Introduction to intellectual property

Most countries provide some form of legal framework to protect the creative design capabilities and output of their population, particularly with regard to innovative products and trademarks. In many cases, it is not the products themselves that are protected but the 'intellectual property', or the concept itself, that is safeguarded. Intellectual property is nevertheless an asset, albeit one that is generally intangible, and many companies build their competitive advantage around the ingenuity or unique nature of their products' design. This is particularly true of companies in the creative industry sector, where the original concept is the product's unique selling point. The decision to sell the goods into new markets therefore raises the question of whether or not the level of protection available overseas is as high as that enjoyed domestically. If a company does not take steps to preserve its intellectual rights, it will quickly find other companies copying the design, marketing the product and setting themselves up as competitors.

A patent is granted to the designer or inventor of a product in order to prevent other individuals or organisations from copying the product and therefore benefiting from the designer's hard work and investment in research and development. Patents are granted for a period of 20 years, running from the date the application was filed, and this is accepted by all members of the World Trade Organisation (WTO) through the terms of the WTO agreement on Trade-Related Aspects of Intellectual Property Rights (TRIPS). Companies that have been granted patents consequently have a 20-year time span in which to commercialise their products and make money from them before they can be copied without legal recourse.

Protecting intellectual property rights (IPR) therefore provides some security against the unauthorised use of a design, product or trademark. However, the protection offered differs from nation to nation and, unless country-specific or worldwide patents are taken out, a patent awarded in one country may offer little protection if the product is copied in another. Some nations recognise the 'first user' of a brand name or trademark as the legal owner of the brand. Others require patents, copyrights and trademarks to be registered for each of the countries in which they are expected to be sold. The international community is, however, moving towards harmonising the different legislative systems, although true integration and harmonisation is still some way off. The EU already operates the Community Trade Mark (CTM) system which grants the registered owner of a patent or trademark protection in all EU member states.

Trade secrets – confidential information that is not in the public domain in the industry or sector in which it is used – can also be protected under the TRIPS agreement. Protection is therefore available for companies that could be adversely affected by their processes, formulae, designs or software becoming public knowledge.

Establishing a presence in an overseas market inevitably means that the company's products are going to be examined by potential clients and competitors alike and it is important to ensure that the risk of products being copied is minimised. This can be achieved by applying for and registering patents in each of the markets that the company aims to target, or by applying for a single, global patent to cover every country in the world. The latter approach may seem excessive, as few companies have the resources to sell to every nation, but the worldwide patent does reduce the threat of designs being copied and sold in markets where they have not yet been registered.

- How much will IPR protection cost?
- How will this affect the financial position of the company?
- How quickly could these costs be recouped from sales in the market?
- How much does the company stand to lose in the event that the product is copied and sold in another market (or even the domestic market)?
- Are the intellectual property rights the basis for competitive advantage?
- Can a value be placed on the IPR's worth to the company?
- What legal recourse will the company have in the event of patent infringement?
- Does the level of recourse justify the registration fee?

Figure 5.2 Questioning value for money in registering intellectual property.

Weighing up the cost

Not surprisingly, there is normally a fee for registering intellectual property. The size of the fee varies from market to market and can be prohibitively expensive in some cases. Companies that wish to protect their designs and brands in several markets will consequently incur substantial expenses in the form of registration costs for each market, unless the worldwide patent is granted (for an even larger fee!).

With this in mind, companies have to weigh up the relative advantages that IPR protection offers against the cost of registering trademarks and applying for patent recognition. Figure 5.2 lists some of the key questions that companies should ask when considering whether or not the cost of safeguarding their designs and brands is both justified and feasible.

Intellectual property rights and the World Wide Web

Chapter 3 demonstrated the role that the Internet can play in the international promotion of goods and services. The World Wide Web is certainly a valuable marketing tool, but its very nature means that it also has its risks. The Internet is simply an international network of computers that is neither regulated nor has a defined geographic location. This clearly has a number of implications for internationally active companies, and especially in the area of IPR.

The facility to email information around the world is one of the greatest advancements in communication technology, but it is also a very public medium. Unless emails are digitally encrypted there is little to stop a determined Internet user from accessing the message and its content, and it is therefore inadvisable to email trade secrets, confidential information and the like, even to trusted colleagues. In the case of information published on a website, the implication is that the owner of the material is prepared for the details to be accessed and used by third parties. Some websites go so far as to publish notices granting limited use of the information contained on their sites.

A good example of this is the *CIA World Factbook* website, which publishes the following guidance:

> 'The Factbook is in the public domain. Accordingly, it may be copied freely without permission of the Central Intelligence Agency (CIA). The official seal of the CIA, however, may NOT be copied without permission as required by the CIA Act of 1949 (50 U.S.C. section 403m). Misuse of the official seal of the CIA could result in civil and criminal penalties.'
> Source: www.odci.gov/cia/publications/factbook.

Legal jurisdiction of the Internet is a contentious subject in itself, with the main focus of the debate being centred on identifying which national law has jurisdiction over contracts and online trading. The principles governing this issue are also of relevance to infringements of intellectual property rights and will be covered in greater detail in Chapter 8.

One final point to bear in mind with regard to IPR and the Internet is that many countries will only approve patent applications for products that have not previously been made available in the public domain. Companies that have developed their products by using the Internet as a forum for discussion, research and feedback may find it difficult to have their patent applications approved as a result.

Further information on IPR and TRIPS can be obtained from the World Intellectual Property Organisation (WIPO) and the World Trade Organisation using the website addresses listed in sources of information.

Exchange controls

Exchange controls are regulations imposed by national governments to limit the inward and outward flow of foreign and domestic currencies. They are no longer as common in 'developed' nations as they once were (certainly, they are not found within the EU), and are nowadays more likely to be found in emerging or developing economies. The UK actually operated exchange controls until 1979, when they were removed, turning the UK into a free market economy. (The Exchange Control Act nevertheless remains on the UK statute book and can be reinstated should the government decide that the flow of domestic and foreign currency needs to be controlled.)

Exchange controls are often used in conjunction with quotas and some of the other non-tariff barriers covered in Chapter 4, although the global movement towards the relaxation of barriers to international trade is also encouraging the gradual cessation of their use. Less-developed countries, particularly those at war, experiencing civil unrest or near bankruptcy, are generally more inclined to make use of exchange controls as a means of controlling their economies.

By imposing controls on foreign and domestic currency movements, governments can monitor the behaviour and development of their economies. To do this, governments operating exchange controls require companies to sell purely in foreign denominations, which will be exchanged by the exporter's national Central Bank at a fixed rate of exchange. Importers are required to obtain permission to buy foreign currency from the Central Bank in order to pay for their purchases. The rate of exchange agreed by the Central Bank will depend on the nature of the product to be imported. If the buyer is importing essential goods, such as healthcare products or raw materials, the government will take a more relaxed view and grant a more favourable rate of exchange than would be the case for the import of non-essential goods and luxury items.

Exchange controls consequently affect buyers and sellers trying to trade in markets where they are in use. Exporters looking at a target market that is subject to exchange controls are likely to have misgivings about the wisdom of trading with a country that limits its currency movements, whilst importers in the same market will find it harder to trade with foreign suppliers. Fortunately, exporters can make use of credit insurance (see Chapter 13) and confirmed, irrevocable letters of credit (Chapter 11) to guarantee receipt of payment, so that exchange controls are not necessarily an insurmountable barrier to trade. It is also possible for the exporter to secure payment by making use of some of the other financing methods covered in Chapter 13 that can be of equal use to importers facing restrictions in the amount of currency they can obtain.

For this reason, companies must be fully aware of whether or not exchange controls have been imposed in the target market and how they are operated. Research into the nature of the controls is therefore essential before the promotional strategy is implemented, sales negotiations get underway and payment methods agreed.

Import licences

An import or export licence may be required before a consignment is permitted to leave the domestic market or enter the buyer's market.

Import licences are another mechanism used by countries to control the inflow of particular goods, especially where they may have a negative impact on the domestic market's indigenous industries. They are therefore most likely to be required by importers in developing countries whose manufacturing industries could be seriously undermined by foreign goods entering the market. Import licences are generally issued by the country's department or ministry in charge of trade and industry, assuming that the importer's application – supported by the exporter's proforma invoice – is approved. If goods are indeed subject to an import licence and the importer has not obtained authority to bring them into the country, then the shipment will be prevented from entering the market and the importer will be unable to receive them.

Activity: Compile a list of products subject to import licensing in the USA. Examine reasons why these products are subject to such controls.

Once an import licence has been granted it is valid for a fixed period of time, meaning that both the importer and exporter must ensure that the goods are physically shipped and received within the timeframe allowed before the licence becomes invalid. Both parties must be aware of the restrictions and time limitations imposed. As far as trade within the developed world is concerned, most importing is carried out under Open General Import Licences (OGIL), which carry no such restrictions.

Comprehensive Import Supervision Scheme

Comprehensive Import Supervision Scheme (CISS) controls often co-exist alongside import licences and are common in several developing markets. CISS is a system that grants the importer's government the right to demand a full inspection of the goods to be imported. The inspection examines the nature, quality, quantity and value of the goods in question, and will often compare the exporter's prices with those of comparable products. This ensures that (a) the goods are of good quality and (b) that they are fairly priced and not taking advantage of the importer.

For the exporter, CISS means allowing an independent inspection agency to examine the goods before they are packaged for shipment. The inspection agency will issue the exporter with either a Special Security Label (SSL) or Clean Report of Findings (CRF) document demonstrating that the inspection has taken place and everything is found to be in order. If the SSL is issued, the CRF is sent to the buyer.

If the inspection is not satisfied with the nature, quality, quantity or value of the goods, the agency will issue the exporter with a non-negotiable report listing its findings, and the consignment is unlikely to be cleared by Customs on entry to the target market. Exporters and importers need to be aware of whether or not CISS controls exist, as well as their individual requirements (which can change from market to market).

Export licences

Export controls are similar in function to import licences in that they restrict what can and cannot be freely moved between countries. Export controls are particularly used to restrict the international sale of goods to organisations and countries that may subsequently pose a threat to the exporting country's security, as well as to countries with a poor human rights record.

Export controls tend to be established by international committees overseeing industries and sectors that pose a threat to international peace and stability. These include the Biological Weapons Convention (BWC), Chemical Weapons Convention (CWC) and Nuclear Suppliers Group (NSG), as well as other organisations. These committees draw up lists of goods that they feel should not be freely traded between nations and require an export licence to be issued by the seller's national government. Whilst trade sanctions and embargoes imposed on individual countries by international agreements restrict the trade in all types of goods for political reasons, export licences are normally only needed for the various 'controlled' goods identified on the lists prepared by governments. In the UK, the Department of Trade and Industry has an Export Control Organisation (ECO) that monitors the trade in sensitive goods and technologies.

Activity: Compile a list of goods requiring export licences before they can be exported from the UK to Indonesia, India and Syria.

Exporters can register with the ECO to make use of an Open General Export Licence (OGEL), which permits the export of specified goods to identified destinations. It is also possible to apply directly to the ECO for an Open Individual Export Licence (OIEL), which permits the export of a range of goods to different destinations. OIELS are valid for up to three years in the case and can cover several shipments without the need to name the overseas buyers when the application is made.

Companies must research the need for export licences in advance of developing a market-specific export strategy. The effort spent in negotiating a contract with a foreign buyer will be wasted if the goods cannot be shipped without a licence that has not yet been approved.

Quality and safety issues

The regulatory controls that exporters and importers need to comply with are not limited to licences and permissions. Most nations also impose regulations on the standard of goods sold in order to provide further protection to consumers and businesses. These requirements are most obvious in demands that products meet a minimum quality and safety standard.

Under international sale of goods conventions and guidelines there is an expectation that products supplied must be of good quality and must not pose any inherent risk to the buyer or user. An exporter supplying substandard goods would therefore be in breach of contract under international law. Even so, individual countries also provide greater protection by publishing minimum requirements for product quality and safety. In the UK, the British Standards Institution issues a mark (the BSI Kitemark) to signify that the goods approved meet the requirements of the standard. Consumer goods sold into the EU will normally carry a CE mark to show its compliance with the EU legislation on quality standards, and other markets have their own national standards organisations that work on similar lines.

Safety standards for products such as toys and other consumer goods are constantly under scrutiny, for obvious reasons, and the international sale of electrical items is, in particular, subject to standards regulations. In these cases, the exporter will be required to provide appropriate certificates of testing and compliance to demonstrate that the products satisfy the minimum standards requirements of the market in which they are to be sold. For UK exporters, the

BSI operates the Technical Help for Exporters service, which can provide information on international standards and market-specific requirements for different products.

Packing

Packing – the materials used to protect the exporter's products in transit, as opposed to the display packaging that the goods are sold in – is also subject to regulations imposed by national governments. The goods may be packed in cardboard boxes, hessian sacks, plastic wrappers, wooden crates or any other recognised method of preventing damage to the consignment. Packing regulations also exist to ensure that the goods are shipped safely and with minimum risk to the cargo handlers. As each nation has its own guidelines on packing for the international movement of goods, research must be carried out at an early stage in order to identify any restrictions that could affect the export sale.

The materials used for packing, as well as the packing process itself, represents a cost to the exporter but it is better for companies to provide adequate packing than to risk damage to the goods in transit through inadequate protection. Specialist export packers and freight forwarders can provide assistance in packing for international transport and it is prudent for companies to consult such organisations to ensure both the safety of the goods and compliance with the target market's requirements. This is particular important if there are any concerns about the facilities for unloading and moving consignments on arrival; it may be necessary to adapt the packing to enable the handling equipment to cope with the package.

The type of packing materials used will also depend on issues such as climate, size, shape and weight of the products and the risk of pilferage, as well the type of transportation used. Packing will be stronger for ocean transport than for air transport in order to compensate for the likelihood of rough seas causing pallets to slide around in the cargo hold, and so on.

> **Activity**: How will the packing requirements differ for the export of electrical goods by sea, a CD-ROM-based software application by air and clay pipes by road?

Environmental restrictions

Businesses have been made increasingly aware of their environmental responsibilities for a number of years but nowadays there is even more pressure on companies to be environmentally aware. This has been especially noticeable since the Kyoto Agreement of 1997, which elicited a commitment from most of the world's developed nations to reduce emissions of greenhouse gases, which affects issues ranging from energy usage to the disposal of refrigerators!

Quite apart from global agreements, individual countries also impose their own restrictions. For example, German legislation has long granted German businesses the right to require suppliers to collect all packaging and to make use of packing materials that are either recycled or from renewable sources. More and more emphasis is being placed on the nature, source and management of packing materials and exporters should be aware of each country's own attitudes to environmentally responsible packing. For further information on packaging requirements and restrictions, British companies can make use of the services offered by PIRA, a specialist organisation that provides consultancy services to the printing, paper, publishing and packaging industries.

Marking and labelling

All exported goods must carry marks and labels to assist carriers, Customs officials and the like in identifying how to handle the consignment appropriately. Yet again, different countries have different marking and labelling requirements that should be complied with to prevent shipments from being delayed or halted.

As a minimum, every product in a consignment should carry a label of origin, for example, 'Made in Britain', together with a mark identifying the producer of the goods. It is not acceptable to place a single mark or label on a crate containing several different packages – Customs officials will need to see marks and labels for each individual item in the crate to ensure that the correct rates of duty are paid for each package.

Labelling is concerned primarily with printing information relating to the product itself on the packaging. Each country has its own requirements as to how ingredients, components and contents should be detailed, as well as companies' claims regarding the product's health benefits, environmental policies, and so on. Labelling can also include warranties and guarantees published on the product's packaging and further information on the specific requirements of each country can be obtained from organisations such as the BSI.

There are five main types of mark used in the shipping process. These are:

1. A standard identification mark designed and issued by the importer. This mark is used by all the importer's foreign suppliers to identify the cases or packages destined for the buyer.
2. The buyer normally provides the exporter with detailed instructions on how to mark the individual packages within a single consignment. For example, a shipment of 10 cases might be marked '1 of 10', '2 of 10' and so on. The pack numbers will allow the cargo handlers, carriers and the buyer to keep track of all elements of the shipment.
3. The port of destination must be marked on the packages.

4. If the export consignment forms part of a larger order, the exporter ought to mark each case with 'component numbers' to enable the buyer to store each package in the right order for use and assembly.
5. Finally, the exporter may include markings to alert handlers to how the goods should be transported safely and without causing damage. Examples of such markings include 'fragile', 'this way up', 'do not stack', 'keep cool and dry' and so on.

Although it is normally the responsibility of the buyer to ensure that the exporter is fully aware of its packing, marking and labelling requirements, the seller should liaise with the importer to make sure that the buyer's requirements are understood.

Dangerous goods

The packing, marking and labelling of dangerous goods in transit is essential to the protection of all parties likely to come into contact with the consignment, as well as those that may be exposed to the contents in the event of an accident. Most of the international regulations governing the carriage of dangerous goods are published by the United Nations in the *Recommendations on the Transport of Dangerous Goods (Model Regulations)*, often referred to as the *Orange Book*. Each method of transport is covered by the legislation, which establishes four key councils to oversee the regulations. The councils are the International Maritime Dangerous Goods Code (IMDG) for the carriage of goods by sea, the Accord Dangereux Routiers (ADG) for road transport, the International Regulations Concerning the Carriage of Goods by Rail (RID) and the International Civil Aviation Organisation Technical Instructions (ICAO) for air transportation.

Figure 5.3 shows how dangerous goods are officially classified, and each classification is further broken down into different divisions, such as Class 1, division 1.1, articles that represent a mass explosion hazard. The different types of dangerous product are issued with a four-figure UN number and a PSN (Proper Shipping Name), which is normally the chemical name for the product in question. The UN number, PSN, classification and division therefore provide a quick means of transmitting the relevant information by an internationally recognised shorthand system.

Class 1	Explosives
Class 2	Gases
Class 3	Flammable liquids
Class 4	Flammable solids/substances that may spontaneously combust/substances that give off flammable gases when in contact with water
Class 5	Organic peroxides and oxidising substances
Class 6	Toxic and infectious materials
Class 7	Radioactive substances
Class 8	Corrosives
Class 9	Miscellaneous dangerous goods

Figure 5.3 Classification of dangerous goods.

It is also obviously important to pack dangerous goods properly, and advice should be sought from suitably qualified dangerous goods safety advisers and similar organisations with expertise in the international carriage of hazardous goods. In the UK, only PIRA can approve and certify packaging for use with dangerous goods. The onus is on the exporter to ensure that all dangerous goods are appropriately marked and accompanied by guidance on handling the goods, emergency procedures and associated health issues. Consignments transported over land must also be accompanied by a Dangerous Goods Note (DGN) or a Shipper's Declaration for Dangerous Goods if transported by air, which provide the same information as the markings and labelling on the packages as well as identifying the buyer and seller.

Conclusions

Regulations, controls and standards are factors that the exporter and importer cannot influence but must learn to take into account. This chapter has explained how and why governments impose restrictions on what can and cannot be imported and exported, as well as the steps they take to protect their citizens from substandard goods. These macro factors are unavoidable and companies should make the effort to fully understand the individual require-ments of the target market.

The chapter has also explored the importance of protecting intellectual property rights, an issue that must be addressed effectively if exporters are to preserve their competitive advantage and prevent other companies benefiting from their hard work and investment.

Once all the market research information has been collected and all the factors affecting trade with the identified target market have been identified, the company can then research the most appropriate means of actually selling overseas. The exporter is now ready to develop an entry strategy, and the different options available will be discussed in the next chapter.

Sources of information

Overview of intellectual property rights and useful links – www.w3.org/ipr/
World Intellectual Property Organisation – www.wipo.org
TRIPS information can be found on the World Trade Organisation website –
    www.wto.org
Example of a country prohibiting and restricting the entry of certain goods (in
    this case, Malta) – www.customs.business-line.com/prohibit.htm
Carriage of Dangerous Goods by Road and Rail (Crown Copyright legislation) –
    www.legislation.hmso.gov.uk/si/si1994/uksi_19940669_en_1.htm
Carriage of Dangerous Goods by Sea (Crown Copyright legislation) –
    www.legislation.hmso.gov.uk/si1996/uksi_19962095_en_1.htm
DTI export controls organisation – www.dti.gov.uk/export.control/
UK Customs and Excise – www.hmce.gov.uk

PIRA – www.pira.co.uk
National Statistics Office trade data – www.uktradeinfo.com
Technical help for exporters – www.bsi-global.com

Further reading

Bennett R, *Getting Started in Export* (2nd ed) (Kogan Page, 1998).

Blackett T, *Trademarks* (Palgrave Macmillan, 1998).

Brake T *et al.*, *Doing Business Internationally: The Guide to Cross-cultural Success* (2nd ed) (Irwin, 1994).

Dew P and Shoult A, *Doing Business with the United Arab Emirates* (Kogan Page, 2000).

Elashnawi F and Harris P R, *Multicultural Management 2000: Essential Cultural Insights for Global Business Success* (Gulf, 2998).

Hart T and Fazzanni L, *Intellectual Property Law* (2nd ed) (Palgrave Macmillan, 2000).

Kettaneh N, *Doing Business in Spain* (2nd ed) (Kogan Page, 2001).

Litman J, *Digital Copyright: Protecting Intellectual Property on the Internet* (Prometheus, 2000).

Nelson C A, *Import Export* (3rd ed), (McGraw-Hill Education, 2000).

Reuvid J and Millar R, *Doing Business with Germany* (3rd ed) (Kogan Page, 2002).

Wilson J R, *Getting Started in Import* (2nd ed) (Kogan Page, 1998).

QUESTIONS FOR CONSIDERATION

1   If English and French are widely accepted as international business languages, why is it nevertheless good practice to communicate in the buyer's native tongue and to understand the cultural influences that affect the buyer's behaviour?

2   What are intellectual property rights and why is it important to protect them? What steps can a company take to protect IPRs in several overseas markets?

3   Why do governments in developing markets establish import controls requiring importers to apply for import licences?

4   How do import controls differ from export controls, and what must the exporter be aware of in each situation?

5   Why is packaging an essential issue to research in advance of developing and implementing an export plan, and how does this affect a company's environmental responsibilities?

 ## Case study: Sutcliffe Play Ltd

Background

Sutcliffe Play Ltd are innovating market leaders in the field of playground equipment, safety surfaces and swing seats. The company is well established with an excellent reputation in the UK and growing international sales. Existing markets include Germany, France and Japan, with sales being achieved through a combination of direct sales and distributors. As part of a defined strategy to expand the company's geographic markets, the company directors took the decision to research the potential of the Polish market for its range of play products.

Secondary research

Sutcliffe Play was in the fortunate position of having an experienced export manager familiar with the requirements and procedures of market research. Consequently, it was decided that there was no need to subcontract the market research exercise to a specialist research agency. Moreover, the manager's knowledge of the company's products and existing markets would be a useful foundation on which to build knowledge of the Polish market.

Secondary market research was therefore made easier due to the manager's industry knowledge and familiarity with competing products. This was supported by in-house records, brochures, fair catalogues and the like that had been collected over several years by the company.

Trade journals proved to be a useful means of identifying further competition and industry trends and the manager also made contact with relevant trade associations in the UK and Poland in order to obtain up-to-date market and industry-specific information.

The Internet also yielded invaluable information. Competitor websites were browsed and researched, whilst websites devoted to company/ product searches (such as Kompass) were used to compile lists of potential clients and representatives. The desk research was then fully supported by information obtained from government departments and offices in the UK and Poland, the British–Polish Chamber of Commerce and the East European Trade Council, all of whom were helpful and keen to assist Sutcliffe Play develop their business. Finally, a visit to a Polish travel agent provided information on the country, travel and accommodation, whilst the manager also took the opportunity to meet with a Polish friend to gain a better understanding of cultural practices and to learn a few words of Polish.

Primary research

The secondary research showed that the market for play equipment in Poland was large enough to be of interest to the company but not sufficiently mature as to preclude attempts at market entry. The market itself was receptive to British goods and services and, as a growing economy keen to join the EU as early as possible, Poland seemed to be an attractive market to do business.

The next stage was therefore to visit the market in order to meet some end users of the company's products to review their requirements. The objectives for the visit also included meeting with academics and leading figures from the world of play in Poland – these contacts would be instrumental for understanding first hand the demands and trends of the market.

Several pre-arranged meetings took place and provided Sutcliffe Play with useful information on issues such as quality, price and after-sales support as well as highlighting other industry contacts who were subsequently approached and met. Interviews with end users revealed who the best and most reliable distributors of play equipment were, and from this information it was simply a question of following the distribution chain back to its source. This resulted in a shortlist of potential distributors who could then be further researched (using some of the criteria outlined in Chapter 6) prior to appointing a representative for the market.

◼ Ṽ **6** Routes to market

Introduction

Having identified the market to be targeted, the exporter must then select an appropriate entry strategy, or route to market. This chapter will show that there is a wide range of channels available to exporting companies, from the investment-based strategies more likely to be considered by larger companies and MNCs to conventional partnering agreements which practically every exporting organisation will make use of. The responsibilities and financial implications associated with each type of entry strategy will be discussed and the chapter will also provide some suggestions on how to identify and appoint agents and distributors around the world.

Each of the routes to market described can be adopted by importers, albeit from a different perspective. The considerations to take into account when deciding which strategy to implement are equally valid for importing companies and the areas covered by the chapter therefore also highlight the different strategies that importers can make use of in their international development.

The need for an entry strategy

Previous chapters have shown the importance of marketing and market research in profiling target markets and the considerations that need to be taken into account if the company is to export successfully to them. Whilst the research report identifies demand for products, barriers to entry and incorporates elements of the marketing mix, it does not necessarily highlight the most appropriate means of selling the goods in the target market.

It is as important to define the channels of distribution for overseas markets as it is for the UK and exporters who assume that they can simply sell in a foreign country without thinking through a market-specific strategy will not get far. An effective entry strategy facilitates the efficient distribution of goods to the end user or consumer. It may make use of locally engaged intermediaries, investments in overseas offices, or perhaps franchising or manufacturing agreements. Equally, the company may decide that the most appropriate route to market is through selling direct to the customer. The company must therefore undertake further research to ensure that it adopts an effective entry strategy, which meets its needs precisely. Clear objectives must be set as inappropriate channels of distribution can be costly and will impede international development.

There are six principal entry strategies that a company might choose to employ, depending on how the exporter anticipates building a presence in the market. These are by selling

1. direct to the end user, or through
2. Aan agent or broker
3. a distributor or dealer
4. a retailer
5. a local office or joint venture
6. or by licensing or franchising

Some of these approaches require substantial investment on the part of the exporter who, in these cases, needs to be fully committed to the target market and convinced that the investment will he justified in the long term. Other channels of distribution rely more on the individual skills and abilities of local intermediaries to secure business. Each type of entry strategy offers different advantages and disadvantages, cost implications and risks as well as allowing the exporter varying levels of control over its overseas markets. It is therefore important to take care in selection. It should be noted that each of these entry methods can be applied by companies in the service sector, the only difference being in the actual structure of the agreements entered into and the nature of the services to be promoted across the target market.

Direct and indirect exporting

Exporting may be classed as either direct or indirect (see Figure 6.1). Direct exporting occurs where the company has direct responsibility for the promotion and distribution of its products in the target market. This might be achieved by selling direct to the client, which places more demand on resources for overseas sales, or through retail outlets that supply goods or services to the end user.

Direct exporting can also be achieved by selling through foreign agents or distributors, who act as sales representatives on behalf of the company. This is the most common approach to developing trade internationally, particularly amongst smaller or inexperienced businesses.

Question: Why is direct exporting often the more popular option for companies embarking on international trade ventures?

Direct	Indirect
To end user	Export management company
Foreign retail outlets	Export trading house
Foreign agents	Confirming house
Foreign distributors	Buying agent (based in the home country)
	Co-marketing

Figure 6.1 Direct and indirect exporting methods.

Indirect exporting removes much of the responsibility and control from the exporter. Typically, this type of exporting is achieved through intermediaries who undertake to promote and distribute products on the company's behalf. The intermediaries, who are likely to be based in the manufacturer's home country, purchase goods from the company in order to sell them on (at a profit) to clients overseas. The manufacturer has little or no control over where and how its products are sold, as the intermediary takes full responsibility for selling the company's goods overseas.

Indirect exporting is generally through organisations such as buying agents who act on behalf of foreign companies or governments, trading houses that purchase goods for resale overseas, export trading companies that offer services to businesses in a particular sector or export management companies, which act as a company's export office and take responsibility for the business' international trade function. Co-marketing, where goods are exported as part of another manufacturing company's product portfolio or as components in a finished product, is also classed as indirect exporting.

In each case, a third party bears the cost, risk and responsibility of exporting. The manufacturing company has the satisfaction of knowing that its goods are being sold internationally but may see the lack of control and influence over where its products are exported to as a major disadvantage.

Even though direct exporting brings greater financial risks, it does permit the exporter to retain more control over the promotion and distribution of the product in the target market. For this reason, direct exporting tends to be favoured over indirect exporting, although each does have its merits. Ultimately, the decision on whether to export directly or indirectly will be based on how comfortable the company is with international trade and how much responsibility it is willing to take on to ensure export success.

Figure 6.2 compares the costs involved using different market entry methods.

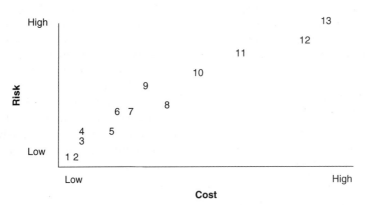

Key: 1 – buying agent, 2 – trading house, 3 – export management company, 4 – distributor, 5 – agent, 6 – direct sales, 7 – retailer, 8 – co-marketing, 9 – licensing, 10 – franchising, 11 – joint venture, 12 – merger/acquisition, 13 – greenfield site

Figure 6.2 Comparison of the costs and risks of different market entry methods.

Export management companies

One of the methods of exporting indirectly is to make use of businesses that provide a complete export management solution. Export management companies can be likened to external export departments that offer a full range of services from market research through to shipping and payment. They are generally employed by companies to represent them in designated overseas markets and may be paid a retainer fee as well as an amount to cover expenses incurred and a commission on sales. The British Exporters Association (BExA) is able to provide details of export management companies operating in the UK.

Although export management companies take on responsibility for every stage of the export process, they do so in the name of the manufacturing company. Thus the manufacturer has the dual advantages of being seen as a competent exporter whilst incurring less costs in administration and other resources. The disadvantage to using this type of intermediary is that the manufacturer gains little real or practical experience of the target market and cannot therefore develop its own skills in international trade. This in turn may mean prolonged reliance on the export management company.

Export trading houses

Export houses, or export merchants, purchase goods from the manufacturer with the intention of selling them on overseas. From the manufacturers' point of view, there is no difference between selling to a domestic customer and to an export house. There are no freight, financial or export sales issues to concern the manufacturer, as the export houses take responsibility for selling the goods overseas. They have no obligation to their suppliers once the goods have been paid for and they are quite at liberty to sell the products on at a profit.

Companies may take the decision to work with export houses in order to reduce the risks and responsibilities of exporting, even if this is at the expense of losing control of how and where its products are sold. Export houses are of particular use to companies with limited resources or international experience as well as to larger companies that are examining the potential of challenging new markets where the cost of undertaking research and sales can be reduced through working with merchants.

The main benefit of established export houses is their international trade experience and knowledge of potential buyers around the world. However, as when working with export management companies, the manufacturer has little opportunity to gain export experience. In the case of export houses, the benefits of international trade fall directly to the merchant and not the manufacturer whose products are being sold around the world.

Confirming houses

Confirming houses are not strictly a route to market, although they do offer a means of securing payment from importers. They exist to provide a service to foreign buyers rather than domestic suppliers and their role is to offer a guarantee of payment to the exporter on behalf of the importer. They are particularly useful in situations where the foreign buyer is either unknown to the exporter or has a poor credit rating, resulting in the exporter being reluctant to offer credit. Under these circumstances, the importer can, for a commission, ask a confirming house to guarantee that the exporter will receive payment for goods purchased. The order from the importer will be endorsed for 'confirmation and payment' and will name the confirming house, which sends a separate document to the exporter confirming that it will accept liability in the event of non-payment by the buyer (see also Chapter 11, Payment).

Buying agents

Many foreign companies, aid agencies and other international organisations employ agents or other representatives to act as their buyers in the exporter's home market. As their role is to purchase goods on behalf of the foreign company, the sale concluded between the exporter and the agent is likely to be on standard domestic terms, with the agent subsequently being responsible for distribution and documentary issues. Buying agents are an attractive option to exporters as they remove the risk of the international trade process. However, companies should not rely solely on being able to sell via buying agents but should develop other routes to market to complement any sales achieved through foreign representatives based in the domestic market.

Co-marketing

There are several types of co-marketing opportunities open to exporters prepared to work with other companies to maximise the potential of overseas opportunities. For example, two (or possibly more) companies might decide to jointly promote their complementary products in an export market in order to reduce the cost of research, sales and distribution. This 'group sales' arrangement can assist the partner organisations in developing market share through mutual co-operation, although the agreement does rather depend on the partners being able to communicate effectively and work well together.

A more formal version of the group sales arrangement is the consortium. This is where several companies come together to offer a portfolio of complementary products to an overseas market, for example in order to tender for a large project or simply to provide a joint export marketing mechanism that represents the interests of all members of the consortium.

Consortia tend to be better organised and managed than informal group sales agreements and they can provide support to companies wanting to expand into new markets. They are, however, only as strong as their weakest member and lack of commitment from one participant may jeopardise the whole venture for the rest. Piggy-backing, where one company (the rider) makes use of the services of another (the carrier) in order to enter an export market, is another common method of co-marketing. Ideally, the two companies should offer complementary products so that each can benefit from promoting a wider range of goods. The carrier company will normally undertake to promote the rider's products alongside its own, using the same channels of distribution. This will be achieved either with the rider paying a commission on sales generated by the carrier or with the carrier purchasing the goods outright from the rider for resale at a profit. In some cases, the companies may agree that the rider's products can be promoted under the carrier's brand name, which clearly has implications in terms of the rider's international exposure and profile. Co-marketing agreements need to be carefully drawn up to ensure that the needs and expectations of all parties are addressed.

> **Example**: In 1998 a group of 10 companies was brought together by an independent management consultancy, Partners in Export Ltd, with the aim of penetrating the petrochemical market in Azerbaijan. The companies were not just selected for the quality of their products or services but for the synergy that they had with other members in the group. In this way, the consortium was able to offer a comprehensive solution to the needs of the petrochemical sector in the market, from welding and pipeline to gases, crewing and environmental consultancy. The consortium, which was made up of a mix of experienced and novice exporters, agreed to share all the costs of the project equally. The interests of the consortium were marketed and represented by the management consultancy over a sustained period of time, leading to three joint ventures being established and several sales opportunities being identified.

Investing as an entry strategy

Investments in overseas markets are a more expensive means of achieving international trade success. They can, however, be more effective in kick-starting trade activity in the target market and investment opportunities should consequently be regarded as useful strategic tools that can quickly assist the company in gaining market share.

There are many different reasons why companies choose to invest in overseas markets. Some do so purely to generate business growth through additional sales and to gain increased market knowledge, others to improve their service and competitiveness, for example by setting up a central distribution centre to service several markets or to benefit from lower production and distribution costs. Investing can also be used to overcome trade barriers imposed in certain markets, particularly those that restrict exports and favour locally manufactured goods.

There are a number of different options available to companies considering investing in an overseas market. These range from setting up a local office to building a comprehensive manufacturing facility on a greenfield site.

Local company

An exporter may decide to invest in establishing a local company in order to permit better access to the target market. The local company may take the form of a joint venture agreement with a partner in the market or a wholly owned subsidiary established with little or no local involvement. The main functions of local offices are to act as manufacturing units, assembly plants, sales offices or stockist of products for distribution in the market.

Local offices or branches are often opened as a result of the inability of the existing agent or distributor to cope with a high level of sales. Investing in setting up a more permanent local presence therefore grants the exporter the facility to manage larger volumes of sales whilst improving distribution within the market. Manufacturing in the target market also helps the exporter to avoid import tariffs and potentially to benefit from lower labour costs and cheaper raw materials.

Activity: Using some of the sources of information listed at the end of this chapter (and throughout the book), identify what regulations and restrictions may affect the setting up of a local office in Germany, the USA, South Africa, Dubai and Malaysia. In particular, what are the requirements for 'local' ownership or involvement?

Not every overseas market welcomes foreign companies setting up branches or offices, and many governments require overseas investors to establish their offices in partnership with local businesses and with local employees. It is therefore always necessary to check the specific regulations in each market before establishing an office overseas.

Joint ventures

A joint venture is an agreement between two organisations to co-operate in several areas and as a result form a third company. Exporters intending to establish a representative local office may have no other choice but to partner with a local company due to government restrictions, but many choose to invest in setting up joint ventures in order to benefit from the partner's local knowledge and contacts. In return, the foreign partner may benefit from the exporter's skills, technologies and products, as well as gaining a means of entry into the exporter's home market.

Joint ventures make use of the combined skills of each company in the development and manufacture of products as well as their promotion and distribution. Consequently, exporters seeking joint ventures look for partners that can offer complementary skills, capital investment and management resources. This type of agreement can be costly in terms of the capital expenditure required in setting up the company, but can nevertheless assist the two partners in working together in several markets at the same time, which may not have been possible individually.

Example: A UK manufacturer of gaskets for the automotive and general engineering industries appointed a distributor to cover the French market in 1997 and the relationship worked well for the first two years. It then became apparent that, as demand grew for the products in France, it would make more sense for the manufacturer and the distributor to enter into a joint venture to produce the gaskets from the distributor's premises in Lille. Although the set up costs were quite high (for tooling, training and so on), these were quickly recouped through a reduction in transport costs. The distributor took on responsibility for production and distribution for the French market, both parties shared the costs and benefited from shared profits.

Joint ventures are not an easy option. They require a lot of work in identifying and negotiating with potential partners, and the agreements themselves are of a comprehensive and detailed nature, covering every conceivable aspect of the partnership from budgets to health and safety concerns. Nevertheless, they are an increasingly common form of overseas investment and a proven means of establishing a company in the target market.

The main factors that should be taken into consideration in the development of a joint venture can be summarised using VENTURE, which covers valuation, equality, neutrality, trust, understanding, relationships and exit strategy (see Figure 6.3).

Greenfield sites

In some cases, exporters may find that there are no suitable investment vehicles that they can use as a route to market. It may be decided that the most appropriate course of action is to identify a greenfield site on which to build a local presence from scratch, thereby eliminating the expense of renovating and redeveloping existing sites to meet the company's purposes. Greenfield investments provide a solid platform for market entry and can allow companies to develop their own corporate culture in the target market. This gives the company the opportunity to design and build a purpose-built manufacturing facility, which meets its needs exactly and avoids many of the legal and environmental obstacles encountered when investing in existing premises. Most greenfield investments are treated as subsidiaries of the parent company but operate under local law.

This level of investment obviously requires considerable capital and commitment. The start up costs are high, and the new facility may not deliver a return on investment for several years. Investments of this type are not a short-term solution to market entry. They are evidence that the company is wholly committed to establishing itself in the target market and has a strategy for the long-term future development of the company in the region. For example, an exporter may take the decision to establish a manufacturing plant in Malaysia in order to meet the needs of the Malaysian market and to act as a distribution centre for other Pacific Rim markets.

Valuation	• The value of the contribution made by each partner to the joint venture should be identified and used as a basis for the agreement.
	• This will identify which partner has majority control over the venture, unless a 50/50 split has been agreed.
Equality	• Joint ventures established on the basis of an equal partnership tend to be more effective than those with an uneven split.
	• Partners who work on an equal footing often have more respect for each other and bring more enthusiasm and motivation to the project.
Neutrality	• The joint venture should be an independent company and should not be seen as part of either partner's existing organisation.
	• Neutral companies are not subject to the daily issues that affect the partner's other businesses.
Trust	• The partners must have total trust in each other's commitment and ability to deliver results for the new joint venture.
	• Lack of trust between partners is not conducive to the successful running of the business.
Understanding	• Joint ventures are invariably established by two different cultures.
	• Understanding each partner's approach to business is essential if common ground is to be identified and a mutual approach developed.
	• It is important to foster strong relationships between the two partner organisations and to maintain effective communication at all times.
Relationships	• Good relationships at all levels of the organisation will help to maintain morale, motivation and commitment.
Exit strategy	• The partners must agree in advance how the joint venture is to be dissolved, should this prove to be necessary.

Figure 6.3   Factors influencing joint ventures.

Unless the government of the target market stipulates that greenfield investments must involve a local partner, ownership of the venture remains with the exporter. Regardless of ownership issues, it is advisable for the parent company to develop a strong management team for the new plant and to include local employees within the management structure. By doing so, the company gains the local knowledge and experience needed to access opportunities and eliminate cultural misunderstandings. Employing a local workforce also wins the approval of the target market's government as this approach demonstrates a responsible commitment to the market. Table 6.1 shows the risk and commitment required by each different entry strategy.

Mergers and acquisitions

The issues surrounding acquisitions and mergers were discussed in some detail in Chapter 2, which showed how companies acquire or merge with foreign companies in order to quickly increase market share or improve their route to market. Whilst these arrangements can bring immediate benefits to each party, they also raise a number of questions that must be resolved before the agreements are reached.

As well as understanding how the potential acquisition conducts its business, culturally as well as practically, the exporter must take steps to understand the legal, regulatory and financial implications of the merger or take-over. For example, the company must be aware of all the tax and environmental liabilities associated with the venture, the full financial position of the company to be acquired and any employment regulations that could impact on the agreement. Assuming that these considerations have been taken into account and the merger or acquisition goes ahead successfully, the exporting company is able to improve its position in the market as well as in the industry sector. The company also benefits from being able to make use of the partner's local knowledge, presence and resources.

Licensing

If a company does not wish to export directly or manufacture in the target market, licensing or franchising could be the solution. A licensing agreement is where a company (the licenser) agrees to sell the intellectual property rights to its products to another manufacturer (the licensee) in exchange for an agreed fee. The agreement may include provision for the licenser to supply materials and technical assistance or training to the licensee for use in the manufacture of the products. In return for the transfer of this knowledge, the licensee undertakes to produce and market the products in the target market and to pay the licenser a percentage commission on sales.

By entering into a manufacturing under license agreement, the licenser is able to establish an overseas presence with the added advantage that a third party is committed to developing the market. The licensee bears most of the risk and costs associated with the venture, and the licenser receives regular payments commensurate with achievements in the market.

To make licensing ventures worthwhile, however, the licenser must ensure that the licensee has the resources to firmly establish the product range in the market and the capacity to manufacture the products to the same standard as those produced domestically. Inferior quality goods in one market may tarnish the reputation of the licenser's goods in other markets and business development may be hampered through an inappropriate licensing agreement.

Franchising

Franchising is a route to market particularly favoured by companies in Western Europe and North America, although developing countries in the Far East and Central Europe are becoming increasingly familiar with the concept.

In many respects, franchising is similar to licensing. Instead of purchasing the rights to a company's products and selling the goods on an exclusive basis in a specified territory as a licensee would, a company in the target market is licensed to sell the franchiser's products. The franchiser also grants the right to make use of its trading name, branding, promotional methods and corporate image, and will also provide training and technical support to the franchisee, who provides the local knowledge, investment and resources to operate the franchise in the target market.

	Franchiser	Franchisee
Advantages		
	• Commitment and enthusiasm from independent franchisees keen to build business	• Established product and business methods can be adopted quickly
	• Fast expansion overseas through a network of franchises	• Availability of training and support from franchiser
	• Franchisee provides capital to operate franchise in the target market	• Advertising and promotion undertaken by the franchiser
Disadvantages		
	• Difficult to monitor how well the franchisee maintains the franchiser's standards and procedures	• Restricted to working within guidelines set by the franchiser, with little room for individuality
	• Loss of control over the sale of the product in the market	• Franchiser retains ultimate control of the business
	• Franchisees unlikely to be interested in product that are not established or proven	• Payment of royalties to franchiser. May also pay a mark up on goods supplied by the franchiser

Figure 6.4 Advantages and disadvantages of franchising.

Activity: Compile a list of well-known franchises in the retail, leisure and service sectors and examine how they are perceived by the public in the market in which they operate.

Franchising offers a faster route to market than would be the case if the franchiser had to invest in recruiting and training its own staff in the target market as well as establishing a presence in the market. In most cases, the franchiser will receive an initial payment or franchise fee as well as royalties on sales generated by the franchisee. The franchiser may also make money from marking up products, services and other supplies that the franchisee is contractually bound to purchase. Figure 6.4 lists the main advantages and disadvantages of franchising from both perspectives.

Table 6.1 The level of cost, risk and commitment associated with different market entry methods

Method	Investment	Risk	Commitment
Buying agent	low	low	negligible
Trading House	low	low	negligible
Export Management Co.	low-medium	low	negligible
Distributor	medium	low	strong
Agent	medium	medium	strong
Direct sales	medium-high	low	reasonable
Direct to retailer	medium	medium	reasonable
Co-marketing	medium	low-medium	strong
Licensing	low	medium	reasonable-strong
Franchising	low-medium	medium	reasonable-strong
Joint venture	medium-high	medium-high	strong
Merger/acquisition	high	high	very strong
Greenfield site	high	high	very strong

Partnering as an entry strategy

Investing in overseas markets can be a costly exercise that demands a serious long-term commitment and may not deliver a financial return for some time. For this reason, many of the common investment vehicles are not open to companies with limited financial and physical resources, and the use of locally engaged intermediaries to establish a presence in the market is more appropriate. One of the most common approaches to market entry is to work through representatives such as agents or distributors. This is particularly true of companies that are reluctant to invest in the target market or work through licensing or franchising agreements.

As an entry strategy, partnering offers several immediate benefits. Foreign representatives possess market knowledge, contacts and relevant experience, which can be made use of as soon as the partnering agreement comes into effect. Even though the roles which agents and distributors play in developing markets on behalf of the exporter are similar, there are a number of key differences that change the precise nature of the entry strategy depending on which type of representative is appointed.

Agents

Agents are appointed by exporting companies to represent their interests and generate business within a defined geographic territory or industry sector. Most agents will represent several complementary, non-competing 'principals' (the companies that engage their services) and will work to win business on their behalf. Their primary function is to achieve sales for the principal, for which they would normally receive a commission (see Figure 6.5). Whilst some agents

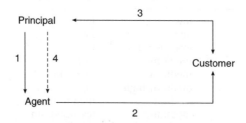

1. Principal engages the services of an agent
2. Agent identifies sales opportunities
3. Principal contracts with, and ships goods direct to, customer
4. Principal pays commission on sale to agent

Figure 6.5 Roles and responsibilities in the agency agreement.

are paid retainers by their principals as well as a commission on sales, most work on a commission-only basis. The commission rates paid vary, depending on the nature of the product and value of the sale, but are generally in the region of between 5 and 10 per cent.

Agents will have promotional materials and samples for the products they are representing but do not take ownership ('title') of the principal's goods at any stage of the transaction. This also applies to agents who provide storage facilities for the goods, although stocking agents will also be paid an agreed amount to cover warehousing and handling costs.

Effective agents do not just look for sales opportunities. They also provide their principals with valuable 'on the ground' market knowledge, experience and contacts, which can be used to improve or refine the export marketing strategy. They can advise on trends and competition, as well as providing practical services such as chasing payments and clearing goods through Customs. In some cases, especially where a relatively unproven agent has brokered a sale for the principal, the agent may even agree to reimburse the exporter in the event that the client defaults on payments. Under these circumstances, the agent is referred to as a 'del credere' agent and the rate of commission is likely to be higher.

Agency agreements

The agreement between a principal and an agent is necessarily detailed as it sets out the duties and obligations of each party. The agreement will specify the goods to be represented by the agent and the precise geographic territory in which they are to be promoted. As the exporter may wish to appoint more than one agent in each market, the territories must be clearly defined. For example, a company that manufactures protective overalls for the medical, electronic assembly and catering industries may appoint an agent for each sector in the target market. If the target market is geographically large and has many potential clients in each sector, as could be the case in Germany, the exporter may decide to appoint six agents: two per sector, one covering Northern Germany, the other covering the South. The agency agreement must therefore ensure that the individual geographic and sectoral territories are specified.

Further restrictions may be placed on the agent in terms of what can or cannot be offered to customers, what service levels are expected, confidentiality and which competing products the agent agrees not to represent.

The agreement will also list the duties of the principal with regard to what support will be provided by the exporter to the agent, what commissions will be paid and so on. Readers are advised to refer to Croner's *Model Business Contracts* for an example of a full agency agreement and the conditions it may contain. It should, however, be apparent that the overriding purpose of the agency agreement is to protect the interests of both parties whilst defining the nature and limits of the principal's and agent's responsibilities and obligations.

European agency legislation

The EU has imposed uniform regulations for the employment and treatment of agents within the EU. In summary, the regulations specify the minimum duties and responsibilities that both principal and agent are obliged to respect when entering into agreement with each other. The regulations also stipulate the notice period required should the agreement be terminated as well as the circumstances under which an agent can expect commission. In spite of the EU Directive, each member of the Union has its own specific regulations and exporters are advised to seek legal advice before appointing an agent. This is even more important in countries outside the EU that are not bound by the Directive.

Distributors

Distributors fulfil a similar role to agents in that they promote the principal's goods in export markets and are a useful means of developing trade in new markets. The main difference between these two types of intermediary is the fact that distributors actually purchase the goods from the exporter, more than likely at preferential rates, with a view to selling them on at a profit in the target market. Agents, as we have seen, do not have this flexibility.

Some exporters have made the mistake of viewing their distributors just as good customers. The reality is that a distributor does much more than simply purchase products. As well as taking title to the goods, the distributor takes on responsibility for every stage of the sales process, from marketing and negotiating to distribution to the client, although the distributor should also receive ongoing support and encouragement from the exporter. No commissions are paid as distributors generate their income through the resale of the goods at a profit.

Types of distributor

There are four main types of distributor, which exporters are likely to engage. An 'exclusive' distributorship is an agreement between the manufacturer and the chosen distributor wherein the exporter undertakes neither to sell to any other consumer or client in the target market, nor to appoint other distributors in that market. In the event that the exporter identifies a potential client in a market where it has an exclusive distributorship in place, the company should refer the prospective customer to the local representative.

'Sole' distributorships are similar to exclusive arrangements in that the supplier agrees to appoint only one distributor for the market. A sole distributorship does not, however, preclude the exporter from selling direct to other clients in the market.

1. Exporter contracts with distributor and supplies product for stock
2. Distributor sells from stock to customer

Figure 6.6 Simple distribution agreement.

'Selective' distributorships generally relate to more technical products or goods requiring a higher level of service and expertise. This type of arrangement is used by exporters to identify the conditions under which distributors can sell their products and to whom. For example, a company might prefer to sell its goods only to technically competent businesses with well-trained staff, and it would be the obligation of the distributor to ensure that the goods are not sold to customers who do not meet the exporter's minimum requirements.

Finally, a 'non-exclusive' distributor is the most relaxed of the agreements, at least from the exporter's point of view. Under the terms of non-exclusive arrangements, exporters have the freedom to sell their goods directly to consumers and to appoint other distributors in the target market if it chooses to do so.

Given that the distributor has much more control over how and where the exporter's goods are sold, the supplier has less control over the distributorship than it would over an agency. The advantage is that the exporter is not normally liable for any losses or claims made as a result of the distributor's activities. It is also likely that the distributor has more inclination to promote the company's products than an agent who represents several different principals does. Having bought the goods from the exporter, the distributor will not make any money until the goods have been sold on in the target market (see Figure 6.6).

Distribution agreements

The written agreements put in place between exporters and distributors are similar in content and function to agency agreements. They exist to set out the responsibilities and obligations of each party, territorial coverage and so on. The agreement cannot fix the price paid by the distributor to the exporter or by the customer to the distributor. Equally, it is unlawful to ban the re-export of the products from the target market to other countries and to make provision against passive sales. In the case of exclusive distributorships, the agreements should not run for more than five years. The legal issues surrounding these agreements can be complicated, particularly in the area of EU competition law. Professional advice should therefore be sought before entering into any sort of partnership agreement.

Both agencies and distributorships have the ability to use their local knowledge to establish exporters in overseas markets. Whether an exporter appoints an agent or distributor depends primarily on the amount of responsibility for promotion, distribution and after-sales service the company wants to take on (see Figure 6.7).

Agent	Distributor
• Does not take ownership ('title') of the exporter's goods	• Purchases goods from the exporter and takes ownership and control of them
• Assumes little or no risk	• Takes on all risks once ownership of the goods has been transferred
• Brokers sales on behalf of the exporter in return for a commission	• Sells the goods on to clients at a profit
• Cannot set the price of goods in the market	• Has direct responsibility for price setting
• Does not necessarily offer after-sales service or guarantees	• Offers customer support and after-sales service unless previously agreed otherwise
• Normally operates with exclusivity in the target market or defined territory	• May be exclusive, non-exclusive, selective or sole distributorships

Figure 6.7 The key differences between agents and distributors.

Question: Under what circumstances might a company decide to use distributors rather than agents? Service companies – having no goods for the distributor to sell on – are more likely to use agents. Explain how such agreements can add value to service companies' export strategies.

Commissionaires

In certain markets, exporters may find it more effective to promote their products through commissionaires, which, in many respects, act in very similar way to agents. Whilst it is not possible to make use of commissionaires to develop trade in the UK, they are relevant within Belgium, France, Germany, Italy, the Netherlands, Spain and Switzerland.

Commissionaires are still the intermediaries between exporters and customers. Whereas agents act on behalf of their principals, commissionaires act on their own behalf in return for a commission on sales. The principal is contractually obliged to deliver the goods sold by the commissionaire, who is in return obliged to pass on payment for the goods from the customer.

Identifying and selecting partners

One of the biggest obstacles to successful market entry is the appointment of effective representation. Many companies fail to achieve their true potential in their target markets as a result of having engaged inappropriate intermediaries. The exporter must therefore take care to ensure that all potential partners are thoroughly researched and profiled to ensure that agreements are reached only with those capable of representing the best interests of the business. Although this exercise may take time and incur additional costs, it is a necessary part of the selection process.

Before a short list of potential partners is drawn up the company must have a clear understanding of what it hopes to achieve in the target market and how it

• Trade association	• Library	• Foreign Embassy
• Recommendation from customers	• Foreign Chambers of Commerce	• Specialist consultants
• Market research companies	• Trade fair catalogues	• Databases
• Chambers of Commerce	• Business Link (UK)	• Euro Info Centres

Figure 6.8 Sources of contact information.

expects the objectives to be realised. This will permit the exporter to develop terms of reference by which to profile prospective agents and distributors. Once the intermediary's role and responsibilities have been identified in this way, the company is ready to begin the selection process proper. This would normally start with further research to compile a comprehensive list of potential partners in the target market, using a wide range of information sources to do so (see Figure 6.8).

PARTNERS

There are eight key issues to consider in profiling potential representatives. Appropriately, they can be summarised using the acronym PARTNERS, denoting products, after-sales service, resources, territory, numbers, experience, reputation and storage facilities. Exporters considering entering an agreement with an overseas partner should take into account the questions listed in Figure 6.9.

Once these questions have been answered, the company will have a much clearer picture of the strengths, weaknesses and requirements of potential partners, and will be able to draw up a shortlist of the organisations most likely to meet its needs. Further discussions with the shortlisted firms will provide the exporter with another opportunity to get to know the potential partners and to confirm whether or not they are suitable. Agreements can then be negotiated and signed with the partner appointed for the market.

Working with foreign intermediaries and partners

It is important to work closely with all types of intermediary and partner, regardless of the nature of the entry strategy, and to develop good relationships with them. Joint venture partners, licensees, franchisees, agents and distributors need to see commitment from the exporter and will not react favourably to a company that signs them up expecting them to get on with the job without any further support. Likewise, staff employed in joint ventures and local offices need reassurance that they are an important part of the company's overall strategy.

Companies that invest time and effort in maintaining effective relationships with their intermediaries and overseas employees are less likely to have concerns about their performance. Agents and distributors who feel valued by

Products	• How comprehensive is the partner's product range?
	• Does the partner specialise in a particular type of product?
	• Are the products already represented by the partner complementary or competitive?
	• How many other principals does the partner work for?
After-sales service	• What level of after-sales service can the partner offer?
	• Will further training be required?
	• Would the partner expect the exporter to undertake the after-sales service?
Resources	• What facilities does the partner have access to?
	• How many employees does the partner have, and how many are employed in marketing or sales?
	• Will further resources be required?
Territory	• What is the geographic territory covered by the potential partner?
	• How is this managed?
	• Does this meet the objectives of the exporter?
Numbers	• How much does the company turn over?
	• What are the projections for the next year?
	• Is the income derived from one or two main sources?
	• How important to the partner would the exporter's business be?
	• What is the minimum quantity or value that the partner would need to sell in order to justify the agreement?
	• What rate of commission would be required by the agent?
	• What discount on purchases would be expected by the distributor?
	• How much is the exporter expected to contribute towards training, marketing and promotional materials?
Experience	• How much knowledge does the partner have of the industry and sector?
	• How much market knowledge can be passed on to the exporter?
	• What contacts does the agent or distributor already have in the market?
	• Does the partner have any previous experience of the exporter's product or competitors?
Reputation	• What reputation does the partner have within the industry?
	• Can reference be obtained from the partner's other principals?
Storage facilities	• What storage and warehousing facilities does the potential partner have?
	• How much warehouse space might be allocated by the partner for the exporter?
	• How are stock levels monitored and controlled?

Figure 6.9 The PARTNERS profiling issues.

their principals will be more enthusiastic and motivated than those that receive little support and encouragement. Regular contact with intermediaries is essential and, thanks to the global developments in IT and communications, there is no reason why, for example, a company in France cannot keep in touch with its Argentinean partner at least two or three times a week. Exporters should also endeavour to visit their partners as often as is practical, or as often as the marketing and travel budget will permit. Again, this helps to strengthen the relationship between the exporter and the intermediary and demonstrates ongoing commitment to the market. Although the exporter's overseas success depends on the nature of the entry strategy adopted, it is ultimately the effectiveness of the relationship between the company and its intermediaries that determines how successful the chosen route to market will be.

Conclusions

This chapter has introduced some of the common routes to market adopted by companies and has shown the advantages and disadvantages of each. Readers will now appreciate the difference between direct and indirect exporting, as well as the roles that investment and partnering have in the development and implementation of the entry strategy. The importance of the selection of appropriate intermediaries has also been highlighted and it should be evident that the key to a successful entry strategy is, as with every other aspect of international trade, accurate and meaningful research.

Sources of information

International Chambers of Commerce – www.iccwbo.org
UK government advice and support for exporters – www.tradepartners.gov.uk
British Chambers of Commerce – www.britishchambers.org.uk/exportzone
Regional International Trade website – www.tradeportalyh.co.uk
British Exporters Association – www.bexa.co.uk
Croner's advice for exporters and importers – www.tradeinternational-centre.net
    and www.croner.cch.co.uk (main homepage)
Links to trade associations – www.martex.co.uk/taf/lookup
The Joint Venture homepage –
    http://home.earthlink.net/~fpearce/Jointventure.html

Further reading

Bartolotti F *et al., The ICC Agency Model Contract* (Kluwer Law International, 1993).
Bennet R, *Getting Started in Export* (2nd ed) (Kogan Page, 1998).
Geringer J M, *Joint Venture Partner Selection* (Quorum, 1998).
Hall R D, *International Joint Ventures* (Praeger, 1997).
Nelson C A, *Import Export* (3rd ed) (McGraw-Hill, 2000).
Sayer S, *Negotiating International Joint Venture Agreements* (Sweet and Maxwell, 1998).
Triantis J E, *Creating Successful Acquisition and Joint Venture Projects* (Quorum, 1999).
Wolf R C, *Effective International Joint Venture Management* (M E Sharpe, 2000).

QUESTIONS FOR CONSIDERATION

    1 What are the key differences between direct and indirect exporting, and what influences their selection as a route to market?
    2 How do export management companies, export houses and buying agents differ? Explain how they fit in to an entry strategy.

3 What are the advantages and disadvantages of co-marketing as an entry strategy?

4 How might even a small manufacturing company consider investing in an overseas market?

5 Describe the roles of agents and distributors as intermediaries and discuss why care needs to be taken in their selection.

Case study: Classic Door Panels Ltd

Background

Classic Door Panels Ltd is a specialist manufacturer of PVCu glazed and unglazed door in-fill panels. The company was originally established in 1988 to serve the Yorkshire area and quickly achieved local success, enabling the company to expand rapidly. By 1993, the company had twice moved to larger premises, but it was not until 1995 that the decision to examine overseas markets was taken.

First steps

Looking back, the company nowadays admits that the decision to start exporting was founded on little more than a belief that it could substantially increase its profits through trading overseas. Classic Door Panels was cash-rich, due largely to good profit margins on the PVCu panels, and the expectation that exports would hold the same margins was the prime reason that international trade was considered. The company started by looking at Europe, recognising that the nature of the product would find little success in warmer climates without costly modifications, which in turn would affect pricing and competitiveness. Classic Door Panels eventually targeted Germany as a primary market. The decision was influenced by the company's German supplier of PVC sheets, whose unique knowledge of the German market would be a useful starting point.

No further effort went into developing the German market. No research into the product's suitability in terms of size and dimensions, the market potential or trends was carried out. The company's marketing literature was adapted only slightly and then only to include different text rather than translating the existing information. The company felt that, as their brochures worked well in the UK that they would be equally effective in Germany.

The company then identified a relevant exhibition to attend in the target market. Although the event was successful in generating leads and enquiries, its success was restricted as no representatives from Classic Doors spoke German.

Recovery

On return to the UK after the exhibition, the company decided to employ an export sales manager with German language ability. Eight weeks later, the new manager took up his position and reviewed company's approach to exporting. He found that:

1. The business was completely unprepared for international trade and had very little idea of what needed to be done to achieve success in Germany.
2. The products marketed by the company in Germany were of the wrong size and dimension and did not meet the style trends in the market.
3. Although the exhibition had generated several leads, none had been followed up, as the company did not have the resources in-house to do so.
4. No follow-up visits to the market had yet taken place.
5. Market research into the potential of the German market was non-existent.
6. Marketing materials were completely inappropriate.
7. There was no coherent policy on pricing for international sales, more a question of trying to get as much as possible out of every situation.

The export manager decided that the first priority was to respond to the enquiries that had been ignored for eight weeks, whilst also trying to resolve some of the other issues by carrying out market research to understand trends, styles and pricing in the market. By carrying out the research, he was able to identify the basic requirements of the market, as well as potential distributors. Further effort, backed by various support providers such as Business Link and the DTI, led to the appointment of a distributor and adaptations to the company's products to suit the needs of the German market.

Progress

Several years on, Classic Door Panels has managed to build up a thriving export business in Germany, France and Hungary, as well as developing sales in other European and Central European countries. The company has learnt from its mistakes and now dedicates time and resources to international trade.

Comprehensive market research lies at the heart of the company's export strategy. For example, a report commissioned from the British Embassy in Hungary provided much of the information the company required to establish a presence in the market. It also contained details of potential distributors that the export manager carried out further research into, even travelling to Hungary to meet each potential partner separately. The company sought to appoint a representative that would be able to take regular quantities of panels and had the financial and physical resources to service the needs of a defined geographic area. A distributor that closely matched Classic Door Panels' criteria was appointed by the end of the visit, largely as a result of the research that had been carried out previously.

The company then attended another international trade fair, but this time in partnership with its German distributor to ensure local knowledge and to demonstrate that the company was prepared to invest in developing both market and distributor. The company prepared new marketing literature to support the exhibition, including brochures tailored to the requirements of the market, and a defined policy on pricing was also in existence by this time. Leads were followed up immediately, in some cases even during the exhibition. The company had pre-prepared correspondence that could be posted at the exhibition post office at the end of each day, meaning that the responses often arrived at the potential client's offices before the contact did. The company also gained credibility and confidence by having a German bank account, invoicing in local currency and engaging a local lawyer to oversee the legal issues.

Conclusions

Classic Door Panels believes that it is older and wiser than when it started to export. The company has the necessary in-house experience and expertise to continue making a success of international trade, but also accepts that it cannot know everything. Classic Door Panels therefore has a policy of working closely with Business Link, the local Chamber of Commerce and other support organisations, many of which have been able to provide grants towards the cost of the company's international expansion.

Summary

This case study shows the importance of understanding a market before trying to export to it. Classic Door Panels learnt quickly that exporting required greater commitment and preparation than had been anticipated. Fortunately for the company, a dedicated resource was brought in to manage international trade and put systems in place to grow the business' overseas sales. Having survived the disastrous first attempts to secure export orders, the company now recognises that the two most important issues to address are market research and, above all, ensuring that agents and distributors are well managed and supported.

◪ ꙮ **7** Basic business finance

Introduction

Any company considering trading overseas should review its financial position carefully before beginning to explore international opportunities. By doing so, the business can understand fully where its strengths and weaknesses lie with regard to overall performance, solvency, profitability and efficiency.

This chapter explains some of the terms and tools used in everyday business finance and introduces a number of basic accounting practices that are as relevant to internationally active companies as to those that are more domestically focused. It is intended as an initial guide to the principles of financial management and by no means does it pretend to be a comprehensive explanation of the subject. Readers who seek a greater understanding of accountancy and finance should be aware that numerous texts devoted solely to this field are readily available.

SLM Trading

The accounts and trading activity of a fictional company will be used to illustrate the financial procedures explained in this chapter. SLM Trading is a small manufacturing company that produces control systems for the food industry. The company employs 18 people and during 2001 sold 210 units to clients around the UK and, to a limited extent, Europe. The company is owned by the managing director and her family, who have provided most of the capital in the company, the rest having been obtained in the form of a bank loan.

Some explanations of terms

Before examining the reporting methods used by companies to keep track of their finances, it is useful to spend a few moments explaining some of the more commonly used terms contained in them.

Fixed and variable costs

There are two generic types of costs that a company would expect to incur. Fixed costs are those that generally do not change even though the volume of sales may fluctuate. They include staff salaries, insurance, rent and rates and the depreciation of equipment and machinery. These costs vary very little from month to month, and it is therefore possible to calculate a figure for the total cost of running the business before any product is made, sold and shipped. It is also prudent to class marketing and promotional costs as fixed, as the monies spent on these activities are irretrievable if sales do not increase. Fixed costs are not governed by timescales and should be therefore seen as a constant in the firm's running costs, regardless of the volume of sales and business activity.

Variable costs, on the other hand, are the costs that do vary in relation to the amount of work carried out. Depending on the nature of the business, these can include the cost of raw materials and supplies, distribution and shipping costs, wages of non-salaried staff and packaging materials. These costs will increase and decrease as the volume of business fluctuates, but each unit produced will carry a percentage of the total variable costs incurred during manufacture, packaging and distribution.

Economies of scale

As a proportion of the fixed costs is also allocated to each unit manufactured by the company, economies of scale can be achieved by increasing production so that the same fixed costs are spread more thinly across a greater volume of products. The variable costs per unit will of course be the same irrespective of quantity. For example, a manufacturer produces 200 000 picture frames per year with fixed costs of £500 000 and variable costs of £300 000. The allocation of fixed costs per unit is £2.50, and variable costs are £1.50 per item produced. The company adds on a margin of £3.50 per unit and sells at a total price of £7.50.

If production is increased to 300 000 units, the fixed cost comes down to £1.66 per unit. The variable costs remain unchanged, but the company now has the choice of selling at £7.50 as before, with an increased profit margin, or reducing its costs to compete more effectively with its competitors. Either way round, the company has generated economies of scale through increased, but more cost-effective, production.

Overheads and direct costs

Indirect costs, also called overheads, are the expenses, which a business incurs that are essential to the effective running of the company but are not attributable to a specific activity. They include costs such as heating and lighting, rent and rates, as well as the cost of running the non-income generating functions of the organisation such as personnel and accounts. It can be argued that none of these cost centres are attributable to any one activity or product, and in these cases it makes good sense to apportion the costs equally across the company so that each department bears some of the indirect costs.

Direct costs are therefore those costs incurred as a direct result of a particular activity. Raw materials needed to manufacture a product, professional services such as legalisation of export documentation, freight charges and even salaries of employees directly involved with the manufacture, packaging, sales and distribution of the product are classed as direct costs.

Assets and liabilities

What a company owes, owns and how it is financed is broken down into the business' assets and liabilities. These can be further distilled into fixed assets, sources of finance (or long-term liabilities) and current assets and liabilities. All have a monetary value, but the fixed assets take longer, and are harder, to convert into cash. They include the physical infrastructure of the company, its buildings, machinery and other fixtures. Internationally active companies that have substantial investments in overseas subsidiaries would also include these under fixed assets.

The company's current assets are generally short-term considerations such as outstanding monies owed by clients, as well as raw materials and stock held ready for sale. The value of the company's cash reserves in the bank is also classed under current assets, as are any payments made in advance to the company's suppliers. Current assets are therefore the funds that the company can access quickly. By the same token, the company's short-term debts, including bank overdrafts, shorter term loans and any monies that the business owes its suppliers are identified as current liabilities.

The longer term liabilities are really the sources of the company's finance, namely any capital invested by the owner or shareholders, long-term loans and profits that the company has reinvested as further capital.

Balance sheet

Having explained the terms, attention can now be given to the reports that they are used in. The balance sheet is one of the main financial reporting mechanisms as it provides a snapshot of the company's current financial position. It is effectively a summary of all the company's assets and liabilities at a specific moment in time and is so called because the value of what the company owns should balance with what it owes. The sum of the company's assets is equivalent to the value of the liabilities and the owner's investment. Effectively, the balance sheet explains what the company has bought and how it has paid for the purchases. Table 7.1 shows an example balance sheet for SLM Trading.

It is impossible to alter one side of the balance sheet without adjusting the other accordingly. Purchases of new machinery will increase the value of the company's assets, but either the liabilities will increase if a loan is needed to pay for the investment, or, if the company pays out of its reserves (cash in the bank), the value of assets will decrease again. As assets and liabilities can change on a daily basis, it is important that the balance sheet is dated to accurately reflect the position of the company at the time of writing.

Table 7.1 SLM Trading – balance sheet at 31st December 2001

Liabilities		Assets	
Sources of finance		**Fixed assets**	
Share capital	£550 000	Machinery	£375 000
Reserves*	(£15 000)	Buildings	£300 000
Long-term loan	£110 000		
Profits reinvested (from 2000)	£10 000		
Current liabilities		**Current assets**	
Creditors	£24 000	Stock	£16 000
Short-term loans/HP	£20 000	Debtors	£15 000
Overdraft	£7 000	Cash	£30 000
Total liabilities:	£736 000	**Total assets**:	£736 000

* Funds taken from the company's bank balance.

Trading and profit and loss account

The 'trading and profit and loss account', usually abbreviated to the P&L account is the other main reporting mechanism employed by businesses to gauge their financial position. It is used primarily to calculate the value of any profit or loss that the company has made in the accounting period covered, and it may give an indication of the reasons behind the profit or loss.

Rather than concentrating on a particular point in time, as the balance sheet does, the P&L account pulls together and summarises the financial changes that the company has undergone over any period of time that the company wants to examine. Generally, companies in the UK will prepare a P&L account on a quarterly basis to coincide with their valued added tax (VAT) returns, although companies may also use a P&L account to show their annual performance when compiling their end of year accounts.

The primary purpose of the P&L is to provide the company with an indication of overall performance over the period. The profit or loss figure reflects the trading position of the company and consequently must be an accurate reflection of all income and expenditure. Where a company has invoiced a client for goods sold and not received payment during the accounting period, the value of the invoice should still be included in the total for the period. Likewise, any invoices from suppliers not received in the period should also be included. All income and expenditure is therefore allocated to the accounting period in which it was generated, assisting management in keeping track of all financial activity that can be attributed to the period under review.

The P&L can be used to work out the cost of sales to the company, that is, how much it costs the company to sell its products once supplier costs, overheads, promotion, travel and so on have been taken into account. The P&L also shows the five levels of profit. These are:

- Gross profit – sales minus cost of goods.
- Operating profit – gross profit minus running costs.

Table 7.2   SLM Trading – P&L account: 1st January to 31st December 2001

Sales revenue		£840 000
Less cost of goods sold		
Raw materials	£428 000	
Less stock held	£16 000	
Cost of goods sold		£412 000
Gross profit		£428 000
Less overheads and running costs		
Salaries	£240 000	
Overheads	£84 000	
Bank charges	£7 000	
Travel	£9 000	
Marketing	£12 500	
Finance costs *	£2 500	
Insurance **	£2 500	
Shipping **	£7 500	
Communications	£5 000	
Professional fees	£14 000	
Misc. other	£2 000	
Total expenses		£386 000
Net profit before interest and tax		£42 000

* See Chapter 13.
** See Chapters 9 and 13.

- Net profit after interest, before tax – operating profit less interest paid to loan or capital providers.
- Net profit after tax – any dividends payable to the company's shareholders are paid from this figure.
- Retained profit – also called reserves. This is the final profit after all deductions have been made.

If the net profit figure actually shows a loss, this reduces the company's assets accordingly, probably in terms of cash in the bank. In the short term, the loss might not appear significant or impact too greatly on the company's future performance. If, however, the company continues to make a loss and eat into its reserves, the longer term outlook for the business is not healthy and corrective action needs to be taken. Table 7.2 shows a P&L account for SLM Trading.

Question: What conclusions can be drawn from SLM Trading's trading and profit and loss account for the year ending 31st December 2001?

Cash flow

Controlling and forecasting the flow of cash within the company is essential. The cash flow forecast is based on the difference between the anticipated volume of sales over a given period – usually six or 12 months – and the operating cost over the same period. The forecast should be reviewed regularly to ensure that the financial information on which it is based is accurate and up to date. The forecast must take into account any projects that the company expects to undertake during the period and all anticipated costs or sales, regardless of origin, should be reflected in the tables. A model cash flow forecast contains three elements. The first section shows projected sales and other sources of income over the period. The second section lists the payments likely to be made. The final section shows the cash balances, either positive or negative, with the bottom line of the table showing how the flow of cash in and out of the company is likely to behave over the period of time examined.

In the example below, SLM Trading has an ambitious forward plan aiming to achieve £1 000 000 in sales revenue during the course of 2002. To facilitate this increase in sales, the company has employed an additional salesman, budgeted for an increase in the cost of travel for sales visits to £12 000 and has allocated a marketing budget of £27 000. Communication costs (telephone, fax, email) will rise in line with the increased sales effort. Research has shown that the cost of materials is not likely to change before the middle of the year, and neither is there likely to be any form of additional financial investment in the company through loans or shares issued.

The price of the goods to the customer will remain unchanged to preserve the company's competitive advantage.

Consequently, when SLM Trading's management draws up a six-month cash flow forecast, the table is structured as shown in Table 7.3.

Table 7.3 SLM Trading – Cash flow forecast, January to June 2002

	January	February	March	April	May	June
Income						
Sales	64 000	68 000	80 000	88 000	96 000	96 000
Loan	0	0	0	0	0	0
Capital	0	0	0	0	0	0
Total	64 000	68 000	80 000	88 000	96 000	96 000
Expenses						
Salaries	21 600	21 600	21 600	21 600	21 600	21 600
Overheads	7 600	7 600	7 600	7 600	7 600	7 600
Bank fees	600	600	600	600	600	600
Travel	1 000	1 000	1 000	1 000	1 000	1 000
Marketing	2 000	2 000	2 500	2 500	3 000	2 000
Comms	450	450	450	450	450	450
Prof. fees	1 000	1 000	1 000	1 200	1 200	1 000
Misc. other	175	175	175	175	175	175
Materials	31 360	33 320	39 200	43 120	47 040	47 040
Total	65 785	67 745	74 125	78 245	82 665	81 465
Balance						
Cash balance	(1 785)	255	5 875	9 755	21 375	22 575
Brought forward	-	(1 786)	(1 531)	4 344	14 099	35 474
Net cash flow	(1 785)	(1 531)	4 344	14 099	35 474	58 049

This is a simplified cash flow forecast, and it does not take into account any funds brought forward from the previous year, meaning that SLM Trading projections are effectively calculated from a standing start from January 1st 2002. Even so, assuming that the company continues with its strategy for the duration of 2002, the projected sales revenue of £1 000 000 looks both achievable and affordable in terms of how it will be financed. Although the first two months anticipate a negative cash flow, the second quarter is increasingly positive and the indications are that costs and income will be very much in line with budgets, generating increased profits over the 12-month period and supporting the company's decision to employ the new sales representative.

Break-even

Break-even is quite simply the point at which a company covers all its costs through product sales, with any income generated over and above this point seen as gross profit. It is important for the company to know how many units must be sold for the business to break-even on the venture – if the break-even point is unrealistically high the company may struggle to achieve the sales needed to reach it. The business is therefore unlikely to make a profit and may not even recoup all its costs.

Break-even volumes can easily be calculated providing that the company is able to put a figure on the price (or net sales revenue) per unit, the variable cost per unit and the total fixed costs. No matter what a company produces, how it sells its products or in which markets it is active, it will always aim to recover enough funds from its activities to cover its fixed costs and to generate a profit. The 'contribution' made from the product sales is effectively what the activity yields financially once the variable costs have been taken into account. For SLM Trading, the price per unit is £4000, of which variable costs are £2122 and the contribution is £1878. Fixed costs are £376 920. The contribution can be used to give the company a precise figure for the number of sales required to recoup the fixed costs of the product. The simplest of several methods of calculating the volume of sales required for the company to break-even is by using the formula:

$$Number\ of\ units = \frac{Fixed\ costs}{Unit\ price - Variable\ cost\ per\ unit}$$

On this basis, the volume of units needed to be sold in order for SLM Trading to achieve break-even is:

$$\frac{£376\,920}{£4000 - £2122} = 201\ \text{complete units}$$

Any units sold over and above this figure generate profits for the company, which, after all, is normally the main objective. To see the volume of sales required to enable the company to reach a certain level of profit, a minor adjustment can be made to the formula so that the target profit is added to the fixed costs as follows:

$$\text{Number of units} = \frac{\text{Fixed costs} + \text{Profit}}{\text{Unit price} - \text{Variable cost per unit}}$$

In 2002, SLM Trading aims to generate profit of £93 000. The volume of sales required to achieve this will be:

$$\frac{£376\,920 + £93\,000}{£4000 - £2122} = 250 \text{ units}$$

Margin of safety

The difference between the break-even point and the volume of product actually sold is referred to as the margin of safety. As long as the company is able to maintain this margin, all its variable and fixed costs are being met and the business is returning a profit. The wider the margin, the less likely the organisation is to experience financial difficulties and the more flexibility the company has to undertake projects or activities it may not otherwise have considered or been able to afford. For instance, the development of overseas markets may not be an option available to companies constrained by a narrow margin of safety as the additional costs and charges may start to eat into the surpluses, reducing the margin and potentially taking the company back to the break-even point or worse. The margin of safety can be represented graphically as shown in Figure 7.1.

The margin of safety is consequently an important element of the financial planning process and should be quantified by companies as a means of reviewing sales performance against costs.

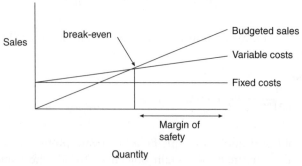

Figure 7.1   Margin of safety.

Working capital

All companies need cash in order to pay for their everyday expenses, supplies and salaries. This is a fundamental requirement as companies that have insufficient working capital are unable to meet their obligations. The company's 'working capital' is also defined as net current assets, which is simply the difference between the current assets and current liabilities.

Working capital is therefore another expression of the company's liquidity, and how much it can afford to spend on developing the business. An organisation that has substantial working capital is in a strong position, whereas companies with negative capital (where current liabilities are greater than current assets) have little or no spending power.

It should be apparent that positive working capital is essential to the successful running of a business. The company still needs to pay its expenses on a daily or monthly basis, and will not find this easy if it is working with minimal or negative working capital.

Setting a budget

Budgets are an essential means of measuring and evaluating business performance. They are set by management, who anticipate the likely costs and revenue for a certain period, for instance a financial year. The budget sets out what the income and expenditure for the company's activities during the year are realistically going to be, thereby giving the company defined financial parameters within which to work. As such, the budget is often seen as the company's business plan from the financial perspective.

The advantages of budgets are that they are generally easily understood, with detailed financial information distilled into category headings under income or expenditure. This in turn can also help management to more closely understand how the company operates and where the main cost and revenue centres are.

As the budget reflects the company's projected activity over the budget period, it is as much a statement of intent as a financial tool. Once the budget has been drawn up, it is stating that its contents are what the business will deliver during the period. Management should therefore review progress against budgeted activity, income and expenditure as part of the overall monitoring of business performance.

Disadvantages of budgets

Although budgets should be drawn up and utilised in every commercial organisation, they should be treated with some caution. If the projected activity does not take place and the budgeted income target will not be met, particularly as a result of a badly managed organisation, this may lead to demotivation amongst staff who feel that their efforts are in vain. Demotivation is even more likely if the budget is used to control costs and is inflexible, offering no room for variation or response to any unplanned difficulties.

These disadvantages notwithstanding, budgets are an integral part of any business and do assist in identifying targets, as well as monitoring progress made towards the company's goals.

Using ratios to evaluate profitability, liquidity and efficiency

Ratios are employed to examine the detail of the formal financial reporting mechanisms, the balance sheet and the profit and loss account. By interpreting key financial indicators and expressing them as simple, numerical expressions, ratios can assist management in focusing on the company's performance or profitability, as well as on the solvency or liquidity of the organisation. Consequently, the accurate use of ratios is an important management process, which identifies certain strengths and weaknesses. The most commonly used ratios are described below and should be considered on a regular basis.

Return on capital employed

The return on capital employed (ROCE) ratio is one of the most often used measures of a company's overall position. The capital employed in a company is the total financial resources that the company possesses, including long-term loans; any profits retained for re-investment as well as the owners' or shareholders' investments in the company. This figure can then be taken in conjunction with the business' profits before interest payments and taxes and expressed as a percentage to give management an indication of the value for money the company is getting out of its investment. The higher the percentage, the better the company is performing. The ratio is therefore expressed as:

$$\frac{\text{Profit before interest and tax}}{\text{Capital employed}} \times 100$$

Return on sales

The return on sales (ROS) ratio is used to give the company an indication of its profitability. By taking the operating profit (gross profit less expenses) and expressing it as a percentage of the sales turnover, the company can see immediately the value that it is getting from sales.

$$\frac{\text{Operating profit}}{\text{Sales}} \times 100$$

The lower the percentage, the lower the profitability and the more sales are needed to ensure that costs are covered and a contribution made. A higher percentage suggests that the company benefits from more profitable sales activity.

Current ratio

The current ratio is a recognised measure of a company's liquidity, that is, cash readily available as money in the bank or assets that can be sold to raise cash. This can also be described as the working capital ratio. It is expressed as current assets over current liabilities and shows how easily the company can meet its liabilities. A ratio of 1:1 is adequate as the company's assets could cover the liabilities if the need arose, but a more desirable ratio of assets to liabilities would be a minimum of 2:1. This would ensure that the company could meet all its obligations whilst being able to retain some working capital.

Acid test

The acid test ratio is also known as the quick ratio. It is used as a measure of the company's liquidity in the face of demands for immediate payment by creditors. The ratio only makes use of assets that can be quickly realised, including cash in the bank and trade debtors and so on. It does not include work in progress or stocks held as there may be no immediate buyer for the goods and hence the company cannot rely on receiving quick payment for them.

The formula for the acid test is written as:

$$\frac{Current\ assets - Stock\ and\ work\ in\ progress}{Current\ liabilities}$$

As for the current ratio, a ratio of 1:1 would enable the company to pay off creditors, but only just, whilst a ratio of 1:0.8 would leave the company in a difficult position were the creditors to demand payment.

Debtors ratio

The average collection period, or debtors, ratio is a measure of the company's efficiency in securing payment from its customers. A company that is owed a lot of money is not as efficient as a company that has more effective credit control procedures in place and consequently has to wait less time to receive payment. The formula is a simple representation of outstanding debts against total sales on account, and is expressed as 'debtor days':

$$\frac{Debtors\ balance}{Sales\ revenue} \times 365$$

Creditors ratio

The opposite of the debtors ratio is the average days' credit, or creditors, ratio. This is used by companies that have bought or borrowed on credit and gauges the average length of the company's debt. The ratio is expressed as 'creditor days' and is written as

$$\frac{\text{Creditors balance}}{\text{Purchases made}} \times 365$$

A high level of creditor days may mean that the company is potentially overexposed in terms of its liabilities. This ratio should therefore be used in conjunction with the acid test ratio and current ratio to monitor the company's overall financial position.

Summary

Ratios can therefore provide a range of useful indicators of a company's performance in key areas. It is the responsibility of management to ensure that these ratios are interpreted accurately so that the results have real meaning for the company. It is especially prudent for the potential exporter or importer to understand the financial position of their business, as buying or selling overseas is likely to bring further pressures to bear. For example, new clients and suppliers will mean new debtors and creditors, which will in turn impact on the company's solvency, efficiency and ultimate performance.

As well as providing management information to assist in the day-to-day running of a business, the ratios are one more process that the company should undertake in advance of its decision to export. Ultimately, the results will show whether or not the company has the financial resources necessary to commit itself to international trade.

Conclusions

This chapter has provided a basic overview of some of the procedures and terms used in standard accounting practice. Readers should now be able to draw up a simple balance sheet, trading and profit and loss account and should be able to understand cash flow forecasts, as well as making use of simple formulae to draw conclusions from financial data. The chapter has indicated that the financial requirements of international trade (for instance shipping, currency and documentary costs) must be taken into consideration alongside existing fixed and variable costs. Exporting and importing should not be seen as separate financial entities, but must be included in the company's overall financial reports. The importance of maintaining accurate, up-to-date financial information for monitoring budgets, performance and efficiency should therefore be apparent.

Sources of information

Chartered Institute of Management Accountants – www.cima.org.uk
Chartered Association of Certified Accountants – www.acca.co.uk
Institute of Chartered Accountants in England and Wales – www.icaew.co.uk
Institute of Chartered Accountants in Scotland – www.icas.org.uk

Further reading

Barrow C, *Financial Management for the Small Business* (2nd ed) (Kogan Page, 1991).
Conlan J, *Principles of Management in Export* (Blackwell, 1988).
Dyson J R, *Accounting for Non-accounting Students* (8th ed) (FT Prentice Hall, 2000).
Eyre E C and Pettinger R, *Mastering Basic Management* (3rd ed) (Macmillan, 1999).
Nicholson M, *Mastering Accounting Skills* (2nd ed) (Palgrave, 2000).
Stickney C and Weilz R, *Financial Accounting: An Introduction to Concepts, Methods and Uses* (9th ed) (Thomson Learning, 1999).
Wood F and Sangster A, *Business Accounting Vols 1 & 2* (8th ed) (FT Prentice Hall, 1999).

QUESTIONS FOR CONSIDERATION

1 Explain the terms fixed costs, variable costs, contribution, assets and liabilities.
2 What is the purpose of the balance sheet, the P&L account and cash flow forecasting?
3 Using the information contained in the balance sheet and P&L account for SLM Trading, what conclusions are reached when the following ratios have been calculated?

   Return on capital employed
   Return on sales
   Current ratio
   Acid test
   Debtors ratio
   Creditors ratio

4 What recommendations could be made to the management of SLM Trading with regard to improving the company's overall performance?

▣ ⱱ **8** Export costing, pricing and the sale

Introduction

Having undertaken the preparatory work necessary to identify the most appropriate route to market to capitalise on overseas opportunities, attention must be paid to how the company prices its products for exporting and to how the sale will be achieved. This chapter will explain how export prices are calculated, taking into account the different financial obligations and other responsibilities that are identified by the internationally accepted delivery terms, Incoterms. Four approaches towards pricing strategies for international trade will be discussed, and the quotation and order process will also be examined in detail. The chapter will give the reader an understanding of how accurate export prices are put together and will introduce the basic principles of international contract law.

Introducing Incoterms

Incoterms (International Commercial Terms) were first introduced by the International Chamber of Commerce (ICC) in 1936 and have been revised on six occasions since, the last time being in 2000. They were developed as a type of internationally recognised shorthand to formally identify the responsibilities and obligations of the buyer and seller in a range of international transport agreements. In particular, they are used to establish beyond question which party incurs the costs and risks of delivery at every stage of the distribution process.

Incoterms were introduced with the aim of eliminating the misunderstandings that often arose between traders in different countries as a result of unfamiliarity with each other's trading practices, which regularly led to misinterpretation of delivery terms or the sales contract. Since Incoterms can avoid this confusion, their use provides an internationally accepted basis for identifying conditions in the contract of sale. They define the conditions that need to be satisfied in order for the exporter to be deemed to have delivered the goods.

The ICC publishes Incoterms as the 'official' interpretation of commercial trade terms, focusing on the exporter's obligations in fulfilling the contractual aspects of the sale of goods overseas. They do not, as many people assume, define the nature of the transport contract. Neither can Incoterms be used in contracts of sale relating to services or other non-physical products.

What Incoterms achieve

The 13 Incoterms are used to cover core aspects of the international distribution process, which fulfil the terms of the export order, such as who is responsible for insuring the goods, where they are to be transported to and when title of the goods passes to the buyer. They also determine who is responsible for transportation and obtaining the export/import clearances.

Incoterms are broken down into four classes, labelled E,F,C and D. Group E (EXW) is the easiest from the exporter's perspective as the goods to be exported are made available to the buyer from the seller's premises, with no further involvement from the seller in the distribution process.

Group F terms (FCA, FAS, FOB) oblige the exporter to deliver the goods to a named carrier arranged by the buyer. The group C terms (CFR, CPT, CIP, CIF) specify that the exporter organises transportation of the goods to a named destination, but does not incur the risks as this is still the buyer's responsibility. The group D Incoterms (DES, DEQ, DAF, DDU, DDP) are least favourable to the exporter, who is obliged to cover all the costs and risks of transporting the goods to their destination.

Each Incoterm has different implications for both the importer and the exporter (see Figure 8.1) and it is important to understand the exact nature of each term before entering into a sales contract with a foreign buyer. It is also important to specify which version of Incoterms the contract is based upon, as the six revisions since 1936 made subtle changes to each definition. The contract of sale should therefore have a clause to the effect that 'any trade terms contained in this contract refer to Incoterms 2000'.

Common issues

The full definition of each term contained in Incoterms 2000 breaks down the responsibilities of both the buyer and seller into 10 sections, which cover:

1. The provision of goods and the price to be paid for them.
2. Who is required to obtain export and import licenses.

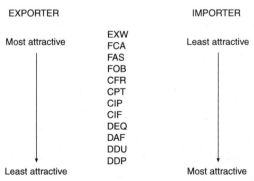

Figure 8.1 Incoterms from the exporter's and importer's perspectives.

3. The contracts for carriage and insurance.
4. When delivery is deemed to take place.
5. When the risk transfers from the exporter to the importer.
6. How the transport costs and other charges are to be split between the two parties.
7. How much notice the exporter and importer need to give when notifying each other of the nominated delivery point and date.
8. What proof of delivery is required – for instance, a bill of lading (B/L) may be used as proof that goods have been loaded onto a ship, constituting delivery under a free on board (FOB) contract.
9. Any specific requirements in terms of packaging, marking and inspection of goods.
10. Other obligations, for instance to assist the other party in obtaining documentation or to provide information to enable the exporter or importer to take out an insurance policy.

Ex Works (EXW)

Under an EXW contract, the exporting company is responsible for making the goods to be transported available for collection by the buyer at an agreed time and location. In the majority of cases, the location will be the exporter's premises. The goods must be appropriately packaged and marked, and should be accompanied by a commercial invoice. The exporter is also obliged, at the buyer's expense, to assist in obtaining any import/export documentation and export licences that the buyer requests help with. There are no other obligations for the exporter to meet and once the goods have been collected by the buyer at the appointed location, the exporter bears no further costs or risk.

As well as paying for the goods and issuing a written (or electronic) acknowledgement of having received them, the buyer is responsible for all costs and risks incurred from the moment the title to the goods has passed from the exporter. The buyer must also undertake to obtain all necessary licenses and other documentary requirements for the onward transportation of the goods. EXW is therefore most appealing to the exporter and least attractive to the buyer.

Free Carrier (FCA...named place)

With FCA contracts, the exporter is obliged to secure all the necessary export licences and pay all the Customs charges in order to clear the shipment for export. The goods must be delivered to the buyer's appointed carrier (the business that is contracted to transport the goods) at the agreed time and until the goods have been transferred to the carrier, the exporter bears all the risks and costs incurred.

Import licences and Customs clearances on arrival remain the responsibility of the buyer, who bears all the costs and risks of transport from the moment the carrier has taken receipt of the goods.

As far as FCA is concerned, delivery is deemed to have taken place either if the goods have been loaded on the carrier's means of transport at the exporter's premises or if the goods have been made available to the carrier at any other agreed location.

Free Alongside Ship (FAS...named port of shipment)

Free Alongside Ship is used when the seller agrees to deliver the goods alongside the buyer's nominated ship at the nominated port of shipment. The exporter is again responsible for making sure that all export licences and clearance authorisation are obtained and must ensure that the buyer receives notification of proof of delivery alongside the vessel.

Again, the buyer is responsible for all import licences and for clearing the goods through Customs on arrival. Where the shipment passes through more than one country, the buyer is also responsible for the fulfilling the Customs requirements of each market. The exporter's obligations therefore cease once the goods have been cleared for export and are unloaded next to the named vessel. The costs and risk from this point until the goods reach their final destination fall to the buyer.

Free on Board (FOB...named port of shipment)

FOB is one of the more commonly used Incoterms, although it is also frequently misused. The term can only be specified when the method of transportation is by sea or inland waterway. There are, however, numerous examples of companies who have specified FOB and named their premises or inland distribution centre as the port of shipment, which hardly reduces the potential for misunderstandings. Whilst a UK citizen would know that Halifax, West Yorkshire, is not a port town, a buyer on the other side of the world may not appreciate that FOB Halifax simply does not make sense. It is important to ensure that the most appropriate Incoterm is used, and that those relating to waterborne transport are not employed for rail or road transport (see Figure 8.2). Under FOB, the exporter is bound to deliver the goods, with all licences and Customs clearances obtained, over the rail of the vessel. Therefore,

Maritime and inland waterway		Any mode of transport	
• FAS	• FOB	• EXW	• FCA
• CFR	• CIF	• CPT	• CIP
• DES	• DEQ	• DAF	• DDU
		• DDP	

Figure 8.2 Differentiating between water-based and multimodal Incoterms.

under the terms of FOB Liverpool, the exporter must place the goods on board the ship at Liverpool docks and the key difference between FOB and FAS is that the exporter must pay for the goods to be placed aboard the ship. The buyer becomes responsible for all costs and risks once the goods have passed the ship's rail.

Cost and Freight (CFR ... named port of destination)

CFR has the same implications as the FOB contract in that the exporter must deliver the goods for shipment across the ship's rail, bearing the costs of transportation from the seller's premises, loading and obtaining the necessary licences and so on. With CFR, however, the exporter is also obliged to pay for the transport of the goods to the destination port. CFR Rotterdam would therefore require the exporter to bear all the transport costs until the vessel docks in Rotterdam.

Although the exporter pays for transportation, the risks remain with the buyer, who should insure the goods during shipping. If the goods are damaged or lost in transit, the buyer has no recourse to the exporter, whose obligations end with the payment for shipping. The buyer's other responsibilities remain the same as for FOB.

Cost, Insurance and Freight (CIF ... named port of destination)

As for CFR, the exporter must also pay for shipment to a named destination port and is seen to have delivered the goods once they have passed over the ship's rail. Whilst the risk of damage or loss during transit still falls to the buyer, the seller is obliged to take out marine insurance to cover the buyer's risk.

The minimum insurance cover acceptable under CIF terms is the value of the goods plus 10 per cent. If the buyer seeks greater insurance cover, this needs to be expressly agreed in the contract of sale with the exporter, or taken out at the buyer's own expense.

The buyer is required to bear all the costs and risks from the moment that the exporter has delivered the goods. Additionally, the buyer is usually responsible for any unloading charges at the port of destination, unless it has been previously agreed in the contract that the cost of unloading is included in overall freight costs.

Carriage Paid To (CPT ... named place of destination)

With the CPT term, the exporter is responsible for delivering the goods to a carrier and for covering the cost of carriage to the named place of destination.

The seller also bears all the risks until the carrier has taken delivery, when risk passes to the buyer. If more than one carrier is used to transport the goods from the point of delivery to the named place of destination, the risk passes from the exporter to the buyer once the first carrier has received the shipment, and the risk remains with the buyer until the goods have arrived at their destination.

The buyer is still responsible for unloading the goods, unless previously agreed with the seller (as under CIF). Export clearances remain the duty of the exporter, the import clearances the duty of the buyer.

Carriage and Insurance Paid To (CIP ... named place of destination)

CIP takes CIF terms a stage further by requiring the exporter to take out cargo insurance to cover the buyer's risks for the carriage of the goods to the named destination.

Delivered at Frontier (DAF ... named place)

The Group D terms imply increased obligations on the part of the exporter. Under DAF, the seller is seen to deliver the goods once they have been made available to the buyer on (not unloaded from) the method of transport on arrival at the named place. The exporter will have cleared the shipment for export, but not import, as this is still the responsibility of the buyer, as are the unloading charges unless previously agreed. Delivery therefore takes place before the Customs control of the neighbouring country. The frontier specified in the term may potentially be the frontier of the exporter's own country where a buyer wishes to take delivery there. Risk passes from the exporter to the buyer once the goods have been delivered at the specified location.

Delivered Ex Ship (DES ... named port of destination)

As DES is one of the Incoterms relating to maritime or inland waterway transportation, it can only be used in conjunction with named ports. Under DES, delivery is seen to have taken place when the shipment is made available to the buyer on board ship at the named port. All the costs and risks of shipping the goods to the port fall to the exporter. The buyer is responsible for unloading the goods, obtaining import clearance and bearing the costs and risks involved from the moment delivery of the goods has been taken. There is no obligation for the exporter to insure the buyer's risks, but the exporter is advised to cover his own risks to the point of delivery.

Delivered Ex Quay (DEQ...named port of destination)

If the buyer and the seller agree that it should be the seller's responsibility to unload the shipment from the vessel, the contract moves from DES to DEQ terms. Delivery takes place once the goods have been unloaded onto the quay or wharf of the port in question, leaving the buyer with the responsibility for import clearance and onward transportation.

Delivered Duty Unpaid (DDU...named place of destination)

DDU requires the exporter to deliver the goods to the buyer at a named destination such as the buyer's premises. This implies that the exporter is responsible for the entire distribution process, from factory to buyer. Consequently, all the risks and costs involved in the transportation of the goods remain with the exporter until delivery takes place at the final destination. The buyer's responsibilities are limited to obtaining import clearance and paying any duties relating to the import of the shipment.

Delivered Duty Paid (DDP...named place of destination)

DDP follows the duties defined for the DDU contract with the exception that the buyer no longer has to obtain import clearance or pay Customs duties and so on. The seller takes full responsibility for all the costs and risks incurred throughout the whole process, with delivery taking place at the buyer's named place of destination. The buyer needs only to take delivery of the goods and to provide written evidence of having done so.

Although DDP is often seen as the least favourable of all the Incoterms from the exporter's point of view, it can be of use as a sales tool. If the company is able to sell on DDP terms, the importer's responsibilities and financial obligations are greatly reduced, which may in turn help to close the sale.

Incoterms from the importer's perspective

Just as the exporter tries to negotiate the most favourable delivery term when contracting with overseas buyers, so the importing company negotiates to secure the most acceptable terms from its perspective. Naturally, this means trying to get the exporter to incur as much financial responsibility and risk as possible. DDP therefore becomes an ideal term for the importer and EXW the term to be avoided, and the importer must take as much care as the exporter in understanding the precise requirements of each Incoterm (see Figure 8.3 and 8.4).

	FAS	FOB	CFR	CIF	DES	DEQ
Seafreight	Buyer	Buyer	Seller	Seller	Seller	Seller
Carriage to ship	Seller	Seller	Seller	Seller	Seller	Seller
Insurance during carriage	Buyer's option	Buyer's option	Buyer's option	Seller's duty	Seller's option	Seller's option
Loading	Buyer	Seller	Seller	Seller	Seller	Seller
Unloading	Buyer	Buyer	Buyer, unless included in freight costs	Buyer, unless included in freight costs	Buyer	Seller
Point of delivery and risk passing to buyer	Alongside ship nominated by buyer at port of shipment	Once goods pass rail of nominated ship at shipment port	On board seller's nominated ship at port of shipment	On board seller's nominated ship at port of shipment	On board seller's nominated ship at port of destination	At quay nominated by buyer at port of destination
Export clearance	Seller	Seller	Seller	Seller	Seller	Seller
Import clearance	Buyer	Buyer	Buyer	Buyer	Buyer	Seller

Figure 8.3 Buyer's and seller's responsibilities under maritime/inland waterway Incoterms.

	EXW	FCA	CPT	CIP	DAF	DDU	DDP
Carriage	Buyer	Buyer	Seller	Seller	Seller	Seller	Seller
Insurance during carriage	Buyer's option	Buyer's option	Buyer's option	Seller's duty	Seller's option	Seller's option	Seller's option
Loading	Buyer	Seller (premises) or buyer (at other location)	Seller	Seller	Seller	Seller	Seller
Unloading	Buyer	Buyer	Buyer, unless if in carriage costs	Buyer, unless if in carriage costs	Buyer	Buyer	Buyer
Point of delivery and risk passing to buyer	At named place – for example seller's premises	Loaded on buyer's carrier at seller's premises/ given to carrier at other location	On delivery to carrier	On delivery to carrier	At a named location at a frontier	At buyer's named location	At buyer's named location
Export clearance	Buyer	Seller	Seller	Seller	Seller	Seller	Seller
Import clearance	Buyer	Buyer	Buyer	Buyer	Buyer	Seller	Seller

Figure 8.4 Buyer's and seller's responsibilities under multimodal Incoterms.

Export costing

Export costing calculations are used to assist exporters in ascertaining how competitive the company's products will be in the target market once all the additional charges and fees have been taken into consideration. Also called 'landed costs', they provide the exporter with a breakdown of how the total cost of the product has been reached, which may then identify areas where savings can be made in order to improve competitiveness. Export costing should be seen as a key part of the company's financial planning activities, especially in conjunction with the cash flow forecast, as an accurate costing sheet will allow the company to take all the costs associated with market entry into account.

The export costing process starts by taking the ex works cost of the company's products, namely the manufacturing costs plus profit margin, packaging and marking costs, export clearance and any commission that may be due to an agent. For an EXW contract, these are the only costs that the exporter need worry about as the buyer incurs the subsequent transport and insurance costs.

Under any other Incoterm, the exporter must ensure that the individual costs specified by each term are included in the costing sheet, as demonstrated

---

Boardman-Murray – export costing sheet, 11th February 2002

Order details

Client	Malay Construction Ltd	
Market	Kuala Lumpur, Malaysia	
Product	Series 3 Drilling Rigs (x4)	
Cost of product per unit	(£2 500)	£10 000
Profit margin (30%)		£3 000
Cost of modifying products to meet market requirements		£1 500
Agent's commission payable (10%)		£1 450
Packing, marking and labelling		£100
Export clearance fee		£200
	EXW cost	**£16 250**
Carriage to port of shipping		£125
Freight forwarder's charges		£35
Unloading costs		£25
Charges levied by port		£20
Storage charges		£0
Other miscellaneous costs		£0
	FAS cost	**£16 455**
Loading onto ship		£350
Documentation charges		£300
Freight charges		£400
Other miscellaneous costs		£0
	CFR cost	**£17 505**
Marine insurance @ 110% of invoice		£1 750
	CIF cost	**£19 255**
Finance fees (*)		£150
Export credit insurance (*)		£100
TOTAL COSTS (CIF)		**£19 505**

*See Chapter 13.

Figure 8.5 Sample export costing sheet.

in Figure 8.5. Once the export costing exercise has been completed, the company can examine all the cost areas to identify those that may offer scope for reduction. For instance, if the cost of clearing customs under a DDP contract is high, the exporter may look to reduce other costs to compensate. This might mean negotiating a cut in the agent's commission, a reduction in marketing expenditure or perhaps reviewing the actual production costs of the product itself. The costing should then be used in consultation with foreign partners and representatives to determine whether it is viable to sell the product at the price arrived at, or whether further work needs to be done to reduce costs in order to preserve competitiveness.

The export costing sheet should be reviewed regularly and used in every sales situation where a buyer stipulates a different or unfamiliar Incoterm. By treating the costing sheet as a fluid document that can take into account different sales volumes and costs as and when the occasion requires, the company will always be able to quickly determine the landed cost of the goods and hence be fully aware of all the cost implications.

Note: Companies in the service sector obviously have fewer costs to consider and are unlikely to require Incoterms. Even so, such companies must be fully aware of all the costs that they are likely to encounter and ensure that any agreement entered into clearly states when the contract is deemed to be fulfilled.

Pricing strategies

As previous chapters have shown, pricing is an essential component in the marketing mix and needs to be considered carefully. By the time the company comes to develop a pricing strategy for a particular market, market research should already have provided information on the exporter's competition and the quality, price and normal delivery terms demanded by their customers. The company will then be able to appraise its own pricing policies in comparison to prices already being offered in the target market.

Pricing strategies go beyond simply adding a profit margin to the fixed and variable costs that make up the total cost of a product, although it is obviously important to make sure that the price set does cover all the costs and delivers a return, or profit, to the company. For instance, the company may decide to adopt a rigid pricing policy and offer its products at the same price to all its customers, regardless of geographic market. Although this approach makes life easier for sales and administration personnel, the inflexibility of the strategy may mean sales negotiations are hampered.

Exercise: Weigh up the relative advantages and disadvantages of fixed and variable pricing strategies and examine the impact that regional variances in economies and currencies may have on pricing policies.

Alternatively, variable pricing allows the exporter to offer the same products to clients at different prices, depending on how the sale is negotiated. This strategy permits the exporter to get as much as possible out of each sales agreement but there is always the drawback that clients may hear that they are paying more than other clients in the same market. This strategy risks the goodwill of the company's customers but can deliver better returns in a shorter period of time. When considering whether to adopt this approach to pricing, the exporter should always examine the ramifications of clients discovering the pricing disparity and ways of preventing them from doing so. Companies may also choose to sell their products into overseas markets either at a consistently high price in order to benefit from greater profits – particularly in markets where competition is limited – or at a low price in the hope that larger volumes will be sold, thereby helping the company to secure a larger market share more quickly. If this last policy is implemented, companies must ensure that they are not contravening any anti-dumping laws imposed by the local government to prevent their market from being flooded by cheap imports, thereby placing indigenous manufacturing companies at a disadvantage.

Research into the prices that competing companies, both foreign and native, are offering their goods at will provide a sound indication of what the market will accept and should offer an insight into the purchasing power of customers in the target market. This information should be used by the exporter as the foundation on which to develop an effective pricing policy that will be both attractive to the customer and rewarding for the company.

Quoting

The purpose of a quotation is to provide the prospective buyer with detailed information on the company's product, its costs and the terms of delivery. Consequently, the exporter should engage all relevant departments within the company in the preparation of the quote in order to ensure that up-to-date and accurate information is used. This process should include production, accounts, sales and marketing and shipping, as well as management.

The quotation, which may be raised either in response to an overseas enquiry or as a result of a foreign buyer making a formal offer to purchase goods from the exporter, will normally contain seven important elements.

1. The quotation should begin by providing a description of the nature and quality of the goods in question, the volume offered for sale and any guarantees or warranties that are applicable.
2. The exporter ought to make reference to how the goods are to be packaged and marked for export in order to show the buyer that every precaution is taken to ensure the safe transit of the goods.
3. The method or methods of transport to be used, for example by road and sea or by any other recognised means of transport.
4. Product price and the currency used in the quotation.
5. The Incoterm used to define the terms of delivery (making reference to Incoterms 2000).

6. How the sale is to be agreed, for instance by letter of credit, open account, cash on delivery and so on.
7. When the goods can be shipped and delivered. Where the quotation covers a large order broken down into several separate shipments, the quotation should show how often the shipments will take place.

A quotation for the provision of services should ideally include a full description of the work to be undertaken, relevant work schedules and details of personnel involved. A description of any indemnity or insurance should also be included.

The quotation can be submitted verbally, although it is good practice to send written quotations so that misunderstandings can be avoided – postal, electronic and faxed quotations are normally perfectly acceptable. The company may prefer to submit quotes in the form of a pro-forma invoice for ease of administration as the pro-forma details can be simply transferred to a commercial invoice when the order is placed. In situations where the exporter is tendering for work overseas through a formal tender procedure, the official tender document will be regarded as the quotation. Once the quotation has been submitted to the buyer, the exporter is committed to fulfilling all the terms contained within the document should an order be placed on the strength of it. When the order is placed, a contract can be drawn up between the two parties to confirm the terms and conditions of the sale.

The need to be realistic

It should be evident from the explanation of Incoterms that there is a wide range of contractual requirements that can be specified in the international trade contract. The company must therefore be careful when quoting or agreeing to any contract terms and must be confident of its abilities to fulfil the demands of the contract. Inexperienced exporters in particular are likely to be guilty of not paying enough attention to their obligations in their eagerness to secure a lucrative export order. For example, a British giftware manufacturer recently agreed to a DDP contract with an American buyer without first establishing the financial viability of the agreement. The result was that the price was agreed before the transport, insurance and import duty implications were checked. The exporter realised, once the contract had been signed, that the deal would cost the company substantially more than the price they were charging and tried to renegotiate the contract. The buyer, understandably, pointed out that the contract had been agreed and that the exporter was bound to its terms. Needless to say, the British company lost money on the sale.

Exercise: History is littered with examples of companies who have entered into contracts on the back of unrealistic quotations and who have subsequently struggled to fulfil their terms. Examine the ramifications of such mistakes, particularly in terms of the long-term market entry strategy. Consider also how such mistakes could affect a company's future development into other markets.

It cannot be stressed enough that the exporting company must always ensure that it has the capacity and resources to meet the terms and conditions of the contract and must be fully aware of its financial and legal responsibilities.

Contracts

The majority of international trade contracts are governed by the United Nations Commission on International Trade Law (UNCITRAL) Convention on Contracts for the International Sale of Goods (CISG) which was established in 1980 and recognises the rules for commercial contracts. UNCITRAL is the United Nations' primary legal institution for international trade and countries that sign up to the Convention undertake to treat its rules as part of their own legal system and, unless they specify that CISG rules do not apply, exporters and importers from signatory countries are bound by the Convention's terms. Outlined below are some of the very basic principles of international contract law, which will provide a useful foundation for further reading. In particular, readers should visit http://cisgw3.law.pace.edu, an online database of international commercial law, to gain a better understanding of the subject. A sales contract does not just identify what is being sold to whom and for how much. It also takes into account the specific terms and conditions of sale (such as delivery dates, currency and payment terms) and will stipulate the country under whose law the contract is governed.

This is particularly important for international trade contracts and it is in the interests of both parties to ensure that they have agreed on the system of law to be used in the event of legal action being taken. This 'choice of law' clause can be used with a 'choice of jurisdiction' clause wherein the buyer and seller agree which country's courts will have jurisdiction over the contract. Hence a contract between a British exporter and Romanian buyer may be 'subject to English law and jurisdiction'.

For EU companies, if no choice of law has been made then EU law provides for the governing law to be seen as that of the country, which has the 'closest connection' to the agreement. Where jurisdiction has not been agreed, the defendant is generally likely to be sued in his native country. Thus a buyer being sued for breach of a sales contract will be subject to the law of the seller's country (closest connection) but may be sued in his home market. The legal footing for the contract must therefore be clearly identified.

Incorporating standard terms and conditions

As contracts tend to rely on the exchange of paperwork, the exporter is advised to prepare some standard terms and conditions of sale that can be incorporated into the documentation in addition to the specific terms of the contract. Difficulties may arise when the purchasing company also includes its standard terms and conditions and tries to gain the upper hand. This is often referred to as the 'battle of the forms' and the two parties must negotiate to agree common ground and the exact terms that will constitute the contract.

The exporter's terms and conditions (T&Cs) should ideally be clearly set out and attached to all documentation sent out to the buyer, including the quotation and the order acknowledgement, which should confirm the buyer's order under the company's standard terms and conditions. It is recommended that the exporter also asks the buyer to sign and return a copy of the T&Cs to acknowledge them and agree to their incorporation in the contract. The seller must take care to check that the buyer does not insert any conditions of his own without prior agreement.

If correspondence received from the buyer indicates that the buyer expects to trade on terms other than those of the exporter, the seller should respond by stating that the sale is under the exporter's T&Cs rather than the buyer's, unless the two parties can reach agreement on the precise terms to be used. Once the terms and conditions have been agreed, the contract can be formed and signed.

As a footnote to this issue, if the standard T&Cs are printed on the reverse of the company's invoices, it can be argued under English law that a regular client who has received several invoices from the exporter is familiar with the seller's terms and that these have been incorporated into the contract 'by default' through previous dealings.

The offer

Every sales contract will contain an offer, which sets out clearly the nature of the goods to be sold and the monetary value that the seller expects to receive for them. The offer must contain details of the type, quantity and quality of the goods to be sold, and may also include a description of the component parts to demonstrate 'origin' (see Chapter 10) or to comply with the buyer's specific requirements.

When stating the price of the goods in the offer, the exporter should explain how the price has been reached and in which currency it is listed, as well as setting out the invoicing and payment terms. Reference to the Incoterm to be used in the contract should also be made at this stage in order to clarify which party will be responsible for the shipping, insurance and other costs.

Ideally, the offer should also contain details of the method of transportation to be used, the ports of shipment and destination and the dates on which the goods will be delivered at each location. It must also be made clear which party is to bear the responsibility for organising the carriers to be used.

In summary, the offer should contain every conceivable detail of the transaction in an unambiguous way so that the terms are instantly under-standable to the buyer.

Promotional brochures and other forms of advertising where goods are marketed to potential buyers do not constitute offers but are considered an 'invitation to treat'. In other words, the promotional materials are designed to generate enquiries from which an offer may subsequently be made and consequently they cannot be used as the basis of a contract.

Counteroffers

Once the offer is made to the buyer, one of three things may happen. The offer may be accepted and the contract agreed, or it may be rejected for whatever reasons the buyer may have for turning it down. The third option is that the buyer responds to the offer by agreeing to it in principle but adding further terms, conditions or qualifying statements. This is considered to be a counteroffer, rather than an acceptance of the original offer. Responsibility is then passed back to the exporter, who must decide whether or not to accept the counteroffer or to maintain that the offer originally made is the only one under consideration. The battle of the forms then begins, with both sides negotiating the exact terms and conditions of the contract.

Alternatively, the exporter may decide to accept the counteroffer but should do so only when wholly aware of all the financial and legal obligations contained in the new offer.

Acceptance

Acceptance of the offer commits both the buyer and the seller to the specific terms of the sale and forms a legally binding contract that cannot be amended unless the two parties agree in writing to make the changes.

Silence, or lack of response to the offer, cannot be considered an acceptance under UK law. Neither can the seller suggest that the offer will be held to be accepted after a given period of time if there has been no response. The acceptance should be made in writing by the person to whom the offer was made and should refer to the terms of the offer. Although offers can be accepted verbally, written confirmation of the acceptance provides both the buyer and seller with the security of having documented proof of the contract.

Breach of contract

As acceptance of the offer creates a legally binding contract, the agreed terms and conditions must be fulfilled if the contract is not to be breached.

Breach of contract occurs either unintentionally or deliberately, and there is legal recourse in each situation. For instance, if the seller is found to have mistakenly sold substandard or defective goods that do not match those specified in the contract, the buyer has the right to demand that the seller replaces the goods with products that do meet the terms of the contract. If, however, it is apparent that one of the parties to the contract has no intention of meeting their obligations this is seen as a deliberate breach of contract and may be considered theft or fraud.

Question: Under what other circumstances might a contract be deemed to be breached?

Summary of the export order process

The following steps summarise the key elements of the export order process, from receiving an enquiry to receiving payment for goods despatched. This is a general approach to the export order and is subject to changes depending on the nature of the sale agreed. For instance, item 6 will not be required if the buyer is prepared to pay cash in advance. Nevertheless, these 11 steps should provide a quick guide to effective export order management.

1. Enquiry received from overseas buyer.
2. Exporter determines whether product modifications will be required and what packaging and labelling requirements are specified.
3. Export costing exercise carried out to ensure commercial viability.
4. Written quotation submitted to buyer.
5. Order placed by buyer.
6. Buyer's Letter of Credit details and credit rating checked by exporter.
7. Exporter accepts order.
8. Exporting company processes order and packages goods for export, making sure appropriate marking and labelling is used.
9. Carriers and transport arranged for shipment of goods.
10. All relevant payment, transport, insurance and customs documentation is raised and checked by the exporter.
11. Exporter ships the goods to the buyer and collects payment.

Buying and selling online

Earlier chapters have looked at the role that the Internet can play in international research, promotion and communication and have shown that every company with a website has the potential to generate international enquiries through the global nature of the World Wide Web. Some estimates suggest that by the end of 2004 the value of business conducted over the Internet will be over three trillion US dollars and there is clearly a need to ensure that all transactions undertaken in 'cyberspace' have a clear legal footing. Admittedly, the proportion of business-to-business trading (B2B), including importing and exporting, is not as great as the amount of trade from business-to-consumer (B2C). However, more and more business is being conducted online and businesses must be aware of the legal and contractual implications of buying and selling via the Internet.

UNCITRAL has published two key Model Laws that are of relevance to online trading. The Model Law on Electronic Commerce sets out to identify the core purpose of paper-based documentation and to define circumstances under which electronic versions will be accepted as equivalent. The Model Law on Electronic Signatures, which came into force in July 2001, takes similar steps to identify what constitutes a reliable legal signature over the Internet. For the purposes of this chapter, the legal implications of contracts agreed via email or website trading will be examined, although exporters and importers should also seek additional legal advice before entering into any form of online international trade agreement.

Electronic acceptance

There are no real issues surrounding online offers and counteroffers as their communication differs only in format. The main issue regarding contracts agreed over the Internet is that of acceptance. We saw earlier that written acceptance of the offer provides both buyer and seller with documented proof of the contract, but this does little to clarify the position with e-commerce. In particular, how does the seller determine when the contract has been accepted and how is the buyer's signature obtained?

In December 2001, the UK's Law Commission produced a paper entitled 'Electronic Commerce: formal requirements in commercial transactions', which provides an in-depth interpretation of UNCITRAL's Model Law's relating to e-commerce from an English Law perspective. The paper highlights four methods of electronic signature, which the Law Commission deems legally binding for Internet trading. Digital signatures and handwritten signatures that have been scanned into a computer and used in emails or other files sent as attachments to emails are generally acceptable, as is an electronic acceptance that bears a typed 'signature'. The final form of electronic signature is the act of 'clicking' on an order confirmation button on a website, as this normally transmits the order details, payment information and buyer's details to the seller. Therefore, as far as online trading is concerned, offers can be accepted in four common ways.

As to when the contract is deemed to be accepted is still under debate. The Law Commission takes an initial view – but does not give specific guidance – suggesting that, in principle, only when the buyer's message communicating acceptance of the offer reaches the seller's ISP is the contract agreed. Under these circumstances, the buyer should ask the seller to confirm receipt of the transmission to ensure that the message has been read and that any attachments have also been transmitted clearly. Companies entering into contracts over the Internet should therefore make provision for identifying precisely when, where and how the contract should be accepted, pending official legal guidance on the subject.

For companies trading within the EU, the Brussels Regulation for Online Consumer Contracts, which was implemented in March 2002, defines the rules for identifying the jurisdiction of commercial contracts, particularly with regard to e-commerce. The basic principles of how jurisdiction is decided were discussed earlier and are as relevant to Internet trading activity as to more traditional forms of contract.

Conclusions

Costing and pricing for international trade and the nature of international sales contracts are disciplines that must be clearly understood by exporters and importers. The use of an inappropriate Incoterm or failure to pay close attention to contractual terms and conditions can bind either party to contracts that prove to be non-viable and costly. The role and purpose of Incoterms in the international sales agreement should now be apparent and, whilst this chapter has given only the briefest of introductions to the complex subject of contract law, the reader should be aware of the main elements of the sales contract.

Sources of information

British Chambers of Commerce international trade support – www.britishchambers.org.uk/exportzone
Croner (for examples of business contracts) – www.tradeinternational-centre.net and www.croners.cch.co.uk (home page)
Electronic Commerce Association – www.eca.org.uk
Incoterms: specific site managed by the ICC – www.incoterms.com
International Chamber of Commerce – www.iccwbo.org
(British) Law Commission – www.lawcom.gov.uk
Online database of international commercial law – http://cisgw3.law.pace.edu

Further reading

Bridge M, *The International Sale of Goods* (Oxford University Press, 1999).
Cartwright R, *Mastering the Business Environment* (Palgrave, 2001).
ICC, *Incoterms 2000: The ICC Official Rules for the Interpretation of Trade Terms* (ICC, 1999).
Kouladis N, *Principles of Law Relating to Overseas Trade* (Blackwell, 1994).
Martin J and Turner C, *Key Facts: Contract Law* (Hodder & Stoughton Educational, 2001).
Poole J, *Casebook on Contract* (Blackstone Press, 2001).
Ramberg J *et al., Guide to Incoterms 2000* (ICC, 2000).
Ramberg J, *Incoterms in the Era of Electronic Data Interchange* (Kluwer Law International, 1989).

QUESTIONS FOR CONSIDERATION

1 What are the advantages of using Incoterms?
2 List the financial responsibilities of both the exporter and the importer under the following Incoterms: EXW, FAS, FOB, CFR, CIF, DAF, DDU.
3 Why is export costing important and how does the costing exercise affect the exporter's pricing strategy?
4 If an exporter accepts a buyer's counteroffer and subsequently realises that the terms contained within it are unfavourable, under what circumstances can the exporter amend the agreement?
5 What are the implications of exporting or importing via the Internet and what legal considerations should the company be aware of when selling online?

■ Y 9 Transport and logistics

Introduction

Once a company has entered into sales or purchasing contract with an overseas organisation, consideration must be given to the physical transportation of the goods from the point of origin to their final destination. Exporters need to be able to transport their products cost-effectively to their clients and logistics therefore plays an important role in the international trade process. The purpose of this chapter is to provide an insight into the way in which transport intermediaries operate and to identify the issues that must be addressed to ensure that the transportation of goods overseas runs smoothly. It therefore has little bearing on exporters of services such as consultancy, finance and training, which clearly have little call for the transportation of goods. On finishing this chapter, the reader will have an understanding of international logistics and the principles of insurance relating to overseas trade. The chapter should be read in conjunction with the sections of Chapter 8 that deal with Incoterms and export costing as well as the sections covering packaging, marking and labelling (Chapter 5) and documentation and Customs procedures (Chapter 10).

The importance of logistics

Logistics is often perceived as simply the transportation of goods from one place to another. In reality, this definition is too narrow and does not reflect the more complex and comprehensive nature of the function. Logistics is really about managing every aspect of a company's business, from sourcing raw materials to production, warehousing, marketing, pricing, sales and ultimately the transportation of the finished goods to the buyer.

The logistics function begins with an understanding of the requirements of the design and development teams and is used to source components and raw materials quickly and cheaply, either domestically or from around the world. It then needs to understand how the product is manufactured in order to take into account any special requirements for packaging, marking and labelling as well as any warehousing considerations. The logistics department must then appreciate how the goods have been priced for sale and which delivery terms (Incoterms) or other contractually binding clauses have been specified that might have a bearing on transportation. Finally, the logistics manager should be fully briefed on where the goods are to be shipped so that the most appropriate method of transport can be identified and arranged.

Logistics is a vital piece of the international trade jigsaw. It is in the company's best interests to make effective use of the process and to ensure that costs are kept to a minimum wherever possible. The majority of exporters will make use of intermediaries such as freight forwarders to facilitate the efficient and cost-effective transport of goods, although it is possible for experienced companies to take on this role themselves. Companies also make use of insurance brokers to insure the shipment during transport and Customs brokers to clear the goods through Customs on arrival.

The role of the freight forwarder

Freight forwarders are transport intermediaries who are contracted to carry out some or all of the elements of the distribution process (see Figure 9.1). It is within the forwarder's remit to ensure that goods are properly packaged and marked for transport and that appropriate documentation is prepared to facilitate shipment. The freight forwarder can arrange for the integrated (or end to end) transport of consignments, from collection at the exporter's factory and carriage to the point of shipment, to consolidating consignments into a larger, more manageable shipment and booking the required cargo space for the voyage to the target market. On arrival, the forwarder can arrange for the on carriage of the shipment to the importer, thereby providing a total solution to the exporter's distribution requirements.

Forwarders purchase space on cargo ships/trucks/trains/aircraft for particular routes and voyages. The cargo space is generally sold on a Freight All Kinds (FAK) basis, meaning that the forwarder is charged a single rate regardless of the type of goods to be shipped. This space is then resold at a profit by the freight forwarders to their clients at a rate per freight tonne or kilogram. As any unsold space must be paid for by the forwarder, freight forwarding is therefore a precise operation. No company wants to pay for something that it is not using and freight forwarders consequently become good judges of how much space they are likely to require and be able to sell on. As the forwarders generally do not possess their own vessels, they are normally termed 'non-vessel owning common carriers', or NVOCCs.

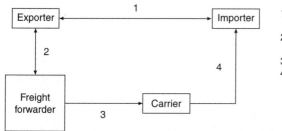

Figure 9.1 Simple freight forwarding illustration.

The main reason why companies choose to work with freight forwarders is for the cost savings that can be achieved by working with experienced transport organisations that have established their own international contacts within the industry. Although forwarders do charge a fee for their services, this can be built into the pricing equation, provided that appropriate research into transport costs was undertaken prior to the quotation. Freight forwarding is a fiercely competitive industry, with each forwarder offering expertise and strengths in different markets. Companies are advised to research potential partners and obtain several quotations for their shipments in order to appoint the most cost-effective and appropriate provider of transport solutions.

Unit load

A unit load is simply palletised freight that can be dealt with as a separate item of freight, as opposed to bulk shipments and containers. Smaller consignments that do not require large containers or bulk vessels for transportation are secured to pallets that can be moved by forklift trucks or cranes with minimum risk of damage. Palletised freight must be properly packaged and secured, and will probably be shrink-wrapped to keep the unit together and offer further protection.

If the unit load is not fragile, it may be possible to stack one or more units on top of each other by placing a wooden layer between the loads. Although this is attractive to carriers looking to make best use of cargo space, it may not appeal to the exporting company to have other loads placed on top of its goods. Companies that are concerned about potential damage caused to their shipments in this way should specify in their export cargo shipping instructions that stacking is not permitted. The ECSI (Export Cargo Shipping Instructions) is a document provided by the exporter for the benefit of the forwarder, as it contains accurate details of the goods to be shipped, their dimensions and weight, which allows for more effective cargo stowage and shipment.

Containerisation

The freight industry quickly recognised that inter-modal transport – the process of shipping goods to their final destination using different modes of transport – offered several advantages over the transportation of consignments via just one method of transport. Inter-modal, integrated transport gives greater flexibility and permits door-to-door deliveries, but it also requires an efficient means of carrying the goods without the need for unloading and repackaging. Consequently, the industry adopted a method of loading consignments into manageable, containerised loads that can be loaded and unloaded with the minimum of effort.

International Standards Organisation (ISO) containers are most commonly used in two sizes, although larger containers do exist and can be used. The standard container is 6.10 metres (20 feet) long by 2.45 metres (8 feet) wide by

2.6 metres (8 feet 6 inches) high. The larger container has the same width and height dimensions, but is 12.20 metres (40 feet) long. However, the load limit of each container is approximately 20 tonnes, even though the larger container can hold larger volume loads.

The transport of goods in containers not only reduces shipping times and loading/unloading costs, but also reduces the risk of theft and damage as the goods should be appropriately packaged and stowed in secure containers. Containerisation can also reduce the amount of packaging required for the consignment, as the metal container itself becomes a part of the packaging. From the ship owner's perspective, containers permit better utilisation of space, and therefore capacity, through their ability to be loaded and stacked in uniform rows.

Containers are a focal part of groupage operations (see below) that combine several unit loads from different exporters into one containerised load, this facility being known as less than container load (LCL) services. FCL is the term used to refer to full container load services that do not make use of groupage.

Bulk freight

Bulk cargoes, or shipments that cannot be carried in conveniently sized containers due to their nature, can be transported in a variety of specialist vessels, depending on the nature of the consignment, whether it be sugar, coal, timber, foodstuffs or vehicles and so on. Bulk freight tends to be loaded directly onto the vessels by operators with specialist knowledge of the goods in question, and the vessels themselves will be tailored for the task in hand. Some vessels are designated O/O, meaning that they are able to transport ore and oil. Others are designated O/B/O (ore, bulk and oil) or LNG (liquid natural gas). Carriers of crude oil have their own labels and will either be listed as VLCCs (very large crude carriers) or ULCCs (ultra large crude carriers/supertankers).

Companies exporting bulk products should take advice from companies that specialise in the transportation of goods, which closely match those being shipped by the exporter. Effective distribution strategies require thought and preparation and the last thing that an exporter wants to deal with is a bulk consignment that is loaded onto a vessel that is patently not built for the purpose.

Groupage

Groupage transport is one of the basic types of freight operation. It is relevant to all methods of transport and is used to consolidate several different LCL consignments belonging to different exporters into a single load, probably the standard ISO container. Groupage works by selling space on a truck or in a container to several companies and combining different consignments bound for the same destination. For smaller consignments, groupage can be a more cost-effective means of transporting goods, although the process may be slower as the forwarder or consolidator will wait until the maximum space possible in the container has been utilised before physically shipping the consignment. This may result in one exporter's goods being held by the forwarder for two or three days until another exporter purchases space for the same journey. The export cargo shipping instructions are essential in groupage operations as they provide the forwarder with the dimensions and weight of the goods to be shipped, which allows the forwarder to plan how best to combine the unit loads. ECSI also provide relevant information on the nature of the goods. It is especially important to notify the consolidator of any goods that the consignment should not come into close proximity with. For example, bleach products should not be transported in the same container as chlorine products. If the two were to mix as a result of damaged packaging they would release a noxious gas, which could endanger the vessel and its crew.

Groupage can also be arranged for road, air and rail freight, making use of specialist containers in each case. Road transport will make use of 12-metre trailer units, rail operations use 18.30-metre wagons and containerisation for air transport is in the form of unit load devices (ULDs), which are also referred to as igloos.

When the goods arrive at the port destination or inland clearance depot (ICD), the forwarder will arrange for the consolidated load to be broken down into its constituent parts for the final leg of the journey.

Transport Internationaux Routiers (TIR)

The transport of goods by road throughout the European Union used to present two difficulties. Firstly, each time a consignment crossed a national boundary it was subject to inspection in order to verify the nature and value of the goods. Although this enabled the monitoring and control of imports and exports, it was time consuming and led to transportation delays. Secondly, a consignment passing through an EU member state prior to reaching its destination in another market was subject to a deposit based on the duty payable on the value of the goods in transit. This was refunded on leaving the country providing that it could be proven that the nature and value of the consignment remained unchanged. Thus a consignment from Belgium to Austria via Germany would be subject to a deposit levied on entering Germany and refunded at the Austrian border.

The European Union recognised that these regulations impeded international distribution and introduced the TIR (Transport Internationaux Routiers) system as a solution.

The main function of TIR is to establish guidelines for the demonstrably secure transport of goods without the need for inspections. Vehicles that can be sealed to prevent goods from being removed or added without the seal being broken, and that have no additional or hidden storage compartments, can be approved by TIR and are exempt from the inspections. In place of the duty deposit, a TIR carnet is used to document the consignment's nature, value and journey. The carnet takes the form of vouchers issued by organisations such as the UK's Road Haulage Association and is a much faster method of expediting the movement of goods across the EU's national boundaries.

Transporting goods without a freight forwarder

Even though it is sensible to work with freight forwarders that can use established international networks to identify the most cost-effective means of transporting a consignment to its destination, it is nevertheless possible for companies to dispense with forwarders and arrange shipping themselves. By doing so, the exporter or importer removes the intermediary from the equation (thereby saving money) and effectively becomes the shipper. Consequently, the company must be prepared to undertake the full range of services normally provided by a forwarder. For this reason, it is not recommended that individual companies make their own shipping arrangements as, in all probability, they will not possess the same level of experience, expertise and contacts as forwarding agents.

Companies that nonetheless proceed with contracting for transportation themselves must, as a minimum, address the following issues:

1. The points of origin and destination of the cargo.
2. The products to be transported.
3. Documentary requirements.
4. Rates and terms of payment.
5. Liability for injury, loss or damage to cargo, damage to property.
6. Performance and penalty clauses.
7. Requirements for specific services or equipment to be supplied by the transport company to ensure the safe loading, unloading and stowage of the consignment.
8. Policy on the replacement value of damaged goods.
9. Clause detailing the circumstances under which the contract can be terminated.
10. Conditions under which the contract may be altered.

Although the shipper should also ensure that the chosen transport company has the capacity to ship the goods in accordance with its wishes, particularly with regard to the arrangements that the carrier has in place at the ports of origin and destination, as well as the ports through which the vessel will pass on route.

Given the amount of research and preparation that has already gone into the development of the international trade strategy, companies may choose to use the services offered by freight forwarders simply in order to reduce the need for further research. The cost savings generated by cutting out the intermediary may well be negated by the cost of researching transport companies and arranging shipping. Although freight forwarders charge for their services, they do at least have well-established international distribution networks that can be utilised cost-effectively, efficiently and with minimum involvement from the importer or exporter.

Carrier's liability

There are few companies that can afford to run a business that does little to minimise risks and the transportation of goods around the world is certainly not without its perils. Consignments may be damaged in transit; containers can be washed overboard in storms or jettisoned if the vessel runs into difficulties. In extreme circumstances, vessels might run aground or even sink. There are many number of ways in which businesses can see their profitability eroded by lost or damaged goods. Whilst it can be argued that the carrier has a responsibility for the safe transportation of the consignment, carriers will generally limit their liability under their bill of lading (see Chapter 10) to a nominal amount per item shipped. The actual value of the goods has no bearing on this amount and the importer or exporter is consequently unlikely to recover the full value of the goods damaged or lost. It is also not unusual for the carrier to specify four common clauses, which effectively exempt the carrier from any liability whatsoever. These are:

- Defect/inherent vice: where the goods have an inherent characteristic that may cause their damage, such as vegetables that are susceptible to decay.
- Act or default of the shipper or owner (exporter): for example, damage caused as a consequence of badly loaded containers or inappropriate packaging.
- Act of God: where damage is caused by the weather and other natural phenomena that could not reasonably have been expected.
- Enemies of the State: covering situations where losses are incurred as a result of terrorism or piracy.

Additionally, the carrier's liability will be limited under the 'Hague – Visby Rules', which govern the legal status of bills of lading and include a method of calculating liability. Companies should make the effort to ascertain the level of insurance provided by the carrier in order to make sure that adequate provision is made to cover the goods during transit.

As carriers will rarely provide adequate cover, additional insurance should be taken out by either the importer or exporter, depending on the delivery terms specified in the contract. Chapter 8 demonstrated the importance of Incoterms in defining the exporter's and importer's obligations in the distribution process and when title to the goods changes hands. Terms such as CIF (where the exporter purchases marine insurance until the shipment reaches its destination) or CFR (where the importer arranges insurance) are instrumental in identifying which party has responsibility for insuring the consignment and when. Under CIF terms, the minimum insurance that exporter is required to purchase for the importer is 110 per cent of the contract value.

Marine insurance

Marine insurance, which covers all distribution methods in addition to ocean-going transport, is designed to remove the financial risk of lost or damaged goods from the exporter or importer. The risk is placed with insurance underwriters that have expertise in risk assessment and managing funds from which claims for compensation can be paid. The reserve funds are made up by insurance premiums paid by other companies for the security of transferring the risk to another organisation. Underwriters may be local company underwriters working for a business already providing marine insurance, or they may be underwriting members of Lloyd's of London. Insurance companies, on the other hand, are commercial organisations that employ the services of underwriters as required. The other type of insurance intermediary likely to be encountered by businesses purchasing insurance is a broker, who shops around for appropriate insurance cover to meet the needs of a client. Brokers endeavour to secure the most competitive premiums by comparing rates across numerous insurance companies. Marine insurance obtained in this way can only be underwritten by a Lloyd's member if the broker is also a member.

Lloyd's of London, perhaps the most famous of all marine insurance organisations, does not itself underwrite any insurance policies. It is instead a membership organisation comprising underwriters (not insurance companies) who work under strict guidelines and controls that are set down by Lloyd's. Underwriters who are members of Lloyd's are personally liable for the risks that they agree to underwrite, whereas those who are contracted by insurance companies are not. The 'London market', which is effectively Lloyd's of London and the insurance companies, is the most important market in the world for marine insurance.

Two principal forms of marine insurance are available to companies to cover their goods in transit (the 'insurable interest'). The simplest is a specific (voyage) policy, also called an individual, one-off or facultative policy, which covers a particular consignment during a single, specified shipment. (The key elements of a marine insurance policy are highlighted in Figure 9.2.) The disadvantage of working under specific policies is that a separate policy needs to be raised and agreed for each individual shipment, and it is unlikely that the cost of purchasing insurance will remain constant across several shipments. Insurance premiums change on a day-to-day basis, depending on, amongst other things, the insurance company's experience of the shipper, the nature of the shipment, its route and final destination and any claims that the shipper has made in the

- Name of insurer
- Policy number
- Name of the assured (company purchasing insurance)
- Goods insured
- Value to be covered (which may include import duty, profits, freight costs and so on)
- Premium paid
- Name of vessel (or other form of transport)
- Details of voyage
- Nature of insurance cover (e.g. all risks)
- Details of the claims procedure and supporting evidence required
- Details of the currency and country in which claims will be paid

Figure 9.2 Elements of a marine insurance policy.

past. Individual policies are therefore not the quickest or most cost-effective option for companies making regular shipments, but may be appropriate for businesses that have fewer consignments.

Open policies are insurance contracts that automatically cover all of a company's shipments over a longer period, normally twelve months. An open policy demands that the company taking out the insurance declare all the shipments made under it. This reliance on the company's honesty extends to declarations of shipments that have already taken place under the policy but which were not notified in advance of shipment. Such policies are therefore issued by the insurance companies in the 'utmost good faith', or *uberrimae fidaes*, to give the term its Latin name. As far as documentation is concerned, the exporter provides a pre-signed insurance certificate, which is tailored for each individual shipment. The cargo insurance policy certificate details the goods to be shipped, their value and the amount of insurance cover purchased.

Institute Cargo Clauses

Marine insurance has its foundations in the UK Marine Insurance Act of 1906, which sets out some core legal guidelines for insurance contracts. The Institute of London Underwriters subsequently defined which risks are covered and under what circumstances they can be insured. These definitions became known as the Institute Cargo Clauses, which provide the main substance of insurance contracts, as the conventional policy is really only an outline document. The insurer will specify one of the following Institute Cargo Clauses in the contract, depending on the perceived risk of transporting the goods to their destination.

Institute Cargo Clauses (C) cover loss or damage due to collision, explosion, fire, sinking, capsizing, derailment, running aground, and so on. This clause also covers jettisoned goods, general average sacrifice and salvage charges. The consignment is also covered if the vessel is forced to unload at a port of distress (port where the vessel is not scheduled to dock but is obliged to do so for emergency reasons).

Institute Cargo Clauses (B) cover all the risk insured under Cargo Clauses (C), but includes loss or damage attributable to volcano, lightning and earthquake, loss of consignment overboard, through loading, unloading or from being washed overboard. Institute Cargo Clauses (A) cover the consignment for all risks in (B) and (C) and may also include additional cover for theft and non-delivery. Institute Cargo Clauses (Air) works on the same premise as (A), but for goods transported by air.

The Cargo Clauses are subject to exclusions that should be checked with the insurer. Typically, these might include war, strikes, riots, insolvency of the shipowner and unseaworthiness of the vessel, as well as issues such as inherent defect and misconduct.

Other Institute Cargo Clauses can be specified to provide cover against some of these risks. For example, Institute War Clauses cover consignments to areas with a high risk of conflict, whilst Institute Strikes Clauses insure goods against damage as a result of walkouts and general strike action.

General and particular average

General average is the intentional loss of part of the vessel's cargo as a direct result of the shipowner's actions in response to a current peril. For instance, jettisoning cargo might be a necessity in order to lighten a ship's load and so raise the vessel off a sandbank that it has run aground on. As this action is undertaken deliberately to save the vessel, and therefore the remaining cargo, contributions to cover the cost of compensation for the lost goods are levied evenly on a pro-rata basis across all the companies whose shipments were saved as a direct result of the shipowner's actions. It is possible for companies to purchase insurance to cover them against the possibility of being liable for general average contributions.

Whilst general average implies that the damage or loss to the goods in question is caused voluntarily, particular average is concerned with unintentional losses, which cannot necessarily be foreseen. This might include a container being washed overboard in transit or being dropped on unloading, and will normally be covered under the terms of the insurance policy.

Making a claim

In the event that goods are lost or damaged in transit, the owner of the goods is obliged to submit a number of documents to the insurance company in order for the insurance claim to be processed. Under Hague – Visby Rules, claims should be registered within one year from the date of the damage or loss occurring, or the date on which delivery of the damaged goods was taken. However, before the claim is lodged with the insurer, the owner should carry out a review of how the goods were packaged, marked and shipped in order to ensure that every aspect of the distribution process took place appropriately and as specified in the contract and shipping documentation. The owner should also ensure that the loss or damage is not as a result of ordinary wear and tear, damage by vermin, delays or an inherent defect as described above, as insurance policies rarely cover these circumstances.

Any claim for compensation under the insurance policy should be based on 'total' or 'partial' loss, as explained in Figure 9.3.

Total loss	Partial loss
• Actual total loss – where the goods are irretrievably lost • Total loss of part – where only a proportion of the consignment is lost • Constructive total loss – where the cost of recovering the goods outweighs their value or where the goods are abandoned as their loss is a foregone conclusion	• General average loss – where the goods are deliberately lost in order to prevent further jeopardy to the vessel • Particular average loss – where damage is caused to a particular container, affecting one company only and the compensation is paid equally by the other insured companies on the voyage

Figure 9.3 Total and partial loss.

Assuming that the owner of the goods is not at fault, a claim against the carrier can be lodged, and must be accompanied by the documents listed below.

- Exporter's commercial invoice.
- Copy of all bills of lading or waybills used during transport.
- Packing list.
- Customs entry documents.
- Insurance certificate or policy (detailing open policy number and declaration number).
- Copy of all written communication to and from the carrier from the point of notification of loss or damage.
- Documentary evidence or report of the nature of the loss or damage.
- Evidence of the condition of the goods on arrival at their destination (inspection report, weight note, and so on).

Clearing Customs

In the vast majority of cases there will be no problems in transit and the consignment will arrive safely in the destination country, where it must be cleared through local Customs before it can be delivered to the importer. The process demands that the exporter prepares a portfolio of Customs, commercial and transport documents for presentation to foreign Customs officers. The types of documentation commonly used for international trade purposes and some of the Customs procedures and reporting requirements that exporters and importers need to be aware of are detailed in Chapter 10.

It is imperative that exporters ascertain what these requirements are in advance of shipping the goods, as missing or incomplete documentation will delay clearance and result in the company incurring additional costs and demurrage (port or depot storage) charges. Assistance on market-specific requirements can be obtained from a number of sources, including the exporter's embassy in the target market, the foreign Customs office and publications such as the *Croners Reference Book for Exporters*. Exporters should also consult their agent or distributor in the market as well as the importing company. It is, after all, in the importer's interests to receive the goods as soon as possible and to avoid delays.

As a brief guideline, the documentation required to facilitate Customs clearance includes a copy of the commercial invoice, a Customs certificate of shipment and reporting sheet, a waybill (a transport document detailing the nature of the goods shipped), a certificate of origin and, depending on the market, a consular invoice. If an import licence is required for the goods, this should also be included in the documentation presented to Customs, as should relevant health and safety certificates, dangerous goods notes and so on.

The core details demanded by Customs to enable them to put a value on the consignment include:

- Name and address of exporter.
- Name and address of importer.

- Description of goods.
- Selling price of goods.
- Information on commissions, royalties, fees or discounts payable to agents and so on that affect the price of the goods.
- Cost of packaging if not included in the price.
- Details of any materials provided by the importer as part of the finished product.
- Information on any costs incurred by the importer in insuring the onward carriage of the goods.
- Country of origin.
- Carrier name and address.
- Quantity and weight of goods.
- Number of packages included in the shipment.
- How the packages have been marked or labelled.

Customs officials then use this information to assess the value of the consignment for duty, which in turn is subject to wider influences such as the preferential rates and agreements explained in Chapter 10. Once all the formalities have been completed and the Customs duty has been paid, the goods are said to have 'cleared' Customs and can continue to their final destination.

The role of the Customs broker

Customs brokers are individuals or organisations based in the target market that advise on all the necessary issues to be addressed before Customs clearance can be achieved. Some markets stipulate that shipments can be cleared solely through Customs brokers, although in the majority of cases there is no such requirement. Nevertheless, it makes commercial sense to make use of brokers as they are generally able to expedite Customs clearance much more quickly than companies with limited experience of the procedures and formalities, and their knowledge and expertise can be invaluable. In the event that a consignment has been opened for inspection at Customs, the broker can also arrange for the cargo to be repackaged and the container resealed. It is therefore worthwhile developing good relationships with the Customs brokers that the company makes regular use of.

The appointment of a Customs broker must be made carefully and the same precautions should be taken as when appointing other overseas partners or service providers. It is not just a question of evaluating the broker's expertise, reputation and competence, but also a question of integrity. Bribery and corruption are not unusual in certain markets, with officials expecting their palms to be crossed before the paperwork is stamped and approved. The exporter should take precautions to ensure that the broker appointed is reputable and will work in the company's best interests, not in the interest of the broker's personal retirement fund.

IT solutions for documentation processing

The documentary requirements of international trade are an essential factor in the success or failure of an overseas transaction. The need to produce accurate Customs, transport and financial documentation makes importing and exporting a paper-intensive activity. Fortunately, modern technology has led to the development of IT systems and software that can improve the control, accuracy and production of all types of international trade documentation, from sales to shipping and banking. In many cases, the documentation produced can be sent electronically to other parties, and the software is also a useful tool for maintaining up-to-date records of shipments made. There are several software suppliers offering a total export management solution for every function of the business and companies that wish to avoid costly administrative errors in their documentation should consider installing one of the IT solutions that are currently available.

Electronic data interchange

The availability of IT solutions for the control and processing of documentation is one area in which information technology can be of use to importers and exporters in the logistics function. The other commonly used system is electronic data interchange (EDI). EDI is the electronic transfer of trade information in internationally recognised formats. It is used particularly for the exchange of commercial documentation such as invoices and purchase orders, although it has great value in international logistics for the electronic transfer of shipping documentation. EDI means that details of invoices, waybills, packing lists and so on can be quickly and efficiently transmitted to the buyer or, for that matter, any other organisation that needs to receive the documentation in order for elements of the transaction to take effect. This not only saves a great deal of time in terms of eliminating the need for retyping the documents; it is also a much more effective means of ensuring that the information reaches its intended recipient so that payment can be made more quickly.

The United Nations' rules for Electronic Data Interchange for Administration, Commerce and Transport (UN/EDIFACT) is the established set of internationally agreed standards for EDI, particularly in relation to goods and services. The standardised format, which works on the basis of a common language, facilitates communication between companies and therefore the rapid processing of commercial transactions. Consequently, EDI has application in the preparation and transfer of documentation between the company and its suppliers, buyers and service providers (including freight forwarders, banks, carriers, representatives and Customs brokers).

Conclusions

It will now be evident that there is a great deal more to the transportation of goods overseas than is necessarily apparent on first sight. Readers should have gained an insight into the role that transport, insurance and Customs intermediaries play in the distribution process, and will recognise that it is important to ensure that service providers are selected and appointed with care.

The basic requirements of the logistics function have been identified in conjunction with an explanation of how the principles of marine insurance are designed to provide cover in addition to the carrier's limited liability, thereby protecting the owner in the event of goods being lost or damaged. The advantages that can be gained through the electronic exchange of documentation have been explained and readers have also been given an introduction to the Customs clearance process, laying the foundations for Chapter 10, which covers the documentary and Customs requirements of international trade.

Sources of information

Links to trade and logistics websites – www.freightworld.com
Links to marine insurance websites – www.insurance-marine.com
Glossary of ocean cargo insurance terms – www.tsbic.com/cargo/glossary.htm
Daily shipping and insurance news – www.llplimited.com/newshome.shtml
National Customs Brokers and Forwarder Association of America –
   www.ncbfaa.ord
Links to international trade websites – http://tradelinks.wfta.org
Directory of freight forwarding services – http://forwarders.com
UK Freight Transport Association – www.fta.co.uk
Legal information and resources for freight forwarding –
   www.forwarderlaw.com
Road Haulage Association – www.rha.net
British International Freight Association – www.bifa.org
International Federation of Freight Forwarders Association – www.fiata.com
International Maritime Organisation – www.imo.org
Web resources for international trade – www.fita.org/webindex
UN/EDIFACT – www.unece.org/trade/untdid
Export documentation software provider – www.export-pro.com
Lloyds of London – www.lloydsoflondon.co.uk

Further reading

Badger D, Bugg R and Whitehead G, *International Physical Distribution and Cargo Insurance* (Prentice Hall/Woodhead-Faulkener, 1993).
British International Freight Association, *The International Freight Guide* (LLP, 1997).
Dover V and Brown R H, *A Handbook to Marine Insurance* (Witherby, 1975).
Felice-Pace J, *Marine Cargo Clauses* (Witherby, 1998).
Luddeke C F, *et al., Lloyds List Guide to Marine Insurance* (LLP, 1996).
Thomas D R and Lord Mustill, *The Modern Law of Marine Insurance* (LLP, 1996).

1 Explain the importance of the logistics function in businesses that trade internationally.
2 What is the difference between a freight forwarder and a carrier, and what are the core services offered by each?
3 What is the difference between an insurance underwriter, insurance broker and an insurance company? Explain how each is involved in insuring goods for international trade.
4 What is the difference between 'general average' and 'particular average', and what are the implications for companies with goods insured for transit in each case?
5 Why is it important to establish good working relationships with Customs brokers in the company's overseas markets?

Case study: Black Rock Logistics Ltd

Background

The purpose of this case study is to provide an example of how a freight forwarder can work with clients to understand their needs and, by doing so, develop tailored solutions for their distribution requirements.

Black Rock Logistics Ltd is a relatively young forwarding company providing groupage and FCL services. The company has a strong reputation for customer care as well as for its established and effective network of agents in Western Europe, which facilitate the transport of goods throughout the European Union. As a consequence, Black Rock Logistics has a growing customer base of companies from a range of industry sectors who are already exporting to Europe.

The problem

Black Rock Logistics was approached by a manufacturer of chemicals that supplies granular surfactants for the industrial detergent industry. The company has a distributor in Germany that purchases 16 tonnes of the product per quarter, stipulating that the goods be palletised on 'euro-pallets' with dimensions of 80 cm × 120 cm. The company has traditionally palletised the consignment in batches of a quarter of a tonne, meaning that 64 pallets are required to fulfil the order.

As the consignment is transported by road, the pallets are loaded onto a standard 13.5 metre trailer with a maximum capacity of 20 tonnes.

The problem that the company encountered with its existing freight forwarder is that only 32 pallets were being loaded per trailer (16 × 2), requiring two trailers to carry the consignment to the German distributor. This obviously increased the distribution costs substantially and affected the profitability of the venture.

The company contacted Black Rock Logistics for a second opinion and advice on the most cost-effective method of transporting the goods to Germany.

The solution

Black Rock Logistics reviewed every stage of the process, from production and packaging to collection, loading and distribution. The key issues highlighted by the review were:

1. Under the current system, each of the two trailers was severely under-utilised, carrying only eight tonnes of the consignment. From the transport operator's point of view, trucks are only at their most cost-effective when at maximum capacity. The cost of unused capacity is likely to be passed on to the client.
2. Consequently, in addition to the utilised space, the company was also paying for unused capacity on two trucks.
3. The granular chemicals were packed in medium-weight cardboard boxes and stacked on pallets. The boxes were not strong enough to support another pallet stacked on top of them. It was also impractical to load other, non-palletised goods due to the risk of damage.
4. The route used by the existing forwarder was not as direct as the routes favoured by Black Rock.
5. The existing freight forwarder had made no effort to try and find a way of reducing the cost of transport.

Black Rock Logistics made two suggestions to the company. Firstly, it was suggested that the packaging used for the goods be made of thicker cardboard and secondly that each pallet be fitted with a wooden 'cap'. The combined affect would provide a firmer, more supportive unit load onto which a second pallet could be stacked. This would then enable a second layer of pallets to be loaded onto the trailer, resulting in all 64 pallets being loaded onto a single trailer ($16 \times 2 \times 2$). Although the maximum weight of the trailer would still not be reached, much better usage would be made of the available space and at least the company would be paying for only one trailer. The company agreed that this was in all probability the best approach and made arrangements for the packaging to be improved and for the wooden caps to be used. The first time that this new approach was implemented, a representative from Black Rock Logistics oversaw the loading of the goods to ensure that the 64 pallets were loaded and stacked as suggested. This left a limited amount of unused space between the second row and the roof of the trailer that Black Rock was subsequently able to fill with a small consignment of wooden panels also being shipped to Germany by a local company.

The consignment duly left for the target market (via the quicker and less costly route identified by Black Rock Logistics). Once the goods had arrived at the buyer's premises in Germany, confirmation was quickly received that they were in good condition and had not been adversely affected from being stacked.

Summary

This case study shows the importance of carefully researching and selecting a freight forwarder to undertake elements, or all, of the distribution function. On the one hand, it has shown that, occasionally, companies will encounter forwarders that are concerned primarily with making money at all costs, rather than with customer care and satisfaction. On the other hand, it demonstrates that a good freight forwarder will always seek to make the most of every opportunity and will endeavour to provide the most cost-effective solution to a client's distribution needs.

Black Rock Logistics not only came up with a viable method of eliminating the need for two trailers, but was also able to keep costs low by consolidating another client's consignment into the same trailer and by working through its network of agents to find the most direct route. The cost of improving the packaging and putting wooden caps onto the unit loads proved to be far less than the cost of an additional trailer for each consignment to Germany. The company is therefore benefiting from more effective transportation and better customer service, yet has reduced its costs at the same time.

■ Ⅴ **10** Documentation and Customs procedures

Introduction

International trade documentation is regularly cited by inexperienced exporters and importers as one of the major obstacles to overseas business. Even companies with substantial experience of shipping and receiving goods may struggle to meet the exacting standards demanded of a variety of documents, perhaps being unfamiliar with their purpose and requirements. This chapter puts the different types of commercial documentation into perspective and explains how and why each is used. The chapter also covers the Customs and Excise procedures followed by companies to ensure that the appropriate levels of import and export duty are applied.

Although there is no substitute for practical experience, this chapter will provide the reader with a solid foundation on which to build further knowledge of the documentary requirements of international trade.

What does international trade documentation achieve?

A wide range of documents passes between importers, exporters and intermediaries to record every element of their international trade transactions. They are used to identify the mode of transport, delivery terms and payment methods agreed, as well as the type of transaction being undertaken. As the documents are raised by all the parties involved in the transaction, from buyer and seller through to forwarder and bank, they fulfil a number of requirements. Firstly, commercial documents are used to provide specific information to the organisations involved in the physical distribution of the goods and are instrumental in ensuring that the international transactions proceed as quickly and efficiently as possible. The documents that relate to payment provide financial security to all parties, and the overall function of the various types of international trade documentation is to reduce risk and maintain evidence of the transactions.

The information provided in the documents must be wholly accurate and appropriate to the particular purpose of each individual document. Inaccurate

Transport	Customs	Insurance	Payment
Bill of lading	Export declarations	Insurance policy	Letter of Credit
Air waybill	Import declarations	Insurance certificate	Bill of Exchange
Invoices	Transit documents	Insurance declaration	
DG Note	ATA Carnet		
CIM	Invoices		
CMR			

Figure 10.1   Type of international trade documentation.

documentation will lead to delays in processing, shipping and receipt of goods, which in turn may lead to contracts being breached through delivery times not being met. This may ultimately have the effect of exporters losing money on the contract and importers not being able to fulfil other orders relying on imported components. It is therefore in the interests of all parties to ensure the accurate completion of all documentary requirements.

Types of documentation

There are four main types of documentation used for international trade purposes (see Figure 10.1). Transport documents are used to confirm aspects of the distribution function, for instance the receipt of goods for shipment and their safe arrival at the intended destination.

Customs documentation ensures that the correct duties are paid on imports, as well as the correct transaction methods used for both importing and exporting. It is also used to demonstrate compliance for Customs warehousing and to prove a company's eligibility for Inward and Outward Processing Relief (see below).

Insurance documentation, which was covered in the last chapter, is the company's reassurance that it will be able to recoup any financial losses that may arise from theft, damage and so on.

Payment documents are the instruments, which help companies to secure payment for the goods sold. They include Bills of Exchange and Letters of Credit, which will be covered in subsequent chapters.

Bills of Lading

The Bill of Lading, often abbreviated to B/L, acts as a receipt from the carrier to the exporter confirming that the consignment has been received 'in apparent good order and condition' for shipment. It also sets out the terms of the contract of carriage between the shipping agent or exporter and the carrier as well as providing evidence of 'title' or the legal right of ownership for the person to whom the goods are being transported (see Figure 10.2).

1. Bills of Lading completed by shipping agent or exporter, naming the shipping line commissioned to transport the goods.
2. ECSI issued.
3. Carrier prints off the Bills of Lading.
4. Goods delivered to point of departure.
5. Carrier or other receiving authority checks the consignment to ensure that they are the same goods as booked for transport.
6. Goods are stowed and booked onto the Ship's Manifest. Bills of Lading signed by Ship's Master.
7. One set of signed Bills returned to the shipping agent or exporter on receipt of payment for freight.
8. Exporter arranges for a 'Signed Original Bill of Lading' to be sent to the consignment destination for presentation.
9. Goods will be released at destination on presentation of the Signed Original B/L.

Figure 10.2 The Bill of Lading process.

Received and Shipped Bills of Lading

The Received B/L really only serves one purpose. It confirms that the carrier has received the goods but that they are still waiting to be loaded for shipping. The Received B/L may become a Shipped B/L if it is stamped with a date showing when the shipment was loaded.

Groupage Bill of Lading

As explained in Chapter 9, Groupage occurs where a freight forwarder combines the shipments of several companies into one container or load. A Groupage B/L can be used to cover the whole load and thereby eliminate the need for separate Bills for each part of the consignment.

Claused Bill of Lading

A Bill of Lading may be 'claused' if the carrier believes the goods not to be in 'apparent good order and condition'. By clausing the B/L, for example as a result of substandard packaging, inaccurate markings or damaged cases, the carrier is able to reduce its liability in the event of claims being made against it.

Stale Bill of Lading

In the event that, for whatever reason, a Bill of Lading is not available for presentation when the shipment arrives, it becomes 'stale', preventing the goods from being cleared until an original copy is presented. This usually causes unnecessary delays and demurrage costs, as well as additional costs for storing the goods pending the arrival of the B/L.

Common and Short Form Bills of Lading

Produced by Simplified Trade Procedures (SITPRO), the Common B/L does not bear the carrier's name in the same way that Bills printed by individual carrier companies do. There is instead a blank space in which the name can be added. The Common B/L is therefore a standard document that can be tailored for each carrier, as opposed to a pre-printed form that can only be used by the shipping line that printed it.

The Short Form B/L replaces the clauses, terms and conditions normally printed on the reverse of the standard Bill of Lading with a simple reference to the 'standard conditions' of the carrier. Both Common and Short Form Bills are acceptable against Letters of Credit unless otherwise specified.

Combined Transport Bill of Lading

Where a single carriage contract is used to cover the movement of goods by means of different methods of transport, a Combined Transport Bill comes into effect. For example, a shipment may be transported by road from Leeds to Hull, where it is offloaded from the truck and stowed on a container ship for the onward journey from Hull to Rotterdam. Another haulage company then picks up the container on arrival and delivers the consignment by road to Antwerp. If the destination is actually named in the Bill, it becomes a Through Bill of Lading covering all the modes of transport from the point of departure to the inland destination.

Transhipment Bill of Lading

It is not unusual for two or more ships to be used to transport goods to their final destination. For instance, a shipment destined for Gdansk in Poland may be shipped from Hull on one vessel, unloaded at Rotterdam and reloaded onto a second vessel for the final leg of the voyage. In these circumstances, the B/L would become a Transhipment Bill of Lading highlighting the port where transhipment will take place.

Air Waybill

For consignments transported by air, the Air Waybill acts almost like a Bill of Lading in that it provides the exporter or agent with a receipt for cargo received and also provides confirmation of the contract of carriage. It does not, however, act as a document of title or offer the security that a B/L can. The carriage of goods by air is governed by the Warsaw Convention of 1929 and its subsequent amendments. (The equivalent governing convention for the carriage of goods by sea is the Hague – Visby Rules.)

Carriage of goods by rail and road

The Rail Waybill and Road Waybill are similar in fashion to the Air Waybill as they are documents from the carrier showing receipt of goods for shipment and evidence of the carriage contract itself. Neither is a document of title. Rail Waybills are governed by the Convention Relative aux Transports Internationaux Ferroviares (COTIF) and Road Waybills by the Convention Internationale des Merchandises par Route (CMR).

Dangerous Goods Note

Chapter 5 described the international regulations governing the carriage of dangerous goods. The export of hazardous or dangerous substances requires that the goods are appropriately classified, marked, packed and can be transported safely. This 'Dangerous Goods Note' (DGN) is used instead of the Standard Shipping Note for surface distribution. In the case of airfreight, the IATA Shipper's declaration must be used.

Invoices

International trade makes use of both pro-forma and commercial invoices, although each has a very different purpose. The pro-forma invoice contains a description of the nature, quantity and value of the goods to be shipped but is not a demand for payment. Under normal circumstances, the importer will request a pro-forma invoice from the exporter in order to provide supporting evidence of the transaction to other parties. For instance, an importer requiring cargo insurance may need to prove to the insurer that the goods exist and the sale has been agreed. The pro-forma can also be useful in assisting the importer when calculating Customs duties. The commercial invoice is the exporter's bill of sale containing details of the goods sold and their value, together with an indication of the trading terms (for example, 30 days). It is essential that the commercial invoice be attached to Customs documentation, not only to facilitate Customs clearance, but also to prove that the sale has taken place and how much the importer has been charged.

In some cases, a written declaration is required to accompany the invoice. The declaration, often in the language of the target market, identifies the destination country and confirms that the prices are correct. (*Croner's Reference Book for Exporters* provides the exact wording required for each country.) An approved issuing body, such as a Chamber of Commerce, can certify the invoice to confirm that the exporter is authorised to make such declarations – resulting in a certified invoice being issued.

> **Example**: Commercial invoices for goods sold to Saudi Arabia must show the country of origin, full description of the goods, net and gross weights, value and any pertinent marks or numbers. The invoice must also carry a signed declaration stating that 'We hereby guarantee that this is a true and correct invoice and that the goods referred to are of the origin, manufacture and production of the United Kingdom.'

Legalisation of the invoices may also be required, depending on the nature of the transaction and the specifications of the Letter of Credit. Certified invoices can only be legalised by the commercial section of the importer's embassy in the exporter's country.

The role of Customs and Excise

Customs and Excise are responsible for the collection of indirect taxes and duties. The taxes that most affect importers and exporters are value-added tax (VAT) and Excise and Customs duties, but the final recipients of the revenue vary. For example, Customs and Excise offices within the EU work on behalf of the European Commission, rather than their native countries, and all import duties collected are paid directly to the Commission. Excise duties on items such as tobacco, alcohol and fuel products purchased and consumed in each member state are collected by Customs and Excise and retained by their national governments. In the same way, VAT is collected by the national revenue department (in the case of the UK this work is undertaken by HM Customs & Excise), and is retained by the national government. VAT and excise duty rates differ between EU member states, hence the need for the trader to be sure in which member state duty or VAT is liable and to provide proof of evidence that the international intra-EU transaction has taken place.

Customs departments the world over therefore play a major role in monitoring imports and exports and ensuring that the appropriate revenue due from them is received and fully supported by accurate documentation. Additionally, Customs and Excise also have considerable responsibility for national security and the protection of citizens from illegal trading and smuggling, and levy severe penalties against such activities.

As far as international trade is concerned, Customs and Excise places many demands and responsibilities on importing and exporting companies, with particular regard to the management of taxes and Customs declarations. Even companies that rely on freight forwarders to complete their documentation must ensure that they themselves submit all the relevant forms and declarations to Customs, regardless of how efficient the forwarders are. In the majority of cases, Customs will focus their enquiries on the company rather than the third-party service provider and it is clearly in companies' best interests to ensure that they are fully compliant and conversant with Customs procedures.

EU trade

The Single European Act of 1986 laid the foundations for the complete abolition of trading barriers across the European Community by the end of 1992. This permitted unrestricted movement of capital, people, services and goods without the need for Customs controls and paperwork, and was further endorsed with the implementation of the 1990 Schengen Agreement, which effectively dispensed with Customs barriers in mainland Europe. The UK did not sign up to this agreement and HM Customs and Excise (HMC&E) retained the right to inspect goods entering the UK from the EU. This remains the case, although in practice HMC&E are more concerned with non-EU exports to the UK.

Customs documentation for trade within the EU has been simplified to facilitate faster movement of goods and is primarily used to provide statistical data on the volume of imports and exports in the EU. The INTRASTAT document is completed by companies that trade with other EU members and is submitted to Customs on a monthly basis. INTRASTAT covers imports and exports valued at over £233 000 per year and does not take into account any intra-EU trade below this figure. For Customs purposes, companies are obliged to provide the following information on their monthly INTRASTAT reports:

1. Tariff commodity code.
2. Value in pounds Sterling.
3. Delivery terms (e.g. FOB).
4. Nature of transaction.
5. Net mass (kg).
6. Supplementary units (where a second quantity is required).
7. Country of consignment.
8. Mode of transport.
9. Country of origin.
10. Number of consignments.
11. Trader's reference.

It is important to supply Customs and Excise with the VAT registration numbers of EU suppliers or customers, depending on the nature of the transaction. This enables EU suppliers to be zero-rated for VAT, with the VAT being collected from the importer at the local rate. VAT registration numbers are submitted to Customs in the form of 'EC Sales Lists' detailing transactions made over a given period. Where the volume of a company's trade with the EU is less than £233 000, the reporting requirements are less stringent. Under these circumstances, the business must supply Customs with details of the shipments made, normally by providing a Customs-endorsed copy of the invoice with the shipping documentation. This then becomes the Certificate of

Shipment and is held by the trading company as part of its VAT record-keeping procedures.

Non-EU trade

Trade conducted with countries outside the EU is subject to a range of tariffs and duties. Preferential trading agreements, such as those discussed in Chapter 4, reduce the level of duty payable on many items imported and exported around the world. Where such agreements do not exist, trade is subject to Normal Trading Relations where the full rates of duties apply.

The main documentary requirement as far as trade under preferential agreements is concerned is the use of the EUR1 Movement Certificate, which is raised and certified in the country of the consignment's origin. The EUR1 is used to prove the origin – and hence the duty-free status – of the goods shipped.

EU companies trading with Turkey require an ATR1 Movement Certificate, which performs a similar function to the EUR1. GSP (Generalised System of Preferences) countries can export their goods to, but not import from, the EU on a preferential basis. A GSP Certificate of Origin must be raised and validated in the GSP country of origin.

Providing that an EUR1, ATR1 or GSP certificate accompanies invoices and shipping documentation, consignments can be distributed duty-free within the EU. Customs and Excise also have their own documentary and reporting requirements for trade outside the EU. The Single Administrative Document (SAD), which is known as the C88 in the UK, covers both imports and exports. The document is made up of eight sheets, which are used by a number of organisations to maintain their records (see Figure 10.3).

It should be apparent from Figure 10.3 that the first three sheets are for export purposes, the fourth and fifth for community transit purposes and the remaining copies are for import procedures. The SAD/C88 document therefore provides information for all relevant parties at every stage of the distribution process. Non-EU goods that pass through EU member states before reaching their final destination must use the SAD document, rather than INTRASTAT. (For example, Japanese goods shipped to the UK via Holland.)

Copy 1	Retained by the Customs Office at the point of export
Copy 2	Statistical copy, retained by the exporting country
Copy 3	Exporter/Consignor copy
Copy 4	(Community transit) Copy for the Office of Destination (where consignment is in transit and not in Free Circulation)
Copy 5	(Community transit) Copy returned from Office of Destination to a correspondent Office in the country of origin to prove receipt of goods at destination
Copy 6	Copy for the importing country
Copy 7	Statistical copy, retained by the importing country
Copy 8	Importer/Consignee copy (also acts as a VAT copy)

Figure 10.3 Recipients of copies of C88 documents.

Rules of origin

The EU, like many other major countries, has published a set of rules and regulations to assist traders in defining the origin of goods imported and exported, as it does not necessarily follow that the goods originate from the market that they have been shipped from. We have already seen that the declared origin of the shipped goods impacts on the level of duty payable, and it therefore follows that the trader must be able to demonstrate the true origin of the products in question. The premise of Article 4(1) of the EU's Basic Origin Regulation states that goods wholly obtained or produced in one country are considered to have originated in that country, and the definitions of 'wholly obtained or produced' are further detailed in Article 4(2).

In principle, products can also be admitted into the EU under preferential status on condition that a minimum of 60 per cent of the content by value has been produced in the country for which the importer is claiming preferential status. The rules governing the origin of products that have been assembled or produced in more than one country are contained in Article 5 of the Regulation, which stipulates that origin shall be from the country which has performed the last substantial process in the manufacture or production of the goods. For example, a component for a particular engineering application might be produced in South Korea (which is not eligible for preferential trade with the EU) and shipped to Hungary where it is assembled with components from other non-preferential markets as well as Hungary. The completed application is then supplied to a British company for inclusion in the end product, which may also include other EU and non-EU goods. The goods are shipped from Hungary to the UK on a preferential basis accompanied by an EUR1. The final product is then sold to a client in France using the INTRASTAT reporting method (see Figure 10.4).

The origin of the goods at every stage of the supply chain will depend on the nature of the preferential agreements between the trading nations. If the majority value of the product (60 per cent) is manufactured in Hungary the goods are classed as of Hungarian origin and the goods can enter the UK duty-free. If the majority value of the product derives from components supplied from South Korea, which has no preferential agreement with either Hungary or the EU, the goods would be of South Korean origin and could not be shipped from Hungary to the UK on a preferential basis.

However, the components may be assembled alongside other components of EU origin in the UK, and the majority of the finished product may be derived from the UK. The end product can be classed as British origin and can be imported by the French client duty-free.

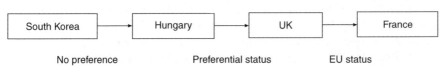

Figure 10.4 Example of how the international supply chain may be subject to different duties.

Preferential status is therefore all about origin and inaccurate classification can lead to heavy fines in the form of import duty payments. Multinational companies in particular are at risk as they increasingly rely on components and materials sourced from supply chains spanning numerous markets. It is essential for companies to correctly identify the origin of all goods shipped if costly fines are to be avoided.

Customs tariffs

Customs tariffs are rates of import duty assigned to every product that could conceivably be imported into a country. Every nation has its own system of Customs tariffs but established trading blocs such as the EU or Mercosur employ a Common Customs Tariff which simplifies the tariff structure for all members of the bloc. The NAFTA countries work together as a Free Trade Area and have not harmonised their tariffs, resulting in varying import duties between the member states. A harmonised system of tariff classification codes has brought many of the world's tariff structures into line with each other, even though individual countries may still charge different rates of duty. The classification consists of eight figures, the first four of which are standard for a particular product regardless of market. The remaining digits vary from market to market and consequently differentiate between the duty levels imposed in each country (see Figure 10.5).

Customs tariffs have an additional purpose. They show which countries have preferential trading status with the home nation as well as identifying and tracking tariff quotas. For example under GSP, less-developed nations are able to export goods on a preferential basis to the EU but some tariff classifications may be restricted to a certain volume during the course of any one year. Once this quota has been reached, the preferential status of those particular products is withdrawn for the remainder of the year and future imports of the goods are subject to duty at the normal rate.

The correct use of the tariff codes is important if accurate information is to be supplied to Customs and clearing agents and all companies involved with international trade should be familiar with the tariff classification for the goods that they are buying or selling.

ATA Carnet

Carnets are used by companies that only temporarily export goods overseas to avoid paying taxes and duties. Circumstances that might require carnets include the shipping of exhibition materials to a foreign market for a company's participation in a trade fair. As the exhibition equipment and samples are eventually brought back to the home market, there is no reason why duty should be payable. The 'admission temporaire' carnet is issued by Chambers of Commerce to companies that are moving materials and samples internationally with the express intention of bringing them back into the domestic market.

Heading number and description	Commodity codes 2A + 2B: imports from non-EC countries		Specific provisions	Unit(s) of quantity	Full rate of duty – non-EC countries	Preferential rates & Accession rates (see KEY)	VAT rate
1	2A: intra-EC imports and ALL exports	2B: imports from non-EC countries					
	2A	2B	3	4	5	6	7
84 10 HYDRAULIC TURBINES, WATER WHEELS, AND REGULATORS THEREFOR: Hydraulic turbines and water wheels:							
Of a power not exceeding 1000 kW[2]	841011 00	00		Kg	4.5%	BG, CH, CS, EE, EEA, GSP, HU, LDDC, LT, LV, MiscP, MX, PL, RO, RY, SM, TR, XC, XL, ZA-Free	S
Of a power exceeding 1000 kW[2] but not exceeding 10000 kW[2]	841012 00	00		Kg	4.5%	BG, CH, CS, EE, EEA, GSP, HU, LDDC, LT, LV, MX, PL, RO, RY, SM, TR, XC, XL, ZA-Free	S
Of a power exceeding 10000 kW[2]	841013 00	00		Kg	4.5%	BG, CH, CS, EE, EEA, GSP, HU, LDDC, LT, LV, MX, PL, RO, RY, SM, TR, XC, XL, ZA-Free	S
Parts, including regulators: Of cast iron or cast steel	841090 10	00		Kg	4.5%	BG, CH, CS, EE, EEA, GSP, HU, LDDC, LT, LV, MX, PL, RO, RY, SM, TR, XC, XL, ZA-Free	S
Other	841090 90	00		Kg	4.5%	BG, CH, CS, EE, EEA, GSP, HU, LDDC, LT, LV, MX, PL, RO, RY, SM, TR, XC, XL, ZA-Free	S

Key to preferential rates
African, Caribbean and Pacific States (ACP)
Overseas Countries and Territories (OCT)
CAC – Costa Rica (CR), Guatemala (GT), Honduras (HN), Nicaragua (NI), Panama (PA), El Salvador (SV)
EEA – Iceland (IS), Liechtenstein (LI), Norway (NO), Svalbard Archipelago (SJ) (including Spitsbergen and Jan Mayen)
EFTA – Iceland (IS), Norway (NO), Svalbard Archipelago (SJ) (including Spitsbergen and Jan Mayen), Switzerland (CH)
Generalised System of Preferences (GSP)
Maghreb (MGB) – Algeria (DZ), Morocco (MA), Tunisia (TN)
Mashraq (MCH) – Egypt (EG), Jordan (JO), Lebanon (LB), Syria (SY)
Others – Andorra (AD), Bulgaria (BG), Ceuta and Melilla (CC), Cyprus (CY), Czech Republic (CZ), Estonia (EE), Faroe Islands (FO), Hungary (HU), Israel (IL), Latvia (LV),Lithuania (LT), Malta (MT), Occupied Territories (OT), Poland (PL), Republic of Former Yugoslavia (RY), Romania (RO), San Marino, (SM), Slovak Republic (SK), Turkey (TR)
CIS – Armenia (AM), Belarus (BY), Georgia (GE), Kazakhstan (KZ), Krygystan (KG), Moldova (MD),Russia (RU), Ukraine (UA), Uzbekistan (UZ)

Figure 10.5 Examples of UK Customs tariff classifications and key to preferential rates (permission to reprint granted by HMSO/Crown Copyright).

Bonded warehousing

Companies may elect to make use of Customs bonded warehousing to avoid paying duty on imported products that will be re-exported to other non-EU countries (and therefore not put into free circulation within the EU). Bonded warehousing can also be used to separate bulk consignments into smaller shipments as well as the preparation, assembly and labelling/repackaging of goods for distribution or resale.

It is not necessary to designate an entire warehouse for bonded purposes, although this will be the case for many companies. It is also possible to secure bonded status for part of a warehouse, storage facility, silo or even a specific room. Free zones and free ports (such as the Port of Southampton and the Port of Liverpool in the UK) undertake a similar role to that of the bonded warehouse, but on a larger scale. As for normal bonded facilities, non-EU goods are classed as outside the Customs remit of the EU whilst stored in an approved area in advance of re-export outside the Union.

Companies that operate a Customs warehouse are obliged to take full responsibility for the security of the stored goods and must maintain an up-to-date system that keeps track of them. Generally, this will include the following data:

- Date goods received and entered in the facility.
- Quantity of goods entered.
- Value of goods.
- Date goods despatched from facility.
- Value of goods despatched.
- Destination (e.g. free circulation in the EU or re-export).

If the goods are released for free circulation within the EU, they must be accompanied by the SAD/C88 document and the requisite level of duty must be paid to Customs.

The effective use of bonded storage for non-EU goods can generate substantial savings for the trader, provided that the appropriate reporting and inventory systems are in place. Customs warehousing is a specialist area of expertise and companies are advised to seek advice when considering making use of this facility.

Inward Processing Relief

Many businesses in Europe import goods for re-export, either in their original state or as components in another finished product. Where the re-exported products are destined for countries outside Europe, the exporter may be eligible for relief from import duty in the form of Inward Processing Relief (IPR).

As this chapter has already shown, companies in the EU are required to pay import duty on goods that are intended for free circulation within the EU whilst goods that are to be re-exported outside Europe are not subject to import duty.

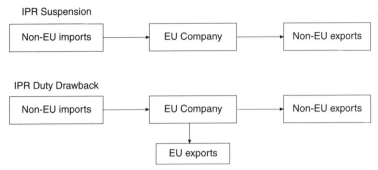

Figure 10.6 IPR Suspension and Drawback flowcharts.

However, many companies do not make the most of the IPR facility, and even those that are part of a larger international supply chain are not necessarily benefiting from the savings that IPR can bring.

There are two types of IPR (see Figure 10.6). If all the imported goods are destined for markets outside Europe, companies may apply for IPR suspension, where the import duty is exempted at the point of import.

If a proportion of the imported goods is released into Free Circulation or is re-exported within the EU as well as outside the Union, the company is subject to IPR Drawback, where import duty is paid on the total value of goods imported. The company can later apply for Drawback on the value of goods re-exported outside the EU.

Question: Identify industries that rely heavily on importing components to be incorporated into finished products and examine the importance of effectively managing IPR and OPR procedures.

It is important for companies working with IPR to retain all invoices, shipping and customs declaration paperwork to provide evidence of all imports and exports. Accurate record-keeping is essential if IPR is to deliver substantial savings for companies that regularly import from outside the EU and re-export to other non-EU markets. Applying for IPR is, however, a relatively complex process and companies should seek advice to ensure that they meet all the necessary qualifying criteria.

Outward Processing Relief

Outward Processing Relief (OPR), as the name suggests, is the opposite of Inward Processing Relief. It allows EU companies to export components and raw materials for modification or finishing and to re-import the finished product, paying import duty and VAT only on the additional value that the original products have gained as a result of the work carried out overseas.

As is the case for IPR there are a number of constraints and qualifying criteria to be overcome before approval for OPR can be granted. Once authorisation has

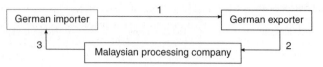

1. Importer obtains OPR authorisation and informs exporter
2. Exporter ships goods to third-party processor
3. Finished products imported under OPRconditions

Figure 10.7   OPR process with more than one EU company.

been given, the company is obliged to maintain accurate records for every transaction for which OPR is claimed. A full set of export documentation, together with copies of the commercial invoices sent to the third-party company that processes the original products must be retained for each shipment.

OPR can also be claimed by the importing company even if it is not the same organisation as the original supplier (see Figure 10.7). For example, a German company may ship components for processing in Malaysia but the finished product may be re-imported into Germany by a different organisation. The responsibility for obtaining OPR authority usually rests with the importer, and confirmation of the authorisation is then sent to the exporter.

The exporter provides the importer with a copy of the invoice sent to the third party, together with a Certificate of Shipment to prove that VAT was zero-rated. When the goods are re-imported, the commercial invoice for the imported goods is attached to the invoice for the exported products. The difference in value between the two invoices is the value-added content inputted by the Malaysian processor. This is the only value of the product that will be liable for import duty. Thus companies can again benefit from substantial savings in duties through good record-keeping and documentation management at every stage of the supply chain.

Customs Freight Simplified Procedures

Customs Freight Simplified Procedures (CFSP) has been implemented to help bring UK duty calculation in line with the SAD requirements of the EU by simplifying non-EU import and warehousing procedures. It has been designed to replace the C88 paper entry and all duties are calculated by Customs and Excise, rather than the company itself.

Information required by Customs, including the supplementary declarations, can be transmitted electronically to the Customs Handling of Import and Export Freight (CHIEF) computer. The appropriate level of duty is accurately calculated and the company is advised accordingly.

New Export System

Businesses in the UK have recently been introduced to the government's 'New Export System' (NES), an electronic reporting system for all export declarations. All the simplified procedures (INTRASTAT, C88, and so on) are submitted in electronic format to CHIEF, although it is still possible to submit paper-based declarations. The paper-based option does, however, take measurably longer to be processed and companies are being encouraged to use electronic reporting wherever possible. The system was introduced as part of the government's commitment to providing electronic services at Dover in March 2002, with all other UK seaports due to adopt the system by October 2002. Airports are due to use NES from 2003.

NES operates in two distinct phases. The first is a short message sent to Customs containing a brief description of the goods to be exported and companies will receive a swift reply, which either grants permission for the shipment to go ahead or requests that the goods be examined.

The second phase is a message containing the supplementary declaration, namely the majority of the information required by Customs following shipment of the goods.

The electronic nature of NES enables immediate clearance of goods for export 24 hours a day, seven days a week and substantially reduces the quantity of paperwork and supporting documentation. The system also provides the exporter with the necessary evidence to support VAT zero-rating, IPR, OPR and temporary imports.

There are a number of organisations in the UK, which supply bespoke software solutions and advice for NES declarations. Their systems provide companies with an effective means of submitting Customs declarations electronically, thereby saving businesses both time and effort.

Online certification

Successful international trade is dependent on accurate documentation supplied at the right time and to the right organisations. In many cases, companies require their documentation to be processed quickly in order to prevent costly shipping delays, and they rely on Chambers of Commerce and other issuing bodies who certify and legalise documents such as Certificates of Origin to provide a fast, efficient service. Generally, documentation is sent through the post or is processed while a company representative waits at the premises of the issuing body.

Exporters and importers are increasingly looking to the Internet to speed up their international trade procedures and communications, and this has now extended to the issue of certifying documentation.

Online international trade documentation has had a troubled history in terms of guaranteeing confidentiality and security of documents transmitted via the Internet. These issues have now been resolved as a result of advances made with digital signature and encryption technologies, and there are now systems in place to facilitate online certification.

In the UK, the British Chambers of Commerce have developed a secure online service that now allows the issuing bodies to verify and certify documents electronically that would otherwise have to be checked and approved manually. The E-Cert service is a major improvement on the traditional approaches and can save companies valuable time.

Conclusions

At first sight, the wealth of documentation required simply to move a consignment from one part of the world to another might seem to be an administrative burden. To many companies it remains an insurmountable obstacle. Nevertheless, it is important to grasp the fact that international trade documentation is there to actually help companies and exists for one main reason: to provide security to exporters, importers and their intermediaries throughout the international transaction and distribution process. Readers will now have a better understanding of the purpose of the different types of documentation for importing and exporting and will be able to put them into their proper context.

Sources of information

Independent Customs & Excise advice and consultancy –
 www.portcullis-isc.co.uk
HM Customs & Excise – www.hmce.gov.uk
British Chambers of Commerce – www.britishchambers.org.uk/exportzone
Croner's handbooks for exporters and importers –
 www.tradeinternational-centre.net
International Air Transport Association (IATA) – www.iata.com
Simplified Trade Procedures Board – www.sitpro.org.uk

Further reading

Bennett R, *Getting Started in Export* (2nd ed) (Kogan Page, 1998).
Bools M, *The Bill of Lading – a Document of Title* (LLP, 1997).
British Chambers of Commerce, *International Trade Manual* (Butterworth-Heinemann, 1997).
ICC, *Incoterms 2000: ICC Official Rules for the Interpretation of Trade Terms* (ICC, 2000).
Rowbotham J M, *A Guide to Importing and Customs Procedures* (self-published, 2001, www.portcullis-isc.co.uk).
Rowbotham J M, *A Guide to Exporting and Customs Procedures* (self-published, 2001, www.portcullis-isc.co.uk).
Sherlock J, *Principles of International Physical Distribution* (Blackwell, 1994).
Wilson J R, *Getting Started in Importing* (2nd ed) (Kogan Page, 1998).

QUESTIONS FOR CONSIDERATION

1 Explain the differences between claused, stale, received, transhipment, combined and through Bills of Lading.
2 Why is it important to include a commercial invoice with import documentation?
3 How might exporters make more effective use of the Internet with regard to international trade documentation?

4   A Malaysian company produces plastic components used in the manufacture of desk lamps. The components are exported to a firm in Poland that includes them in the assembly of the base unit. The base units are then exported to a company in Holland where they are incorporated into the finished product. The Dutch company then exports the lamps to businesses in Germany and the UK. Given that the Malaysian components cost £1.20, the base unit £3.50 and the finished product is exported to the UK at a price of £7.80 per unit:

(a)   What is the origin of the product and where will import duty be paid?
(b)   Explain whether IPR or OPR is applicable and what the UK importer must demonstrate to be eligible.

Case study: Examples of export documentation

The following pages provide examples of export documentation covering different stages of the fulfilment of an export order. The documentation was prepared by ExportPro Limited, one of the UK's leading suppliers of export management software.

The case study is based on an order for computer hardware and peripheral accessories to be supplied by ExportPro Limited to ExportPro SA in France. The documentation includes:

- The initial quotation
- Order acknowledgement
- Pro-forma invoice
- Commercial invoice
- Packing list
- Shipping instructions
- Standard Shipping Note
- CMR international consignment note
- C88
- Bill of exchange
- Letter of credit documentary presentation

and should provide readers with a better understanding of how export documentation is set out and what each form contains.

			QUOTATION		

Seller   VAT no.   GB 523 3557 59

ExportPro Limited
Tower Court
Oakdale Road, Clifton Moor
YORK YO30 4XL

Tel: +44 (0)1904 557642   Fax: +44 (0)1904 557643

QUOTATION Number	Amendment Number
200	

Date(Tax Point)	Seller's Reference
02/01/2002	DEM0000001

Buyer's Reference	Validity
EMAIL12345230102	02/04/2002

Consignee   VAT no.   FR 12 456789012   Buyer (if not consignee)

ExportPro S.A.
18 rue Viville
60530 Neuilly-en-Thelle
FRANCE

Notify
Beran Industrie-Consulting GmbH
Spaldingstr 210, Soltau 7650
Neidersachsen, Germany

Country of Despatch	Currency
United Kingdom	British Sterling

Country of Origin	Country of Destination
UNITED KINGDOM	France

Vessel/flight no and date   Port/airport of loading
          GB LIVERPOOL

Port/airport of discharge   Place of delivery
FR MARSEILLE   FR NEULLY EN THELLE

Method of Transport   Sailing on or about

Terms of delivery and payment
Carriage Paid to Marseille, France
Open Account
40 days after receipt of goods

Item	Part Number	Description	Quantity	Unit	Unit Price	Extended Price
		COMPUTER HARDWARE				
1	P1600	Pentium 4 1600 IBM Thinkpad i PC	30	Each	846.00	25,380.00
		40 Gigabyte Hard Disk.				
		256 Mb RAM.120x DVD, CD Rewriter				
2	P2000	Pentium 4 2000 IBM Thinkpad i PC	20	Each	975.00	19,500.00
		80 Gb Hard Disk. 256 Mb RAM.				
		120x DVD, CD Rewriter				
						44,880.00
		220/240 VOLT ELECTRICAL COMPONENTS				
3	ECABLE	PC Power CABLE 3Mtr Black, Moulded Plug.	50	Each	2.46	123.00
		external fuse CE Spec 4567/el				
4	EPLUG3	3 Pin Plug 13 amp RED TOP, Sealed Unit	50	Each	0.50	25.00
		CE Spec 12345/el				
						148.00

EX WORKS London	**GBP 45,028.00**
Inland Freight to Port in UK	234.00
TOTAL FOB UK PORT	**GBP 45,262.00**
Transport Insurance	339.47
Ferry Charges and On Carriage to Destination	345.00
DELIVERED DUTY UNPAID Neuilly-en-Thelle	**GBP 45,946.47**

OUR BANKERS ARE HSBC BANK PLC 100 KING STREET, MANCHESTER M60 2HD, U.K.
SORT CODE 40-31-24 A/C NO 41648020

We hereby declare that the above mentioned goods are in free circulation within the European Union and that the prices shown are true and correct at time of print (date also shown).

Name of Authorised Signatory
Alan Raimes

Place and date of issue
York, 02/01/2002

Signature

ExportPro - ExportPro Limited

			ORDER ACKNOWLEDGEMENT		

Seller VAT no. GB 523 3557 59

ExportPro Limited
Tower Court
Oakdale Road, Clifton Moor
YORK YO30 4XL
Tel: +44 (0)1904 557642   Fax: +44 (0)1904 557643

Order Acknowledgement Number	Amendment Number
400	
Date(Tax Point)	**Seller's Reference**
04/01/2002	DEM0000001
Buyer's Reference	**Other Reference**
EMAIL12345230102	

Consignee VAT no. FR 12 456789012	**Buyer (if not consignee)**
ExportPro S.A. 18 rue Viville 60530 Neuilly-en-Thelle FRANCE	

Notify	**Country of Despatch**	**Currency**
Beran Industrie-Consulting GmbH	United Kingdom	British Sterling
Spaldingstr 210, Soltau 7650	**Country of Origin**	
Neidersachsen, Germany	UNITED KINGDOM	

Country of Destination
France

Vessel/flight no and date	**Port/airport of loading**	**Terms of delivery and payment**
	GB LIVERPOOL	Carriage Paid to Marseille, France
Port/airport of discharge	**Place of delivery**	Open Account
FR MARSEILLE	FR NEULLY EN THELLE	40 days after receipt of goods
Method of Transport	**Sailing on or about**	

Item	Part Number	Description	Quantity	Unit	Unit Price	
		COMPUTER HARDWARE				
1	P1600	Pentium 4 1600 IBM Thinkpad i PC	30	Each	846.00	
		40 Gigabyte Hard Disk.				
		256 Mb RAM.120x DVD, CD Rewriter				
2	P2000	Pentium 4 2000 IBM Thinkpad i PC	20	Each	975.00	
		80 Gb Hard Disk. 256 Mb RAM.				
		120x DVD, CD Rewriter				
		220/240 VOLT ELECTRICAL COMPONENTS				
3	ECABLE	PC Power CABLE 3Mtr Black, Moulded Plug.	50	Each	2.46	
		external fuse CE Spec 4567/el				
4	EPLUG3	3 Pin Plug 13 amp RED TOP, Sealed Unit	50	Each	0.50	
		CE Spec 12345/el				

THANK YOU FOR YOUR CONTINUED BUSINESS, PLEASE NOTE
CONFIRMATION OF RECEIPT OF YOUR ORDER AS DETAILED ABOVE
WE WILL INFORM YOU OF OUR DELIVERY SCHEDULE IN DUE COURSE
PLEASE DIRECT ANY IMMEDIATE QUERIES TO OUR EXPORT SALES DESK

	Name of Authorised Signatory
We hereby declare that the above mentioned goods are in free circulation within the European Union and that the prices shown are true and correct at time of print (date also shown).	Alan Raimes
	Place and date of issue
	York, 04/04/2002
	Signature

ExportPro - ExportPro Limited

PROFORMA INVOICE

Seller   VAT no.   GB 523 3557 59

ExportPro Limited
Tower Court
Oakdale Road, Clifton Moor
YORK YO30 4XL

Tel: +44 (0)1904 557642   Fax: +44 (0)1904 557643

Proforma Invoice Number	Amendment Number
200	
Date(Tax Point)	Seller's Reference
02/01/2002	DEM0000001
Buyer's Reference	Validity
EMAIL12345230102	02/04/2002

Consignee VAT no. FR 12 456789012	Buyer (if not consignee)
ExportPro S.A. 18 rue Viville 60530 Neuilly-en-Thelle FRANCE	

Notify		
Beran Industrie-Consulting GmbH Spaldingstr 210, Soltau 7650 Neidersachsen, Germany	Country of Despatch	Currency
	United Kingdom	British Sterling
	Country of Origin	Country of Destination
	UNITED KINGDOM	France

Vessel/flight no and date	Port/airport of loading	Terms of delivery and payment
	GB LIVERPOOL	Carriage Paid to Marseille, France
Port/airport of discharge	Place of delivery	Open Account
FR MARSEILLE	FR NEULLY EN THELLE	40 days after receipt of goods
Method of Transport	Sailing on or about	

Shipping Marks; container no	No. and kind of packages; description of goods	Commodity Code	Total Gross Wt(kg)	Total cube (m³)
ExportPro SA	15 Pallets+Shrinkwrap, 1 Shipping Carton	55004200705		
18 Rue Vivielle	holding 150 Carton(s) of	45006702 56	1,002.50	
60530	Computer Hardware			
Neuilly-en-Thelle	System Units, Peripherals		Total Net Wt(kg)	17.778
FRANCE	& Cabling Components.			
Imported from	& Misc. Electrical Goods		882.50	
UNITED KINGDOM				

Item	Part Number	Description	Quantity	Unit	Unit Price	Extended Price
		COMPUTER HARDWARE				
1	P1600	Pentium 4 1600 IBM Thinkpad i PC 40 Gigabyte Hard Disk. 256 Mb RAM.120x DVD, CD Rewriter	30	Each	846.00	25,380.00
2	P2000	Pentium 4 2000 IBM Thinkpad i PC 80 Gb Hard Disk. 256 Mb RAM. 120x DVD, CD Rewriter	20	Each	975.00	19,500.00
						44,880.00
		220/240 VOLT ELECTRICAL COMPONENTS				
3	ECABLE	PC Power CABLE 3Mtr Black, Moulded Plug. external fuse CE Spec 4567/el	50	Each	2.46	123.00
4	EPLUG3	3 Pin Plug 13 amp RED TOP, Sealed Unit CE Spec 12345/el	50	Each	0.50	25.00
						148.00

EX WORKS London	**GBP 45,028.00**
Inland Freight to Port in UK	234.00
TOTAL FOB UK PORT	**GBP 45,262.00**
Transport Insurance	339.47
Ferry Charges and On Carriage to Destination	345.00
DELIVERED DUTY UNPAID Neuilly-en-Thelle	**GBP 45,946.47**

OUR BANKERS ARE HSBC BANK PLC 100 KING STREET, MANCHESTER M60 2HD, U.K.
SORT CODE 40-31-24 A/C NO 41648020

It is hereby certified that this invoice shows the actual price of the goods described, that no other invoice has been or will be issued, and that all particulars are true and correct.

Name of Authorised Signatory
Alan Raimes
Place and date of issue
York, 02/01/2002
Signature

ExportPro - ExportPro Limited

Seller	VAT no. GB 523 3557 59	**COMMERCIAL EXPORT INVOICE**	

COMMERCIAL EXPORT INVOICE Number	Amendment Number
500	

ExportPro Limited
Tower Court
Oakdale Road, Clifton Moor
YORK YO30 4XL
Tel: +44 (0)1904 557642   Fax: +44 (0)1904 557643

Date(Tax Point)	Seller's Reference
30/01/2002	DEM0000001

Buyer's Reference	Other Reference
EMAIL12345230102	Account No. EXPRO1

Consignee	VAT no. FR 12 456789012	Buyer (if not consignee)

ExportPro S.A.
18 rue Viville
60530 Neuilly-en-Thelle
FRANCE

Notify	Country of Despatch	Currency
Beran Industrie-Consulting GmbH	United Kingdom	British Sterling
Spaldingstr 210, Soltau 7650	Country of Origin	Country of Destination
Neidersachsen, Germany	UNITED KINGDOM	France

Vessel/flight no and date	Port/airport of loading	Terms of delivery and payment
	GB LIVERPOOL	Carriage Paid to Marseille, France
Port/airport of discharge	Place of delivery	Open Account
FR MARSEILLE	FR NEULLY EN THELLE	40 days after receipt of goods
Method of Transport	Sailing on or about	

Shipping Marks; container no	No. and kind of packages; description of goods	Commodity Code	Total Gross Wt(kg)	Total cube (m³)
ExportPro SA	15 Pallets+Shrinkwrap, 1 Shipping Carton	55004200705		
18 Rue Vivielle	holding 150 Carton(s) of	45006702 56	1,002.50	
60530	Computer Hardware			
Neuilly-en-Thelle	System Units, Peripherals		Total Net Wt(kg)	17.778
FRANCE	& Cabling Components.			
Imported from	& Misc. Electrical Goods		882.50	
UNITED KINGDOM				

Item	Part Number	Description	Quantity	Unit	Unit Price	Extended Price
		COMPUTER HARDWARE				
1	P1600	Pentium 4 1600 IBM Thinkpad i PC	30	Each	846.00	25,380.00
		40 Gigabyte Hard Disk.				
		256 Mb RAM.120x DVD, CD Rewriter				
2	P2000	Pentium 4 2000 IBM Thinkpad i PC	20	Each	975.00	19,500.00
		80 Gb Hard Disk. 256 Mb RAM.				
		120x DVD, CD Rewriter				
						44,880.00
		220/240 VOLT ELECTRICAL COMPONENTS				
3	ECABLE	PC Power CABLE 3Mtr Black, Moulded Plug.	50	Each	2.46	123.00
		external fuse CE Spec 4567/el				
4	EPLUG3	3 Pin Plug 13 amp RED TOP, Sealed Unit	50	Each	0.50	25.00
		CE Spec 12345/el				
						148.00

EX WORKS London	**GBP 45,028.00**
Inland Freight to Port in UK	234.00
TOTAL FOB UK PORT	**GBP 45,262.00**
Transport Insurance	339.47
Ferry Charges and On Carriage to Destination	345.00
DELIVERED DUTY UNPAID Neuilly-en-Thelle	**GBP 45,946.47**

OUR BANKERS ARE HSBC BANK PLC 100 KING STREET, MANCHESTER M60 2HD, U.K.
SORT CODE 40-31-24 A/C NO 41648020

Name of Authorised Signatory
Alan Raimes

It is hereby certified that this invoice shows the actual price of the goods described, that no other invoice has been or will be issued, and that all particulars are true and correct.

Place and date of issue
York, 23/01/2002

Signature

ExportPro - ExportPro Limited

Seller	VAT no.	GB 523 3557 59	**PACKING LIST**	

ExportPro Limited
Tower Court
Oakdale Road, Clifton Moor
YORK YO30 4XL

Tel: +44 (0)1904 557642   Fax: +44 (0)1904 557643

Packing List Number	Amendment Number
500	

Date(Tax Point)	Seller's Reference
23/01/2002	DEM0000001

Buyer's Reference	Other Reference
EMAIL12345230102	Account No. EXPRO1

Consignee	VAT no.	FR 12 456789012	Buyer (if not consignee)

ExportPro S.A.
18 rue Viville
60530 Neuilly-en-Thelle
FRANCE

Shipping Marks; container no	No. and kind of packages: description of goods	Commodity Code	Total Gross Wt(kg)	Total cube (m³)
ExportPro SA	15 Pallets+Shrinkwrap, 1 Shipping Carton	55004200705		
18 Rue Vivielle	holding 150 Carton(s) of	45006702 56	1,002.50	
60530	Computer Hardware			
Neuilly-en-Thelle	System Units, Peripherals		Total Net Wt(kg)	17.778
FRANCE	& Cabling Components.			
Imported from	& Misc. Electrical Goods		882.50	
UNITED KINGDOM				

Item	Part Number	Description	Quantity	Unit	Packing Type

Pack ID	Pack Type	No of Packs	Dimension (cms)	Net Wt (kgs)	Gross Wt (kgs)	Volume (m³)
1-10	Pallets + Shrinkwrap	10	120 x 80 x 112	49.00	55.75	1.075

Item	Part Number	Description	Quantity	Unit	Packing Type
1	P1600	Pentium 4 1600 IBM Thinkpad i PC	2	Each	Carton(s)
		40 Gb Disk. 256 Mb RAM.120x DVD, CD Rewriter			
2	P2000	Pentium 4 2000 IBM Thinkpad i PC	1	Each	Carton(s)
		80 Gb Hard Disk. 256 Mb RAM. 120x DVD, CD RW			

Pack ID	Pack Type	No of Packs	Dimension (cms)	Net Wt (kgs)	Gross Wt (kgs)	Volume (m³)
11-15	Pallets + Shrinkwrap	5	120x 80 x146	71.00	80.60	1.402

Item	Part Number	Description	Quantity	Unit	Packing Type
1	P1600	Pentium 4 1600 IBM Thinkpad i PC	2	Each	Carton(s)
		40 Gb Disk. 256 Mb RAM.120x DVD, CD Rewriter			
2	P2000	Pentium 4 2000 IBM Thinkpad i PC	2	Each	Carton(s)
		80 Gb Hard Disk. 256 Mb RAM. 120x DVD, CD RW			
3	ECABLE	PC Power CABLE 3Mtr Black, Moulded Plug.	4	Each	Carton(s)
		external fuse CE Spec 4567/el			
4	EPLUG3	3 Pin Plug 13 amp RED TOP, Sealed Unit	4	Each	Carton(s)
		CE Spec 12345/el			

Pack ID	Pack Type	No of Packs	Dimension (cms)	Net Wt (kgs)	Gross Wt (kgs)	Volume (m³)
16	Carton(s)	1	30 x 25 x 24	37.50	42.00	0.018

Item	Part Number	Description	Quantity	Unit	Packing Type
3	ECABLE	PC Power CABLE 3Mtr Black, Moulded Plug.	30	Each	Carton(s)
		external fuse CE Spec 4567/el			
4	EPLUG3	3 Pin Plug 13 amp RED TOP, Sealed Unit	30	Each	Carton(s)
		CE Spec 12345/el			

Part Number	Pack ID	Quantity
ECABLE	11-15	4
ECABLE	16	30
EPLUG3	11-15	4
EPLUG3	16	30
P1600	1-10	2
P1600	11-15	2
P2000	1-10	1
P2000	11-15	2

We hereby certify that this consignment has been shipped in accordance with the above mentioned details.

Name of Authorised Signatory
Alan Raimes
Place and date of issue
York, 23/01/2002
Signature

SHIPPING INSTRUCTIONS

Freight Forwarder/Carrier		Number	Customs Reference/Status
B. Brown Forwarders Ltd		500.SIN	

	Date(Tax Point)	Exporter's Reference
156 High Street	26/04/2002	DEM0000001

	Booking Reference	Forwarder's Reference
Shipley BD18 7TF	BRF14762002	FFR75548

Consignor

ExportPro Limited
Tower Court
Oakdale Road, Clifton Moor
YORK YO30 4XL

Documents — Send to

Bill of Lading 3 Originals / 3 Copies — Exporter
Certificate of Shipment — Consignee

Consignee

ExportPro S.A.
18 rue Viville
60530 Neuilly-en-Thelle
FRANCE

Charges — Charge to

All Freight Charges — Exporter

Notify

Beran Industrie-Consulting GmbH
Spaldingstr 210, Soltau 7650
Neidersachsen, Germany

Vessel/flight no and date	Port/airport of loading	Notify	By	Event
	GB LIVERPOOL	Exporter	E-Mail	Transport Delays
Port/airport of discharge	Place of delivery	Consignee	Fax	Arrival
FR MARSEILLE	FR NEULLY EN THELLE			
Method of Transport	Sailing on or about			

Shipping Marks; container no	No. and kind of packages: description of goods	Gross Weight	Measurement
ExportPro SA	15 Pallets+Shrinkwrap, 1 Shipping Carton	1,002.50 kgs	17.778 cbm
18 Rue Vivielle	holding 150 Carton(s) of		
60530	Computer Hardware		
Neuilly-en-Thelle	System Units, Peripherals		
FRANCE	& Cabling Components.		
Imported from	& Misc. Electrical Goods		
UNITED KINGDOM			

Carriage Paid to Marseille, France
Open Account
40 days after receipt of goods

Special Instructions

Please position 1 x 20 ft container, clean, dry and odour free
on .27th APRIL 2002
at 7.30 hrs at SHED 7, GOOLE FREEPORT, HUMBERSIDE.
Driver Accompanied, direct to consignee address as above

Name of Authorised Signatory	Place and date of issue	Signature
Alan Raimes	York, 23/01/2002	

Please issue the Transport Document EXACTLY as in the bold outlined section

STANDARD SHIPPING NOTE - FOR NON-DANGEROUS GOODS ONLY

IMPORTANT USE THE DANGEROUS GOODS NOTE IF THE GOODS ARE CLASSIFIED AS DANGEROUS ACCORDING TO APPLICABLE REGULATIONS SEE BOX 10A

Exporter	1	Customs reference/status		2
ExportPro Limited **Tower Court** **Oakdale Road, Clifton Moor** **YORK YO30 4XL** Tel: +44 (0)1904 557642 Fax: +44 (0)1904 557643		Booking number 3 BRF147622002	Exporter's reference 4 DEM0000001	
			Forwarder's reference 5 FFR75548	

Consignee	6
ExportPro S.A. 18 rue Viville 60530 Neuilly-en-Thelle FRANCE	

Freight forwarder	7	International carrier	8
B. Brown Forwarders Ltd 156 High Street Shipley BD8 7TF		For use of receiving authority only	

Other UK transport details (e.g. ICD, terminal, vehicle bkg. ref, receiving dates)	9

The Company preparing this note declares that, to the best of their belief, the goods have been accurately described, their quantities, weights and measurements are correct and at the time of despatch they were in good order and condition: that the goods are not classified as being hazardous by reference to relevant national and international regulations applicable to the intended modes of transport.   **10A**

Vessel/flight no. and date	Port/airport of loading	10
	GB LIVERPOOL	

Port/airport of discharge	Destination	11
FR MARSEILLE	FR NEULLY EN THELLE	

TO THE RECEIVING AUTHORITY - Please receive for shipment the goods described below subject to your published regulations and conditions (including those as to liability).

Shipping marks	Number and kind of packages; description of goods: non-hazardous special stowage requirements	12	Gross wt (kg) of goods	13A	Cube (m3) of goods	14
ExportPro SA 18 Rue Vivielle 60530 Neuilly-en-Thelle FRANCE Imported from UNITED KINGDOM	15 Pallets+Shrinkwrap, 1 Shipping Carton holding 150 Carton(s) of Computer Hardware System Units, Peripherals & Cabling Components. & Misc. Electrical Goods		1,002.50		17.778	

For use of shipping company only	Total gross weight of goods	Total cube of goods
	1,002.50	17.778

Container identification number/ vehicle registration number	16	Seal number (s)	16A	Container/vehicle size and type	16B	Tare (kg)	16C	Total gross wt. (including tare) (kg)	16D
W426 BCP		RS235678 RS235679		20ft Container		7,560.00		8,562.50	

DOCK/TERMINAL RECEIPT

HAULIERS DETAILS	RECEIVING AUTHORITY REMARKS	Name and telephone number of company preparing this note	17
Haulier's name	Received the above number of packages/containers/trailers in apparent good order and condition unless stated hereon.	ExportPro Limited ExportPro+44(0)1904557642	
Vehicle reg. no.		Place and date	
		York 23/01/2002	
Driver's signature	Receiving authority signature and date	Name of contact Alan Raimes	

630   Non-completion of any boxes is subject for resolution by the contracting parties

ExportPro Ltd. - SITPRO Approved Licensee No. 34

LETTRE DE VOITURE INTERNATIONALE   CMR   INTERNATIONAL CONSIGNMENT NOTE

Sender (name, address, country) Expediteur (nom, adresse, pays) 1	Sender's/agent's reference Reference de l'expediteur/de l'agent 2/3
ExportPro Limited **Tower Court** **Oakdale Road, Clifton Moor** **YORK YO30 4XL** Tel: +44 (0)1904 557642 Fax: +44 (0)1904 557643	DEM0000001

Consignee (name, address, country) Destinataire (nom, adresse, pays) 4	Carrier (name, address, country) Transporteur (nom, adresse, pays) 5
ExportPro S.A. 18 rue Viville 60530 Neuilly-en-Thelle FRANCE	B. Brown Forwarders Ltd 156 High Street Shipley BD8 7TF

Place & date of taking over the goods (place, country, date) Lieu et date de la prise en charge des marchandises (lieu, pays, date) 6	Successive carriers Transporteurs successifs 7
MARSEILLE, FRANCE,	Compagnie Maritime Generale Norbert Dentressangle

Place designated for delivery of goods (place, country) 8 Lieu prevu pour la livraison des marchandises (lieu, pays)	
Neuilly-en-Thelle,France	This carriage is subject, notwithstanding any clause to the contrary, to the Convention on the Contract for the International Carriage of Goods by Road (CMR) Ce transport est soumis nonobstant toute clause contraire a la Convention Relative au Contrat de Transport International de Marchandises par Route (CMR)

COPY 1 SENDER
COPY 2 CONSIGNEE
COPY 3 CARRIER

Shipping marks; no. & kind of packages; description of goods* Marques et nos; no et nature des colis; designation des marchandises* 9	Gross weight (kg) 10 Poids brut (kg)	Volume (m3) 11 Cubage (m3)
ExportPro SA 18 Rue Vivielle 60530 Neuilly-en-Thelle FRANCE Imported from UNITED KINGDOM	15 Pallets+Shrinkwrap, 1 Shipping Carton holding 150 Carton(s) of Computer Hardware System Units, Peripherals & Cabling Components. & Misc. Electrical Goods	1002.5	17.778

*NB FOR DANGEROUS GOODS SPECIFY: 1. Substance identification number (if applicable) 2. Substance description 3. Class 4. Item number and letter (if any) 5. The initials 'ADR' or 'RID' 6. Other statements as required by ADR or RID.

Carriage charges Prix de transport 12	Senders instructions for customs, etc... Instructions de l'expediteur (optional) 13
£928.47	

Reservations Reserves 14	Documents attached Documents annexes (optional) 15
	Special agreements Conventions particulieres (optional) 16

Goods received Marchandises recues 17	Signature of carrier Signature de transporteur 16	Company completing this note Societe emettrice 21
		ExportPro Limited
		Place and date; signature Lieu et date; signature 20 York, 23/01/2002

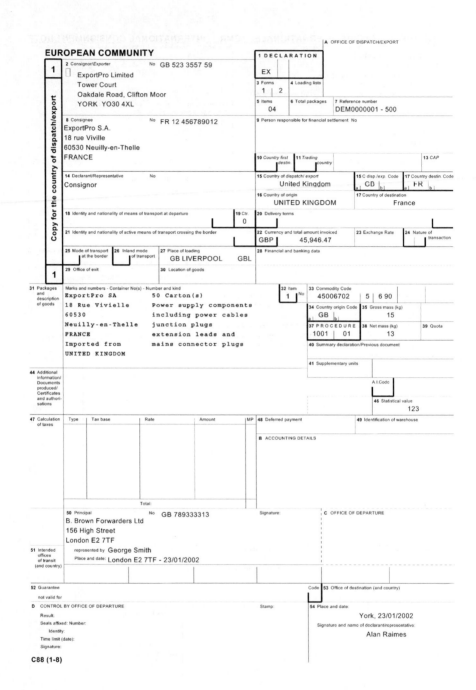

EUROPEAN COMMUNITY

1 Copy for the country of dispatch/export

2 Consignor/Exporter No GB 523 3557 59
ExportPro Limited
Tower Court
Oakdale Road, Clifton Moor
YORK YO30 4XL

8 Consignee No FR 12 456789012
ExportPro S.A.
18 rue Viville
60530 Neuilly-en-Thelle
FRANCE

14 Declarant/Representative No
Consignor

18 Identity and nationality of means of transport at departure **19** Ctr. 0

21 Identity and nationality of active means of transport crossing the border

25 Mode of transport at the border **26** Inland mode of transport **27** Place of loading
GB LIVERPOOL GBL

29 Office of exit **30** Location of goods

A OFFICE OF DISPATCH/EXPORT

1 DECLARATION
EX
3 Forms 1 | 2 **4** Loading lists
5 Items 04 **6** Total packages **7** Reference number DEM0000001 - 500
9 Person responsible for financial settlement No
10 Country first destin. **11** Trading country **13** CAP
15 Country of dispatch/ export United Kingdom **15** C disp./exp. Code CD a| b| **17** Country destin. Code FR a| b|
16 Country of origin UNITED KINGDOM **17** Country of destination France
20 Delivery terms
22 Currency and total amount invoiced GBP 45,946.47 **23** Exchange Rate **24** Nature of transaction
28 Financial and banking data

31 Packages and description of goods
Marks and numbers - Container No(s) - Number and kind
ExportPro SA
18 Rue Vivielle
60530
Neuilly-en-Thelle
FRANCE
Imported from
UNITED KINGDOM

50 Carton(s)
Power supply components
including power cables
junction plugs
extension leads and
mains connector plugs

32 Item 1 No
33 Commodity Code 45006702 5 | 6 90
34 Country origin Code GB **35** Gross mass (kg) 15
37 PROCEDURE 1001 | 01 **38** Net mass (kg) 13 **39** Quota
40 Summary declaration/Previous document
41 Supplementary units

44 Additional information/ Documents produced/ Certificates and authorisations
A.I.Code
46 Statistical value 123

47 Calculation of taxes
Type	Tax base	Rate	Amount	MP

Total:

48 Deferred payment **49** Identification of warehouse
B ACCOUNTING DETAILS

50 Principal No GB 789333313
B. Brown Forwarders Ltd
156 High Street
London E2 7TF
represented by George Smith
Place and date: London E2 7TF - 23/01/2002

51 Intended offices of transit (and country)

Signature: C OFFICE OF DEPARTURE

52 Guarantee
not valid for
Code **53** Office of destination (and country)

D CONTROL BY OFFICE OF DEPARTURE
Result:
Seals affixed: Number:
Identity:
Time limit (date):
Signature:

Stamp:

54 Place and date:
York, 23/01/2002
Signature and name of declarant/representative:
Alan Raimes

C88 (1-8)

ExportPro Limited
Tower Court
Oakdale Road, Clifton Moor
YORK YO30 4XL

Bill of Exchange

for: GBP 12,722.60

No: DEM0000004 - 501

York, 23/01/2002

At 30 days from date of arrival of shipment pay this Sole Bill of Exchange (First of the same tenor and date unpaid) to the order of Trading Bank of Brazil the amount of:

Amount in words	Millions	Hundred Thousands	Ten Thousands	Thousands	Hundreds	Tens	Units	1/10
	*******	*******	One	Two	Seven	Two	Two	Six

Drawn under Documentary Credit Number CVB/FGT/O1/076582 dated 20th January 2002 of Bank of Dubai.
Shipped According to your Purchase Order VB5485

To: ABC Pipe Limited
      2732 King Faisal Avenue
      Alkhobar
      Saudi Arabia
      Account No. ABC123

for and on behalf of
ExportPro Limited

Alan Raimes - Shipping Manager

LETTER OF CREDIT DOCUMENT PRESENTATION

Drawer	Our Reference
ExportPro Limited **Tower Court** **Oakdale Road, Clifton Moor** **YORK YO30 4XL**	DEMO - 547

	Value of the drawing
	FRF 399,709.42

To	Your Reference
Barclays Bank Plc Bank Road London NW10 2EB England, UK	BARC/1998/LOC/57

Issuing Bank	Letter of Credit No
Union Bank of Switzerland Grand Places 1701 Fribourg 1 SWITZERLAND	LOC No.1998/1/DEMO

Dear Madam/Sir,
We enclose herewith the following documents related to the Letter of Credit referred above. In case you discover any discrepancies, please contact us BEFORE taking any action.

Bill of Exchange	Commercial Invoice	Certified Consular Invoice	Certificate of Origin	Packing List	Insurance policy/Certificate	Transport Document	Letter of Credit for Endorsement
1	4		1	2	1	1	1

Other Documents being submitted
NONE

Payment Instructions
PLEASE REMIT 10% of proceeds TO MYB PERSONAL A/C IN JERSEY
Transfer rest by Electronic transfer to Arbuthnot & Latham, 40-47-31, Account No. 61347000

Discrepancies/Term Drafts/Special Instructions
In case of discrepancies please refer to buyer,
all charges to account of drawer.

Contact Details	Place and date of issue
Alan Raimes Chief Accountant ExportPro+44(0)1819640527	London, 23/01/2002
	Signature

▓ M █ Payment

Introduction

All the effort put into marketing, market research, pricing, logistics and documentation will be for nothing if the exporter does not receive payment for the goods or services sold. Getting paid is the most important aspect of international trade and companies that do not take the time to ensure that payment is guaranteed are likely to run into difficulties sooner or later. This chapter therefore aims to explain the different types of payment methods used in international transactions, including the mechanisms that exist to facilitate the actual transfer of funds between buyer and seller, and will highlight the relative safety of each. The payment methods outlined can be used by service providers as well as conventional manufacturing companies.

Readers will also be shown the importance of accuracy in letter of credit transactions and the courses of action available when difficulties arise through discrepancies and fraudulent acts. On completion of the chapter, the reader will be able to identify the most commonly used approaches to securing payment from overseas buyers and will understand the procedures required under each method.

Payment options

Securing payment from an overseas buyer is one of the fundamental requirements of international trade. It is also one of the most important issues to fully understand as the risk of not receiving payment is much greater than it is for domestic trade. The chances of an exporter being able to trade with buyers in the same language, with the same business culture and the same financial/legal infrastructure are slim and the potential for misunderstandings arising between the two parties is not to be underestimated. This is particularly true when the cultural issues addressed in Chapter 5 are taken into account.

There are four main methods of payment in common usage for international trade, although each has a number of variations depending on the circumstances in which it is used. The payment options (prepayment, documentary credits, documentary collections and open account trading) offer varying levels of security and risk to both the exporter and importer, and both parties must therefore ensure that they fully understand the payment terms agreed and the obligations that the arrangement entails (see Figure 11.1).

Exporter's perspective

Least risky   Most risky

Prepayment   Documentary   Documentary   Open
                        credits   collections   account

Most risky   Least risky

Importer's perspective

Figure 11.1 The payment risk scale.

Prepayment

Prepayment, or payment in advance, is the most favourable payment method from the seller's point of view and least favourable to the buyer (see Figure 11.2). Consequently, in order to be able to agree on these terms, either the exporter is in a very strong position, as would be the case if the seller were a sole supplier, or the buyer is in a very weak one, perhaps as a result of bad credit ratings. Cash in advance of receiving the goods is a high-risk option for the importer, but this may be the only feasible method of payment open to buyers who are not in a firm enough position to negotiate better terms. Prepayment may take the form of cash with order or on shipment, although it is not uncommon for the exporter to request a deposit on ordering, with the balance subsequently paid at an agreed date.

Advance payments can be a useful source of finance for the exporting company, particularly if payment is received far enough in advance to allow the company to purchase the materials, components or stock required to fulfil the order rather than replenish stock on completion of the order. Under these circumstances, especially those involving machinery or capital equipment as opposed to readily available consumer goods, the buyer may demand that the seller provides an advance payment guarantee (APG). This grants the importer a certain degree of security in the event that the exporter does not supply the goods in question.

Advance payments can be useful to both parties if they are part of the same group of companies, in which case the degree of trust between buyer and supplier will be high and the buyer will have no concerns about prepayments being used by the exporter to fund the venture.

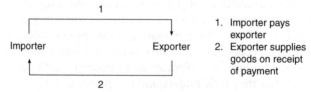

1. Importer pays exporter
2. Exporter supplies goods on receipt of payment

Figure 11.2 Simple prepayment model.

Note: Prepayment can present different problems for both the exporter and the importer. For instance, the importer may pay in advance for services, which are subsequently not delivered. It is also possible that prepaid funds will be used to finance manufacture of the goods in the first place, leading to delays in production and delivery. This in turn could place the exporter in breach of contract and neither party is satisfied.

Open account

Trading on open account terms is practically the opposite of prepayment terms in that the importer takes title to the goods shipped by the exporter before any payment is made for them (See Figure 11.3). This therefore leaves the exporter exposed to the risk of non-payment for 30, 60, 90 days or longer, depending on the credit period agreed. The buyer benefits from not having to pay for the goods for a given period of time and, as a result, from having the purchases financed by the exporter for that period. The exporter, however, must be prepared to take the risk that the importing company is unable to meet its financial obligations.

Due to the level of risk taken by the exporter in allowing a buyer to trade on these terms, open account trading normally only occurs in situations where the buyer has a particularly good credit rating or is well known to the supplier. Open account terms are also common within the EU, due largely to the relaxed trading conditions in the EU and easy access to credit information.

Bills of exchange

Before discussing the more complex payment methods – documentary credits and collections – it is useful to first examine the nature of the bill of exchange, which is one of the most important international trade documents.

The internationally accepted definition of a bill of exchange is that it is an unconditional order in writing addressed by the person giving it (the drawer) to another person (the drawee) and signed by the drawer. It requires the drawee to pay on demand (or at a fixed and determinable future time) a specific sum of money to, or to the order of, a named person or the bearer (the payee). The bill of exchange is therefore proof of the buyer's obligation to pay and is one of the key financial documents used in collections. For example, SLM Trading enters into a

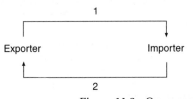

1. Exporter ships goods and documents of title to importer
2. Importer pays exporter at an agreed date

Figure 11.3   Open account trading.

```
No.      87

Exchange for £42 600.............................................30th APRIL 2002
AT SIGHT...........................................of this FIRST BILL of Exchange
(SECOND..............of the same tenor and date being unpaid) pay to the
order of SLM TRADING LTD........................................the sum of
FORTY-TWO THOUSAND SIX HUNDRED POUNDS ONLY

                                          FOR AND ON BEHALF OF
To:      CHEAP AND CHEERFUL FOOD CO       SLM TRADING LTD
         TENNESSEE, USA                   (Signature, position)
```

Figure 11.4 Sight draft/bill of exchange.

contract of supply with the Cheap and Cheerful Food Company in the USA. SLM Trading draws up a bill of exchange payable to itself and sends the bill to the importer's bank, instructing the bank to pay the specified amount on receipt of the bill ('sight draft' – Figure 11.4) or at an agreed later date ('term draft' – Figure 11.5).

The importer's bank sends the bill of exchange to the buyer who, on signing the bill, accepts it and agrees to make the payment as specified. Depending on the date agreed, this might still mean that the exporter has to wait to receive payment for the goods, thereby prolonging exposure to the risk of non-payment through buyer defaults or insolvency.

This risk can be reduced by obtaining a guarantee of the buyer's acceptance from the importer's bank. The resulting 'avalised' bill of exchange covers the exporter for the buyer's reluctance or inability to pay for the goods shipped, but does not guard against the possibility of the bank itself being unwilling to make payment. To reduce this particular risk, the exporting company can 'discount' the bill of exchange to a bank in its own country (probably its own bank). What this effectively means is that the bill of exchange is sold to the exporter's bank for its full value less an administrative or handling charge levied by the bank (the discount). The exporter therefore receives payment quickly and the bank takes on the transaction risk.

If the exporter expects to make use of this facility, the cost of discounting must be taken into consideration when pricing the sale in order to avoid incurring charges that cannot be recouped from the transaction.

By purchasing the bill of exchange the bank is entering into what is called an 'acceptance credit' transaction and becomes the 'holder in due course',

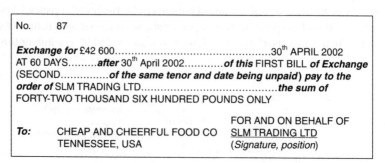

Figure 11.5 Term draft/bill of exchange.

meaning that the bank has a legal right to receive payment when the bill of exchange matures, providing:

1. that the bill of exchange was neither overdue nor dishonoured prior to the bank taking possession of it; and
2. that the bank purchased the bill in good faith and was unaware of any issues affecting the value or validity of the bill at the time of purchase.

Missing documentation

The examples of sight and term drafts above include the phrase '(SECOND .... of the same tenor and date being unpaid)'. These are often included in the drafts to avoid costly delays due to a bill of exchange being lost. For instance, the bank may decide to mail out two versions of the same draft. The first bill asks the receiver to ignore the second bill, which in turn requests that the first be dismissed. This procedure guards against the possibility of the bill being lost in the post and so minimises the risk of the buyer being unable to collect the shipping documents. If both copies of the draft arrive on the buyer's desk one copy is deemed to be surplus to requirements, providing that the accepted bill is the same one that is transferred to the collecting bank.

Protesting a bill of exchange

In the event that the buyer refuses to honour or accept a bill of exchange when presented, the exporter can resort to a course of action known as 'protest'. This is a formal legal procedure, which goes some way towards protecting the seller's rights but does not guarantee that the exporter will eventually receive payment. Protesting a bill of exchange requires the involvement of a notary who re-presents the bill to the importer in person. Assuming the bill is still not accepted or honoured, the reasons given by the buyer are listed and then subsequently published, for example in the commercial press. This has the dual effect of shaming the importing company and warning other companies that trade with it of the unreliability of the company. The logical consequence of this is that the buyer starts to lose further business and the protest note is therefore something that most buyers would rather avoid.

The impact of protested bills of exchange does vary from country to country and it is in the exporter's interests to research the process, costs and likely impact in advance of requesting that a bill be protested. Exporters should also be aware that, unless specifically requested in the collection, banks are under no obligation to issue a protest, even when a bill has clearly been dishonoured.

Documentary letters of credit

Letters of credit (L/Cs) are the most commonly used method of payment in international trade, although as bank charges can be quite high for this method, it is more likely to be adopted for transactions over £10 000. L/Cs are one of the safest payment instruments available to the exporter, but they also provide a certain amount of security to the importer as well.

Documentary letters of credit depend on the co-operation of banks that, in brief, take receipt of the shipping documentation and authorise payment to the exporter. Before the importer takes ownership of the goods the exporter's bank checks to make sure that effective systems are in place to facilitate transfer of payment. At the same time, the importer's bank makes sure that the importer has taken title to the goods before releasing any payment to the exporter. This system allows both importer and exporter to reduce the risk of non-receipt of goods and non-payment. The buyer is guaranteed to take ownership of the goods prior to payment and the seller is guaranteed to receive payment once the specified commercial and shipping documents have been presented to a named bank.

If, however, there are discrepancies between the documents specified in the L/C and those that are actually presented, the issuing bank may refuse to accept the credit until the discrepancies have been remedied. This clearly has implications on the length of time taken to process the credit, and banks will also charge for re-presentation. This really confirms what has been said in earlier chapters about the need for accuracy in all import/export documentation.

Letters of credit offer different levels of security depending on the exact nature of the credit. A 'revocable' letter of credit can be cancelled or altered by the issuing bank without necessarily having to inform the exporter. The revocable L/C is therefore little more than a bank guarantee to accept the exporter's documents unless the seller's bank has been notified of the L/C's cancellation. This method offers least security to the exporter.

The opposite of the revocable L/C is the irrevocable letter of credit, which cannot be amended or cancelled without prior agreement from both buyer and seller. It also carries a guarantee from the importer's bank that the exporter's bills of exchange (see below) will be honoured and payment will be made. The irrevocable L/C is a much more secure method for the exporter, but the safest option from the exporter's perspective is to have the irrevocable L/C confirmed by a bank in the seller's country, thereby securing the promise of two banks that payment will be made. For a fee, the confirming bank provides proof of confirmation and undertakes to pay the exporter in the event that the issuing bank fails or is unable to, providing that the exporting company has fulfilled its requirements by providing the requisite goods and documentation. The confirming bank may differ from the exporter's 'advising' bank, although there is no obligation for this to be the case. In some cases, the overseas office of the issuing bank may confirm the letter of credit, although for obvious reasons the exporter is advised to seek confirmation from a financial institution that is not connected to the issuing bank (see Figure 11.6).

Letters of credit are governed by the 'autonomy principle', meaning that the issuing bank will pay the beneficiary of the L/C on presentation of the requisite documentation, regardless of other issues such as breach of contract, defective goods, non-performance or any other factor with the exception of fraud (see below). The L/C should be regarded as an independent contract, the terms of which must be met by both parties so that payment must be made against compliant documentation.

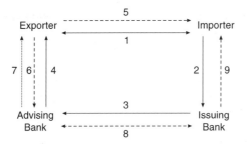

1. Contract agreed by exporter and importer
2. Importer arranges for their bank to open L/C
3. Issuing bank advises correspondent bank in the exporter's country
4. Correspondent bank advises exporter of the L/C's requirements and adds its confirmation
5. Exporter ships goods to buyer
6. Exporter send relevant documents to advising bank
7. Advising bank transfers payment
8. Advising bank notifies issuing bank of transfer and sends documents. Issuing bank reimburses advising bank Issuing bank passes documents to importer

Figure 11.6 Standard letter of credit transaction.

Example: Wanderer's Glassware of Middlesborough, UK, contracts to supply Lavender Tiger of Sydney, Australia with £45 000 of crystal tableware, specifying CIF Sydney and payment through a confirmed, irrevocable letter of credit in pounds Sterling.

Lavender Tiger request their bank in Australia to issue them with a letter of credit to meet their needs, specifying the nature of the L/C and the documents that need to be received before payment can be authorised. The company also deposits a sum of money with the bank as security for the credit.

Lavender Tiger's bank approaches a correspondent, 'advising' bank in the UK and requests that Wanderer's Glassware be told that the irrevocable L/C has been opened and what conditions the company must meet before payment is authorised. The issuing bank also asks the advising bank to confirm the letter of credit.

Wanderer's Glassware collates the requisite shipping documents, including four copies of the commercial invoice, certificate of origin, bills of lading, packing list and inspection report, and arranges shipment. The documents are then passed to the advising bank, which checks each document against the requirements of the credit to ensure that all conditions have been complied with. Assuming that everything is in order, the advising bank provides Wanderer's Glassware with payment for the goods and forwards the documents on to the issuing bank in Australia, which in turn passes them to Lavender Tiger to enable the company to take ownership of the goods.

The irrevocable letter of credit raised by the Australian bank would be laid out along similar lines to the example in Figure 11.7.

Date   1st May 2002   Irrevocable documentary credit no. 1234

Beneficiary   Applicant

Wanderer's Glassware Ltd   Lavender Tiger
Middlesborough, UK   Sydney, Australia

Advising bank   Amount

High Street Bank plc   UK £45 000
Middlesborough   (FORTY-five thousand pounds Sterling)

Available by your draft(s) in duplicate at sight drawn on the advising bank for the full invoice value and accompanied by the following documents:

1. signed commercial invoice in quadruplicate
2. certificate of origin showing U.K. origin
3. bill of lading providing proof of shipment
4. packing list
5. inspection report
6. insurance policy in assignable form for 110% of invoice value, claims payable in Australia, covering Institute Cargo Clauses 'A' (including War and Strikes).

Proving shipment of crystal tableware CIF Sydney.

Partial shipments permitted/prohibited   Transhipment is permitted/prohibited

Shipment from UK port to Sydney no later than 30th June 2002. All documents must be presented within 10days from date of shipment. This credit is irrevocable and valid until 31st July 2002. This credit is subject to the International Chamber of Commerce Uniform Customs & Practice for Documentary Credits (1993)(UCP500).

Authorised signature

Figure 11.7   Sample letter of credit.

Types of L/C

There are a number of different types of documentary letter of credit that can be raised depending on the circumstances and nature of the transaction to be concluded. For instance, a 'red clause' letter of credit allows for a percentage of the value of the credit to be paid to the exporter up front, perhaps to cover production costs or purchases of components and raw materials needed to fulfil the contract. The advance payment is made before shipping documents are submitted, normally in conjunction with a bank's advance payment guarantee (APG) and/or the exporter's written undertaking to refund the payment if the order is unfulfilled or the goods are not shipped. The red clause L/C clearly has advantages for the exporter in terms of being able to part finance production prior to receiving full payment, which will assist cash flows. It is also referred to as an 'anticipatory' or 'packing' L/C, although red clause is by far the most commonly used term.

The opposite of the red clause L/C is the green clause credit, which makes provision for the importer to withhold a percentage of the credit value after the shipping documentation has been presented. The purpose of the green clause L/C is to provide the importer with security in the event that the goods supplied do not meet the terms of the contract, for example through inferior quality. Assuming that the goods are acceptable, the importing company can authorise payment for the withheld monies by submitting confirmation that the goods meet its requirements to the issuing bank. The other main types of letter of credit likely to be encountered by companies during the course of their international activities are revolving, standby and transferable L/Cs.

Revolving letter of credit

The revolving L/C is used in situations where several similar shipments are to take place that can be covered by a single L/C, as opposed to raising a series of separate L/Cs (and incurring the administrative and financial charges for doing so). Revolving credits can be used to cover a number of specified shipments over a given period, even if the value of each shipment varies. There are three principal types of revolving documentary letter of credit.

The 'revolving L/C through value' exists for an agreed period of time and is reinstated whenever the limit of the credit value has been reached. The credit cannot be 'revolved' until payment for each transaction has been received. The nature of the credit ensures that the exporter cannot send one large shipment, potentially causing the buyer financial difficulties in meeting a single payment for the full order. It provides the importer with the security of knowing that a series of shipments will be made and that the total cost will be split into several smaller and more manageable payments governed by one credit.

Revolving L/Cs through time (cumulative) indicate that the credit revolves after a certain amount of time, rather than when the credit limit is reached. Any outstanding credit is then brought forward onto the revolved credit. For example, a buyer raises a revolving credit for €30 000 to cover four shipments of different values with a total contract value of €120 000. The first time the credit is paid, it is for the full €30 000. The credit is revolved and, after the second shipment, payment is made for only €20 000 as the exporter only ships two-thirds of the consignment. At the next revolution, the credit is for €40 000 (€30 000 plus the balance of €10 000). The buyer makes payment for €35 000, meaning that the final revolution is for €35 000 (€30 000 plus the balance of €5000), that the buyer clears with a last payment. This type of credit is riskier for the importer as the L/C revolves without necessarily coinciding with the presentation of shipping documents, leaving the buyer exposed to the risk of having to make larger payment instalments than originally anticipated. By the same token, the credit is more favourable to exporters who cannot guarantee that the scheduled shipments will be of the same size or value.

Revolving credits through time (non-cumulative) do not carry forward the outstanding balances in this way and prevent the importer from being obliged to make payment for more than one credit at a time. Consequently, these credits are more appropriate for shipments of equal (or similar) value.

Standby letter of credit

The standby L/C is generally raised as a form of protection against the possibility of breach of contract. Standby credits tend to be used to guard against buyer default, particularly when trading on open account terms, and rely on an undertaking from the importer's bank to pay in the event that the buyer fails to do so.

This type of guarantee also exists for the buyer for cases where the exporter has failed to deliver the contractually promised goods. 'Performance bonds' can be written into contracts with the aim of providing the buyer with financial compensation for any costs incurred in pursuing fulfilment of the contract. Such bonds typically specify a figure of 5 or 10 per cent of the total contract value, which will be guaranteed by a bank or insurance company.

Transferable letter of credit

Transferable or 'back-to-back' letters of credit can be of use in financing production of goods to meet an international order. For example, an exporter enters into a contract to supply an overseas buyer but to fulfil the order needs to purchase raw materials and components from a foreign supplier. The exporter's client raises a L/C to facilitate payment for the goods purchased and the exporter subsequently uses this 'prime' L/C as a guarantee for a second credit (for a smaller amount) raised in favour of the exporter's supplier. The seller is seen by the banks as the intermediary, or middleman, in the transaction. In some cases, the transferable L/C permits the exporter to either transfer a percentage of the prime L/C to the supplier instead of simply acting as a guarantee for a second credit.

Doctrine of strict compliance

Documentary letters of credit are, by their very nature, guarantees that the exporter will receive payment and the importer will receive the goods. All documentation specified in the credits will be rigorously checked by the advising and confirming banks to ensure that the terms of the credit are being fully met. The banks work under the 'doctrine of strict compliance', which demands that all documentation presented with a letter of credit has to wholly comply with the terms of the credit. It is therefore in the exporter's interests to ensure that all the requisite documentation is both accurate and available for presentation with the credit.

In an ideal world, the banks would find no discrepancies or errors and would make payment with no hesitation. Unfortunately, this is not the case. The banks are meticulous in their checking procedures and in the UK alone, over 60 per cent of all letters of credit presented are found to have discrepancies and are rejected. The documents must then be amended and resubmitted. Not only does this mean additional costs (the banks will charge a fee for each presentation of the documents), but it also increases the amount of time needed to complete the transaction. What, then, can the exporter do if discrepancies are found?

Firstly, if the end of the credit's operating period is not imminent, the exporter can make the necessary amendments to the documentation and re-present the credit, thereby incurring the extra bank charges. Secondly, the advising bank may be asked to send the shipping documents to the issuing bank to be used on a collection basis, which means that the buyer can only take title to the goods if payment is made. This passes the responsibility for acceptance of the documents to the buyer, discrepancies and all. Thirdly, the advising bank can ask the issuing bank for authority to make the payment regardless of the discrepancies. This course of action is more common for minor discrepancies such as spelling mistakes, which the banks may be more inclined to forgive and overlook than they are for incomplete or inaccurate documentation. Finally, the advising bank can be asked to make payment 'under reserve' with recourse to the exporter if the issuing bank does not accept the documentation. Each of these options will carry a financial charge levied by the bank and, prevention being better than the cure, it makes more sense to pay close attention to the detail of the credits in the first place and so avoid discrepancies.

A brief note on fraud

If an exporter sets out to deliberately defraud the importer by forging documentation in order to convince the bank that the contract has been fulfilled, and succeeds in doing so, the importer has no recourse to the bank and is obliged to sue the exporter. If, however, the forgery is self-evident and the bank has approved the L/C, the buyer can sue the bank for making the payment in the face of an obvious fraud.

If, on receipt of the goods, the buyer discovers that fraud has taken place (by the exporter shipping cases of wine bottles filled with vinegar, for instance), it may be possible to halt payment of the letter of credit. This can be done by quickly obtaining a court order to prevent the bank from transferring the funds. If payment has been made, the buyer cannot sue the bank and must try and secure payment from the seller.

Documentary collections

The purpose of documentary collections (see Figure 11.8) is to ensure that the goods remain the property of the exporter until the collecting bank has received payment from the importer in exchange for the commercial and financial documentation. When documentary collection is agreed as the method of payment for a particular transaction, the exporter is obliged to ship the goods to the buyer and post all the relevant commercial documentation to a 'collecting bank'. This includes documents of title (such as the bill of lading), invoices, insurance and shipping documentation, and may also include financial documents – bills of exchange, promissory notes and so on.

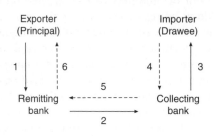

1. Exporting company passes documents to a bank in its own country
2. Remitting bank forwards documents to a bank in the importer's country
3. Collecting bank presents documents to the importer
4. Importer makes payment or accepts bill of exchange
5. Collecting bank advises remitting bank of acceptance or payment
6. Exporter receives payment or notice of acceptance

Figure 11.8 Documentary collections.

Documentary collections are more secure than 'clean' collections, which occur when only the financial documents are required to authorise payment, as the bank will not release the documents of title to the importer unless payment has been received ('sight draft') or promised ('term draft'). In general, banks will only pass the documentation to the importer when payment is made (DOP/documents on payment), although in some cases documents may be transferred on the buyer's acceptance of a bill of exchange (DOA). The collection presented to the bank will detail the documents transferred by the exporter and will set out the terms under which the collection is to be made.

Once the collecting bank has presented the documents for collection, the remitting bank must be informed of the outcome, regardless of whether the importer makes or refuses acceptance or payment. This 'advice of fate' should be sent immediately to the remitting bank, which will then inform the exporter of the position.

The roles and responsibilities of the banks in the collection process are laid down in the International Chamber of Commerce publication, *Uniform Rules for Collection* (ICC No. 522).

In many respects, documentary collections are similar to letters of credit in that there is a dependence on the banks to exchange documentation and secure payment. However, documentary collections are less secure as the exporter bears the full risk of the transaction until payment is received and is consequently financing the sale until the importer makes the payment.

Receiving payment

Modern banking provides companies with a variety of methods for the international transfer of payments. As with every other aspect of international trade, the choice of payment mechanism will be based on research to identify the most appropriate method to meet the company's needs.

Cash payments are rare in import/export transactions and it is unlikely that a facility to cope with this method will be required. On the other hand, cheques drawn on the buyer's own account may be acceptable but they can also cause additional problems as well as incurring bank handling fees.

The cheque will be drawn on an overseas bank to which it must be presented for payment. The exporter's bank may either 'collect' the cheque by presenting it to the foreign bank for payment or may be prepared to 'negotiate' the cheque by crediting the exporter's account and subsequently presenting the cheque to the buyer's bank. If the cheque is not honoured, the seller's bank can reclaim the monies paid to the exporter. Either way can result in a delay in receiving payment, assuming that the buyer does not stop the cheque in advance of payment being made!

Companies may agree to make payment through a bankers' draft, which is a more secure payment mechanism than a buyer's cheque. Bankers' drafts are raised by the buyer in favour of the seller, normally in the exporter's currency and drawn on a bank in the seller's country. Drafts are paid into a bank account in the same way that cheques are, but banks will charge for handling them if they are made out in a foreign currency. The main disadvantage of the bankers' draft is that it tends to be submitted by mail and is therefore subject to delays and being 'lost in the post'.

Fortunately, the wide availability of electronic communication has been instrumental in reducing delays in payment processing. The Society for Worldwide Interbank Financial Transmissions (SWIFT) is a well-established global network of banks, which exists to facilitate payment instructions to be transmitted electronically across the network. SWIFT offers a fast, efficient and secure method of transmitting payments in most major currencies, with urgent payments being made by the next working day. There is a fee for using SWIFT, particularly for urgent transmissions, but it is perhaps the most effective mechanism available to companies.

The Internet has also improved the speed at which payments can be made. Transfers can be arranged and carried out online quickly and easily, 24 hours a day, through the growing network of Internet banking websites that has spring up over recent years. The majority of payments made over the Internet are credit card transactions but commercial organisations are increasingly looking to online applications to improve all aspects of their operations, including finance and payments for their international trade activities. The main consideration to bear in mind when accepting or making Internet payments is the issue of security. It is essential to preserve the integrity of the transaction and companies should only enter their financial details onto a website if they are 100 per cent satisfied that the website is secure and that the details entered will not be accessible by anyone else.

Pricing issues

From this brief introduction to the most common methods of payment it should be evident that each has its own merits and disadvantages, both from the buyer's and seller's perspectives. Prepayments, whilst being the most secure option for the exporter, are the riskiest method for the buyer. Likewise, open account trading is most attractive to the importer.

In the same way that companies are able to use Incoterms (see Chapter 8) to influence pricing and the offer, payment terms can also be used to the same effect and may even be the decisive factor as to whether or not the exporter is awarded the contract. For example, in a market where the exporter's main competitor is well established, there may be little to differentiate between the two companies in terms of delivery, lead time, after-sales service and pricing. The company that can offer the more attractive payment terms will stand a much better chance of being successful. Being able to offer credit terms to a foreign buyer may be the competitive advantage that the exporter needs to win sales, but it may also mean increased exposure to bad debt and cash flow difficulties.

Depending on the type of payment method agreed, there are also numerous cost implications to be aware of, which can affect the true cost of the international transaction. These include fees charged by banks for opening and confirming letters of credit as well as bills of exchange. There will also be subsequent charges if the L/Cs are found to have discrepancies.

Regardless of whether it is the importer or exporter who is liable for these charges, they impact on the cost of the sale. After all, if the exporter is liable for any costs associated with securing payment, these will be built into the price of the transaction. If the importer incurs such costs, they will be in addition to the cost of goods purchased. Consequently, it is vital that the exporter researches the costs of each payment method and evaluates how they will affect pricing. From the importer's perspective, the cost of arranging payment may be useful in negotiating better prices with the exporter.

Each company will adopt its own approach to payment terms and there is ultimately no right or wrong way, providing that appropriate steps have been taken to satisfy the company that payment will be received when expected. The decision as to which method of payment to use is not based on financial considerations alone. It is also influenced by the marketing, sales and promotional strategies implemented by the company. As such, substantial thought must be given to the likely benefits and repercussions of the different payment methods on every function within the business.

Conclusions

This chapter has introduced the principal methods of payment used in international trade transactions and has demonstrated the nature and security of each. The importance of accuracy in the preparation of documentation used to secure payments from overseas buyers has been stressed and the role of the importer's and exporter's banks in approving and making payment on their client's behalf should also be apparent. Readers are advised to make sure that this aspect of international trade is fully understood as there are substantial repercussions in terms of cost, delay and even non-payment, which can easily arise as a result of misunderstanding the requirements of international methods of payment.

Sources of information

Regional international trade website for Yorkshire and the Humber –
  www.tradeportalyh.co.uk
Simplified guide to letters of credit –
  www.credit-to-cash.com/letter_of_credit.htm
International Chamber of Commerce – www.iccwbo.org
'Small business knowledge' – www.bizmove.com/export/m7m.htm
Website dedicated to Internet payments and security – www.commerce.net

Further reading

Briggs P, *Principles of International Trade and Payments* (Blackwell, 1994).
British Chambers of Commerce, *International Trade Manual* (Butterworth-Heinemann, 1997).
Bugg R and Whitehead G, *International Trade and Payments*, (Prentice Hall/Woodhead-Faulkner, 1994).
del Busto C, *Guide to ICC Documentary Credit Operations for the UCP* (ICC, 1994).
ICC, *Bills of Exchange* (ICC, 1990).
ICC, *Uniform Customs and Practices for Documentary Credits* (ICC, 1993).
ICC, *Key Words in International Trade: The International Chamber of Commerce's Unique Business Language Handbook* (ICC, 1996).

QUESTIONS FOR CONSIDERATION

1 What are the main risks for the importer and the exporter under prepayment and open account trading terms?
2 What are the main differences between documentary collections and documentary credits, and what are the responsibilities of the importer and exporter in each case?
3 What is the difference between red clause L/Cs, green clause L/Cs, transferable L/Cs and standby L/Cs?
4 What is the role of the remitting bank in bill of exchange transactions?
5 Why might an acceptance credit transaction be of value to an exporter and what is meant by 'holder in due course'?

☑ 12 Making the most of currency

Introduction

Foreign exchange rates represent both an opportunity and a threat to international traders. This chapter provides an introduction to the nature of exchange rates and the factors that influence them as well as explaining some of the methods used by companies to manage currency in order to reduce their exposure to adverse exchange rate fluctuations. The chapter also discusses the European single currency, the euro, and examines the impact it will have on international trade, as well as the arguments for and against membership of the single currency.

On completion of the chapter, the reader will understand the role that currency movements play in international trade and will be able to take steps to ensure that the import/export strategy takes account of the risks associated with foreign exchange.

Foreign exchange rates

A foreign exchange rate is simply the value of one currency expressed in terms of another, such as 1 pound sterling being the equivalent of 1.5 US dollars. Outside the commercial world, most people will be familiar with exchange rates from purchasing currency for a foreign holiday and comparing the cost and value for money of goods between the foreign and domestic markets. The management of currency for international trade works along very similar lines but the potential risks for companies trading in foreign currencies are much greater than they are for travellers on a short overseas break.

If an exporting company sells its products in a foreign currency there is a risk that the value of the currency may fall and therefore reduce the sales revenue to the exporter. Likewise, if an importer agrees to purchase goods priced in the seller's native currency, the company runs the risk of seeing the value of his national currency depreciate against the seller's currency, thereby increasing the cost of the goods. Equally, if the value of the currency rises, then the importer will get a better deal and the seller loses out. For example:

1. An American buyer contracts with a UK management consultancy in order to review productivity in his Chicago factory. The project is valued at £50 000 at a time when the exchange rate is £1 = US$1.5 and the buyer agrees to pay the UK consultant in pounds sterling 30 days after completion of the exercise.

The value of the order in US dollars is therefore $75 000. On the payment date, the exchange rate has changed to £1 = US$1.55. The seller receives payment for the agreed £50 000, but the cost of purchasing sterling for the transaction has risen to $77 500, costing the buyer an extra $2500.

2. A British importer of automotive components from the USA enters into a contract to purchase goods worth US$60 000 and agrees to pay in US dollars. The sterling value of the transaction at the time the order is agreed is £40 000 (£1 = US$1.5). When the buyer authorises payment on receipt of the goods, he finds that the exchange rate has increased to £1 = US£1.55 and is pleased to discover that he now only needs to purchase £38 710 worth of dollars in order to pay the seller, a saving of £1290.

Fluctuations in currency exchange rates, however small, can therefore have a major impact on the financial viability of an international trade transaction. The changes are influenced by a range of factors including inflation and interest rates. Countries that have a higher rate of inflation than others, particularly those with whom they are trading, will find that their exports are more expensive as a result of higher production costs and so on. As exports become less competitive, fewer goods will be sold overseas, which in turn affects the value of the country's currency.

If a country is subject to higher interest rates, its currency is likely to appreciate in value as a result of the increase in foreign investors seeking to benefit from the greater financial returns that the interest rates generate. Investment in a country is also affected by economic performance, political stability, taxation and government borrowing.

Ultimately, these issues are reflected in the country's balance of payments (BOP), a table showing the country's overall financial position with foreign countries. The balance of payments shows the credits and debits generated by the international trade of goods and services, as well as any profits or interest from overseas assets. It also tracks inward and outward investments, grants and loans. Profits and interest accruing to overseas countries deriving from their assets in the country in question are deducted and the balance of payments is therefore the net result of all the income received from overseas less all the payments made to other nations. If payments exceed income, resulting in a BOP deficit, the country will see a reduction in its foreign reserves (the amount of foreign currency that the country owns) and the value of its currency may fall. If the BOP shows a surplus, the country's foreign reserves will grow and its currency is likely to increase in value.

The structure of the balance of payments reporting method is set out by the International Monetary Fund (IMF), which was established in 1944 to encourage international co-operation and to facilitate a relaxation in foreign exchange rate restrictions. The IMF also assists member countries to cover any sustained deficit in their balance of payments and thereby prevent major fluctuations in exchange rates. Members requiring use of this facility can obtain foreign currency from the IMF in exchange for their own currency in order to shore up their foreign reserves, on the condition that the national currency is repurchased within three to five years.

Exchange rates are also influenced by every country's national central bank. The central banks have the authority to determine interest rates, which, as we have seen, affect the level of foreign investment. They also buy and sell foreign currencies as well as setting the exchange rate for their own national currency by operating either a fixed or floating rate of exchange with a foreign country, or by operating a 'managed float'. The fixed exchange rate policy predetermines the rate at which the national currency is exchanged for foreign currencies, whereas the floating policy permits the exchange rate to be determined by open market currency trading. The 'managed float' – also known as the 'dirty float' – is the most common form of exchange rate policy. It requires greater involvement by the central banks, which intervene to support their national currencies as necessary. For example, if the value of the national currency is increasing as a result of demand, the central bank may sell off some of its own reserves in order to make more currency available and keep the exchange rate steady. On the other hand, if the central bank sees its national currency depreciating in value due to there being more sales than purchases of the currency, it may choose to buy – again to maintain a steady exchange rate. The central banks can exercise a great deal of control over currency value and it is one of the main aims of the G8 group of countries to co-ordinate their activities in order to ensure that their influence does not adversely affect the course of international trade.

Question: Why do exporters and importers choose to price, quote and invoice in foreign currencies?

Calculations

Calculating foreign exchange transactions is not a difficult process. There are really only two calculations that the exporter or importer needs to understand. The first, and easiest, exchange calculation simply multiplies a value of the domestic currency by the rate of exchange to give an equivalent value in the foreign currency. For example: What is the value of a transaction in euro if the pound sterling value is £91 500 and the exchange rate is £1 = €1.63?

$$£91\,500 \times €1.63 = €149\,145$$

The other type of exchange rate arithmetic is the cross rate calculation, which is used to work out the exchange rate between two countries from the known exchange rate of a third, common currency. For instance: what is the exchange rate between US dollars and the euro if the euro/sterling exchange rate is €1 = £1.63 and the dollar/sterling rate is $1 = £0.70?

$$\$1(£0.70) = €1(£1.63)$$
$$\$1 = €1(£1.63) \times (£0.70)$$
$$\$1 = €1.14$$

Spot and forward contracts

Earlier examples have shown that whilst currency fluctuations can work to the advantage of the exporter or importer, they can also threaten the financial viability of a transaction. The decision to invoice foreign clients in their currency, or an acceptable third currency, can have far-reaching consequences and careful consideration must be given to the potential risks (see Figure 12.1). Some businesses prefer not to get too involved in managing currency issues and will quite happily risk unfavourable currency movements. Most companies, especially those with more experience of international trade, will take steps to cover the risk by buying or selling currency at 'spot' or 'forward' rates, the most basic currency contracts used to manage foreign exchange risks.

The 'spot' rate is the market rate of exchange between two given currencies at a specific point in time. In a spot transaction, the currency purchased will normally be available for collection within two days, or payable in two days if being sold. Wherever a spot rate is quoted, the assumption is made that the rate of exchange is valid for purchases or sales made within the two-day period.

Spot rates differ depending on whether the currency is being purchased or sold. Companies buying foreign currency in order to pay an overseas supplier will be sold the currency at a lower rate than companies converting foreign currency into their native currency. The difference between the two rates is called the 'spread'. The exact rates of exchange vary in accordance with every movement of the international currency market and it is not unusual for an exporter to purchase currency at one rate, only to see the rate change for better or worse later in the day. For this reason, companies should not rely on being able to generate a return on their foreign currency transactions as fluctuations in the global currency market have the potential to eliminate any initial gains.

Spot rates should not be seen as the final solution to currency management. They fulfil a short-term need to purchase or sell currency and consequently should be used primarily for small, irregular or one-off contracts. Companies that work in foreign currencies for larger, more regular contracts are advised to make use of 'forward' contracts as a more appropriate means of covering foreign exchange exposure. Forward rates are used for the exchange of currencies at any date or time other than that which would be covered by the two-day spot rate. They are contractual agreements entered into by commercial banks and customers, effectively fixing the exchange rate for a given period and therefore offering greater security and guaranteeing a return. The banks will build a margin into the contract and, as a consequence, the forward rate will be more

---

- What is the unit of currency to be sold (normally the native currency)?
- What is the unit of currency to be bought (the foreign currency)?
- How much currency is to be bought (and therefore sold)?
- When will the exchange contract come into effect?
- What will the exchange rate be?

Figure 12.1 Information required in every foreign exchange contract.

expensive than the spot rate. However, this type of contract is not subject to currency movements once it has been agreed. The customer, having paid for the privilege of guaranteeing an exchange rate for a future transaction, is secure in the knowledge that the exchange rate negotiated will neither be higher nor lower at the time the exchange is made. For example: a German company purchases clothing from a British supplier for £30 000 and agrees to pay in 60 days. The exchange rate at the time the contract is agreed is €1 = £1.625, meaning that the contract value is €48 750. The company orders the required amount of sterling from the bank at a forward contract of €1 = £1.63 (contract price €48 900) but at the time of payment, 60 days later, the exchange rate is actually €1 = £1.64. The new contract price would consequently have been €49 200 and the importer has therefore saved €300 – not a large amount in the scheme of things, but for a company undertaking 40 or 50 international trade transactions per year, the potential savings are much greater.

Premiums and discounts

The rate quoted for forward contracts takes into account the length and value of the contract and is also dependent on the difference in interest rates between the domestic and foreign currency. If the interest rates in the country of origin are higher than in the target market, the forward contract is quoted at a 'premium'; meaning that the exchange rate is reduced slightly to reflect the domestic currency's projected growth against the foreign currency over the period of the contract. If the target market's interest rate is higher, the forward contract will be quoted at a 'discount' and an appropriate value is added to the exchange rate.

Premium and discount contracts take into account the interest that the company would have earned by either keeping its cash in the domestic currency or transferring it to a foreign currency. Hence companies are better off retaining domestic currency if premium rates are quoted and exchanging for foreign currency if domestic rates are quoted. In this way, the company is compensated for the difference in interest rates. The rates quoted will depend on the amount of currency being purchased and the length of time covered by the contract. Examples of premium and discount rates are shown below.

Although forward contracts may prove to be more expensive due to the additional margins added by banks and the risk of losing out on a more favourable exchange rate at the point of exchange, they do offer a greater level of security that in many cases save companies money.

Examples: (NB, illustration only)

1. Interest rates in the USA = 1.5 per cent. Interest rates in the UK = 4 per cent. Forward contract will be quoted at a premium.
   Exchange rate: £1 = US$1.520
   Premium rate: 0.015 (to be deducted from spot rate)
   Rate quoted on forward contract: £1 = US$1.505

---

2. Interest rates in Brazil = 6.3 per cent. Interest rates in the UK = 4 per cent. Forward contract will be quoted at a discount.
   Exchange rate: £1 = 4.443 Brazilian reals
   Discount rate: 0.021 (to be added to spot rate)
   Rate quoted on forward contract: £1 = 4.464 Brazilian reals

Currency options

Forward contracts may be at 'fixed' or 'option' rates. Fixed rates specify the date on which the exchange will take place and the company has no leeway to exchange before or after that date. Contracts arranged on an option basis have more flexibility as they permit the exchange of currency during a given period between two specified dates. Companies with limited experience of currency management are advised not to make use of option contracts until they are more familiar with the nuances of international exchange rate behaviour as options are a more complex approach to managing exchange risk.

In options contracts, a premium is charged by the bank based on the agreed rate of exchange for the transaction, the current forward rate offered by the bank, the desired length of option period and the anticipated changes in the exchange rate. Having taken these factors into account, the option contract can be agreed. The company then has the facility to make the exchange either at the current spot rate at the time of exchange or the agreed rate specified in the option contract, the decision depending on the most favourable rate. Again, the company pays for the privilege of maintaining this window in which to exchange currency, but the benefits will normally outweigh the cost of entering into this type of contract.

Currency accounts

Companies that regularly work in foreign currencies can avoid having to change currency for each individual transaction by setting up currency accounts. Being able to receive and make payments in the foreign currency without having to worry about foreign exchange risk can bring many benefits to the trader, not least because currency accounts normally carry all the advantages of a normal business account such as overdraft facilities and so on. It is inadvisable to use forward contracts in conjunction with currency accounts as charges for both are based on the interest rates of the foreign market. A forward contract used with a currency account therefore results in the company paying twice for the same interest rates.

Currency accounts can be opened for most of the world's convertible currencies – that is, currencies, which can be traded on an established market – but such accounts should really only be opened in cases where a company regularly trades in the currency. For example, a British company that exports worldwide may accept payment primarily in US dollars and euro in addition to occasional payments made in other currencies. Under these conditions, the company may choose to open a dollar account and a euro account to manage the currency transactions more effectively, but may still rely on sporadic transactions carried out on an individual basis for other currencies. Whilst the company may at some stage wish to transfer funds from the currency account to its own business account, it has much more control over when to exchange the currency and can therefore opt to make the exchange when rates are favourable.

Measuring exposure

Foreign exchange risk does not just impact on the viability of international transactions but can also affect businesses in other ways. It is therefore useful for companies to be able to quantify the exact nature (and value) of their exposure to exchange risk in order to recognise all the financial ramifications of an unfavourable rate of exchange.

The most apparent form of exposure is the risk that companies take in buying and selling goods overseas. 'Transaction exposure' typically occurs when a company is owed a certain amount of foreign currency, which subsequently loses its value before the buyer makes the payment. The company consequently receives less currency for the transaction than it expected, reducing income and profitability.

Any changes in exchange rates affecting currencies held, or due to be received, by a company also affect the balance sheet as the company's assets and liabilities change accordingly. Such changes therefore need to be reflected in all financial reporting mechanisms to provide management with an accurate picture of the company's financial position. The potential impact of exchange rate fluctuations on the balance sheet is referred to as 'translation exposure', showing how the foreign currency exchange risk moves from simple transaction exposure to the wider financial perspective.

Finally, 'economic exposure' measures the effect that changes in exchange rates can have on cash flow forecasting and the future growth of a company. For example, a manufacturing company based in Germany might export 60 per cent of its production to Poland, leaving the company susceptible to depreciation in the value of the zloty. The consequent rise in value of the euro against the zloty reduces the company's competitiveness, as its products become more expensive to export to Poland. The economic exposure is the impact that this eventuality could have on income projections and the company may be forced to look at different ways of preserving market share. This could be achieved by adopting different pricing or promotional strategies to try and maintain the 60 per cent of production capacity destined for Poland or the company may decide to spread its international trade activity more evenly across new markets and research previously untapped opportunities.

Companies should recognise that an adverse exchange rate does not simply reduce the profitability of a transaction but also has an effect on the business' financial planning processes. If a company has budgeted to do £500 000 in export sales but achieves only £420 000 as a result of not managing currency transactions effectively, the shortfall of £80 000 will affect profitability, reinvestment into the company (for example for research and development or capital equipment) and overall growth. Currency management must therefore be tightly controlled if it is not to work against the business.

A brief history of the euro

Whilst the Treaty of Rome in 1958 began the formation of the European Common Market, with the aim of reducing trade barriers and increasing prosperity between the member states, subsequent treaties have taken the ideal of a united Europe further (see Figure 12.2). European Economic and Monetary Union (EMU) was seen as a core objective of what was then called the European Community and in 1969, a conference at the Hague launched an initiative which effectively paved the way for EMU. By 1970 the committee with responsibility for establishing a timetable for monetary union published a 10-year plan which would achieve this goal. The plan was then put on hold as a result of the oil crisis of the early 1970s, as well as different economic policies being adopted across Europe and a comparatively weak US dollar affecting world trade.

EMU was revived in 1979 by the creation of the European Monetary System (EMS), a stable method of defining the exchange rates for European currencies against a new currency, the European Currency Unit (ECU). EMS had the effect of controlling exchange rate fluctuations, lowering inflation and encouraging investments within the member states. By the mid-1980s, the European Commission judged that the time was right to pursue EMU further.

The Single European Act (SEA) of 1986 was the first EU treaty to stipulate the objective of achieving complete economic and monetary union within Europe. This was followed in 1988 by the European Council of Hanover, which established a committee (under Jacques Delors) to review the requirements of

1958	Treaty of Rome establishes the European Common Market with the aim of increasing co-operation and integration across Europe.
1969	The Hague conference sets out an objective to achieve economic and monetary union.
1970	Ten-year plan published, outlining a three-stage approach for achieving EMU.
1979	European Monetary System and the European Currency Unit introduced.
1986	Single European Act sets out the main aims of EMU.
1988	Council of Hanover undertakes to review what steps will be required to achieve EMU, leading to the Delors plan recommending the creation of a single currency and the European Central Bank.
1992	Treaty of Maastricht identifies economic convergence criteria required for membership of EMU.
1995	European Council in Madrid publishes a timetable for implementing the single currency.
1996	European Council in Dublin sets out the legal framework for monetary union.
1997	European Council in Amsterdam signs the Stability and Growth Pact.
1998	European Central Bank introduced.
1999	The euro is officially introduced as the European single currency.
2002	ECB issues euro notes and coins for the first time as 12 legacy currencies are phased out.

Figure 12.2 The euro timeline.

EMU and to submit a proposal for the actions necessary to enable monetary union. The proposal included a recommendation for a single currency to be developed and operated by a European Central Bank.

The Maastricht 'Treaty on the European Union', which was signed in 1992, set out the economic requirements (also called convergence criteria) that each member state would have to meet in order to be accepted into EMU. The Treaty of Maastricht also changed the name of the European Community to the European Union. A timetable for the implementation of the European single currency was subsequently agreed at the European Council meeting in Madrid in 1995. It was at this meeting that the name of the currency was confirmed as the euro. The European Council meeting of 1996 (Dublin) set out the legal infrastructure for the transition to a single currency and in 1997, the European Council met in Amsterdam to discuss long-term economic convergence in EMU member states, leading to the adoption of the Stability and Growth Pact.

The European Central Bank (ECB) was established in 1998 to monitor and control monetary policy in the euro-zone. It is also responsible for issuing euro notes and coins. The ECB is based in Frankfurt but is the executive body for the European network of national Central Banks, collectively known as the Eurosystem.

The final stages of EMU began on 1 January 1999 when the European single currency, the euro, was introduced in the participating EU member states. The currency co-existed with the national, 'legacy' currencies of the member states for a three-year transitional period before the final exchange rates between the 'legacy' currencies and the euro were fixed and the euro became the sole currency for 12 EU countries on 1 January 2002 (see Figure 12.3). The euro has also been adopted by Madeira, the Canary Islands, the Azores, Reunion, Martinique, French Guyana and Guadeloupe as well as by other former colonies of EU states and smaller European principalities such as Monaco, San Marino, Andorra and the Vatican City.

The British, Danish and Swedish positions

Three full members of the EU are, at the time of writing, currently not participating in the economic and monetary union. Britain negotiated an

€1 =		
	13.7603	Austrian schillings
	40.3399	Belgian francs
	1.95583	Deutschmarks
	2.20371	Dutch guilders
	5.94573	Finnish markka
	6.55957	French francs
	340.750	Greek drachmas
	0.787564	Irish punts
	1936.27	Italian lire
	40.3399	Luxembourg francs
	220.482	Portuguese escudos
	166.386	Spanish pesetas

Figure 12.3 European currency conversion rates when the euro came into effect.

'opt-out' of joining the single currency, which was incorporated in the Maastricht Treaty in 1992. The clause allows the UK to adopt the euro when the government believes that the economic conditions are right for it to do so, although UK membership of the single currency will also be subject to a referendum. The euro debate, which has raged in Britain for many years, is one of the most emotive of recent times. Even though more information on the supposed benefits and disadvantages of monetary union is becoming available to the British public, the argument seems to be increasingly dominated by whether or not to keep the pound than the wider issues of EU trade, production costs, pricing and transaction costs.

Although a date for the referendum on Britain joining the euro has yet to be fixed, the pro-euro and anti-euro lobbies are gathering momentum and the British public is gradually becoming better informed about the implications of monetary union. Several high-street retailers, especially in London, will accept payment in euro and there is a hint of a growing acceptance of the currency within the UK. It is to be hoped that, by the time a referendum takes place, the British will have all the information and facts that they need to enable them to cast a meaningful vote and not one based solely on sentiment.

Denmark is in a similar position to the UK. The Danish government held a referendum on whether or not to accept the Maastricht Treaty in 1992, which resulted in a surprising and unexpected rejection of the Treaty. Denmark subsequently negotiated an opt-out clause to preserve the facility to join the euro at a later stage. However, a second Danish referendum in September 2000 also rejected entering into EU monetary union, with 53 per cent of the vote against membership. In January 2002, the Danish government committed itself to yet another referendum on the issue, which is likely to take place during 2003.

Sweden became a member of the EU in 1995, three years after the signing of the Maastricht Treaty, but to date has not committed itself to membership of the single currency. The Swedish government is also to hold a referendum in 2002 to gauge public support for entering the euro.

For the time being, Britain, Denmark and Sweden remain outside the euro-zone. As result, their companies must still take steps to manage their currency transactions for intra-European trade whilst continuing to run the risk of being subject to adverse exchange rates.

The pro-euro argument

The EU is the UK's largest trading partner and it is more often than not the first export market targeted by companies new to exporting. Western Europe actually accounts for approximately 60 per cent of the UK's exports and when the states of Central and Eastern Europe eventually meet the criteria set out for their accession to the EU, the European Union will become the largest single free trade area in the world. The importance of the EU for British trade cannot therefore be underestimated.

Trading solely in a single currency across the euro-zone should, logically, reduce the administrative and financial burdens of managing foreign currencies.

British companies no longer have to work in 12 separate currencies and can therefore work effectively with a single euro account for trade within the EU. Sterling will, however, continue to move up and down against the euro, and the potential exchange risks have only been reduced to those rising from dealing in a single foreign currency as opposed to several. The British pro-euro lobby argues that the UK should join the single currency in order to benefit from the fixed exchange rate with the other members. By adopting the euro, British companies will be able to more effectively anticipate their production costs and final selling price as the need to cover exchange rate risks is eliminated. For example, a British company that imports components from Germany to incorporate into finished goods for re-export to France will not be concerned with currency exchange at any stage in the process. The overall sales value will not be subject to movements in the exchange rate, meaning that companies will no longer have to deal with transaction exposure. Currently, British companies must treat the euro as they would any other currency.

The most visible effect of European monetary union is likely to be increased competition within the EU member states. A German buyer can instantly compare the prices and value for money offered by EU suppliers, as each will quote in euro. Whereas exchange rates previously influenced export costings, the euro permits a very high level of pricing transparency. Companies trading in the euro-zone will therefore have to be able to compete on price as well as on quality and service. British companies are consequently at a disadvantage as to quote for contracts in the EU, exchange rates are still an issue, with currency charges and transaction costs increasing the price of goods. The impact of the euro will not just be felt in Western Europe: the EU's major trading partners around the world will also have to learn to cope with the new currency and in some areas the euro may even replace the dollar as the preferred currency for international trade. This is especially true of countries across Central and Eastern Europe preparing to join the EU (see Chapter 4).

The anti-euro argument

On the reverse side of the coin, the anti-euro lobby points out that, as an existing member of the EU, Britain has the right to enjoy free trade within the Union no matter what other agreements the other members may enter into. The introduction of the euro should not, therefore, be seen as an insurmountable obstacle that will ultimately kill off British trade within the EU.

There are also doubts as to whether adopting the single currency will significantly affect British/EU trade. The UK is currently a net importer of goods from the EU and it has been suggested that other EU states are hardly likely to want to see a reduction in their volume of exports to Britain. After all, UK importers can make payments in euro and as long as the EU exporter receives payment for the goods sold, both parties will be happy.

Another compelling argument against joining the single currency is the fact that a large proportion of the UK's overseas trade is carried out in US dollars, rather than European currencies. This tends to suggest that the benefits of eliminating exchange risk for British/EU trade will not be as great as the pro-euro lobby maintains. Since the euro was introduced, sterling has also proved to be more stable against the dollar than the euro, which has weakened quite substantially against the pound.

Pricing in euro for the whole of the euro-zone is likely to be difficult. Disparities between pricing policies in different markets will be all too evident and British companies may find it hard to develop a pricing strategy that allows them to set a consistent price across the zone.

The anti-euro lobby therefore concludes that the continued international trade success of British companies will be dependent primarily on the UK being able to produce products that are competitively priced, rather than on membership of a currency union that, in their view, offers few advantages.

Conclusions

Foreign currency management is an integral part of effective international trade. If it is well managed, exporters and importers will benefit from the security of knowing that the exchange risk has been minimised, even when transactions are susceptible to volatile exchange rate fluctuations. This chapter has demonstrated the pitfalls of ineffective currency management and readers should now be familiar with the principles of currency exchange as applied to international trade.

It should also be evident that the euro presents a number of opportunities and threats for British, Danish and Swedish companies. The introduction of the European single currency gives rise to many other issues that need to be given serious consideration if all businesses across the EU are to trade on equal terms.

Sources of information

National Statistics Office (UK) – www.statistics.gov.uk
International Monetary Fund – www.imf.org
EU official website for the euro – http://europa.eu.int/euro
UK Treasury euro website – www.euro.gov.uk
Information on EU monetary issues – www.ecu-activities.be
Homepage of the UK network of Euro Info Centres – www.euro-info.org.uk
A balanced UK perspective on the euro can be found at
    www.thesinglecurrency.net
Pro-euro argument – www.britainineurope.org
Anti-euro argument – www.no-euro.net

Further reading

Beetham R, *The Euro Debate* (Kogan Page, 2001).
Bennett D, *Managing Foreign Exchange Risk* (Pitman, 1996).

Coyle B and Graham A, *Introduction to Currency Risk* (AMACOM Currency Risk Management Series, 2000).

Hicks A, *Managing Foreign Exchange Risk Using Currency Options* (Woodhead, 2000).

Randall Henning C and Padoan P C, *Transatlantic Perspectives on the Euro* (Brookings Institution Press, 2000).

Rosenberg M R, *Currency Forecasting* (Irwin, 1995).

Stringer C, *Preparing for the Euro* (FT Prentice Hall, 2001).

QUESTIONS FOR CONSIDERATION

1   Describe the function of foreign exchange rates and how their values are influenced.
2   What is the exchange rate between the Danish krone and the euro if the sterling/euro conversion rate is £1 = €0.61 and the sterling/krone rate is £1 = 12kr?
3   What are the main differences between exchange rates quoted at spot and forward rates? How do premiums and discounts affect these rates?
4   What are the financial implications of ineffective foreign exchange management?
5   How has the introduction of the euro affected trade within the EU and trade with non-EU countries?
6   What are the opportunities and threats that the euro presents to the UK, Denmark and Sweden?

▌ ⍓ **13** Finance for international trade

Introduction

This chapter explains how companies are able to finance their international trade activities through a variety of methods and why they need to do so. It demonstrates that international trade finance forms part of the financial planning process and impacts on other areas of the export strategy, such as costing and the ways of securing payment described in Chapter 11.

The risks associated with international trade finance are also explained in conjunction with the steps that companies can take to cover credit risk and by the end of the chapter readers will be able to identify the issues to be borne in mind when considering which form of financing most closely meets their requirements.

What is financing?

Financing is the method by which companies are able to meet their cash needs when there are insufficient funds or revenues to cover expenditure for the day-to-day operation of the business. Although it is separate from the company's financial planning and operations functions, financing does have a bearing on them. In an ideal world, a company's income and expenditure would always be proportional and the cash flow forecast would have a regular pattern. In reality, payment may be received up front and the costs incurred subsequently or vice versa. Under these circumstances, the cash flow forecast has an irregular pattern and may highlight periods where there is a shortage of cash to cover short-term needs.

For example, Charlie Horse, a small manufacturer of soft toys, has a positive cash flow for the first six months of the year. In August, the company receives a substantial order, for which payment will be made in October even though the costs of materials and production are incurred in August. An order of similar size is then placed in September, with payment due in November. In the simplified six-month cash flow forecast illustrated in Table 13.1, the company realises that the cost of producing goods to fulfil the two orders will cause Charlie Horse to incur a negative cash flow, especially in September. In this position, the company needs to find financial support if it is to meet its short-term obligations. This might be achieved by agreeing an overdraft with the bank or by any of the other methods described later on in this chapter (see Chapter 7 for further examples).

Table 13.1 How receiving payment after incurring production costs impacts on the cash flow forecast – Charlie Horse: six-month cash flow forecast (2002)

	July	Aug	Sept	Oct	Nov	Dec
Income	25 000	23 000	23 000	29 000	31 000	26 000
Expenditure	23 000	29 000	30 000	25 000	25 000	21 000
Cash balance	2 000	(6 000)	(6 000)	4 000	6 000	5 000
Brought forward	5 000	7 000	1 000	(5 000)	(1 000)	5 000
Net cash flow	7 000	1 000	(5 000)	(1 000)	5 000	10 000

Exporting companies in particular are likely to make use of finance options as payment for the goods sold may not be received for several weeks after the production and shipping processes have been completed. As suggested in Chapter 11, payment terms of 60, 90 or even 120 days are not unusual in international trade, which consequently means that the exporter bears the full cost for the production of the goods until payment is received. Equally, exporters of services such as consultancy, training and so on may use financing in order to cover salaries, travel and material costs prior to securing payment from overseas clients.

As previously demonstrated, there are several additional costs associated with international trade that are not necessarily to be found in domestic trade. These include export packing and labelling, distribution, shipping and insurance costs, documentation charges, translation fees, agent's commissions and so on (see Chapter 8). Exporters are likely to be liable for these costs prior to receiving payment, which again affects cash flow and (potentially) solvency.

Financing is a means of covering these costs until the exporter is paid for the goods, or for situations where an importer has paid for goods received but has not yet sold the goods on. It is therefore a useful option to consider when cash flow forecasts appear to be unhealthy or require a cash injection.

There are a number of different financing options available to companies on a short, medium or long-term basis. The type of financing method used will depend on the company's interpretation of its requirements in terms of how much finance is required, what for and for how long a period. When considering making use of the various finance options to cover a particular project, companies should be able to answer the following questions:

1. What expenses will be incurred?
2. What is the cost of each of these expenses and can the costs be better controlled?
3. Can the company cover any of these costs from existing reserves?
4. Could the shortfall be made up in other areas (for example, pricing structures)?
5. How much additional financial support does the company require?
6. When will the finance be required (for instance, up front or a series of regular payments)?

Short-term finance

Short-term financing is most commonly accessed for basic international trade transactions in situations where the credit period for goods purchased or sold is less than a year. The type of financing used under these circumstances is dependent on the payment method specified and the financing of the venture may be the responsibility of the exporting or importing company, their banks or potentially other organisations that are prepared to bear the financial responsibility in the short term.

Previous chapters have highlighted the different payment methods available to companies trading overseas. Some, such as cash in advance and confirmed irrevocable letters of credit provide the seller with a great deal of security whilst others, such as open account, are less secure. The various methods of securing payment can also be used as a means of financing international transactions.

Financing through payment terms

Figure 13.1 Lists the various payment terms. Cash in advance, for example, provides the exporter with revenue up front; either on acceptance of the contract or before the goods are shipped to the buyer, thereby enabling the company to cover its costs sooner. This method of payment shifts the responsibility for financing the venture to the importer and is therefore the most favourable form of international trade financing available to the exporter.

Letters of credit, as demonstrated in Chapter 11, provide exporters with a guarantee of payment underwritten by at least one bank. Although the banks levy a fee in return for their backing, documentary credits remain one of the most frequently used payment methods for international trade. A 'sight draft' permits the exporter to receive payment on presentation of the document to the bank, whilst 'term credits' make provision for payments at specified times such as 30 days after delivery, 60 days from the date of shipment and so on. In certain situations, letters of credit can also be made to work for the exporter by providing a form of finance. For instance, the exporter may be able to negotiate with the importer to include a payment schedule in the L/C so that 25 per cent of the contract value is payable on signing the contract, 25 per cent part way through production, 25 per cent on shipping and 25 per cent on delivery. This method ensures that the exporter receives a regular income for the duration of the project and can minimise the negative impact on the company's cash flow.

Equally, rather than waiting for 60 days after shipment to receive payment, the exporter may negotiate payment on the date of shipment or delivery, thereby securing the revenue and recouping costs earlier.

- Cash in advance
- Letter of credit
- Documentary/clean collections
- Open account
- Discounting foreign receivables
- Bank operating lines of credit

Figure 13.1 Short-term finance options.

Collections, such as bills of exchange, normally require the exporter to finance the export sale until the buyer makes payment, which will either be CAD (cash against documents) or DOA (documents on acceptance) as described in Chapter 11.

Documentary collections – where a bill is accompanied by commercial documents transferring title of the goods from the exporter to the importer – and clean collections (unaccompanied bills) are less secure than a letter of credit but are nevertheless a common method of payment. As a short-term means of generating finance for the sale, collections are less effective from the point of view of the exporter as payment is received after the costs have been incurred. Collections are therefore a more attractive option for the importer.

Open account terms are common within Europe and between the USA and Canada. Trading under these terms is most favourable for the importer as the exporter is required to completely finance the International trade venture until the buyer pays at an agreed date – normally 30 days after the goods have been delivered and an invoice raised. This is the least secure method of trading for the exporter, as revenues are not protected by a bank and the exporter trusts the buyer to make the payment.

Other short-term finance options

Conventional methods of payment can therefore be used as finance instruments to a greater or lesser extent, although in most cases the exporter will still have to wait for a certain period of time before receiving payment. In cases where the exporter struggles to maintain a positive cash flow and cannot afford to wait for payment, other forms of short-term finance are available.

Firstly, the company may apply to a bank to arrange an operating line of credit, which is simply a short-term loan to cover the cost of the international trade process pending payment from overseas. The operating line of credit is easier to arrange for domestic trade due to the reduced risk of trading in the same country and is harder to secure for international transactions as a result of the increased risks that are associated with overseas trade. However, if export credit insurance (see below) is taken out by the exporter to cover the risks, the banks will take a more favourable view and will be more inclined to set up the operating line of credit. It must be remembered that there will be a fee for this facility and companies must ensure that any advantage they gain in receiving short-term finance is not outweighed by the charges levied.

The other short-term finance option is for the company to sell its foreign receivables, or payments due from export sales. Using this method, the exporter is able to convert the receivables into hard cash, simply by selling them to a bank. For example, Charlie Horse sells £10 000 of goods to a French customer, who agrees to pay in 60 days. In the meantime, the company needs to purchase materials and components for another order but is limited by the lack of available funds. The company approaches its bank, which agrees to purchase the commercial invoice issued to the French company and to pay Charlie Horse the value of the invoice, less a fee to cover the bank's financing charges and risks. The bank then receives payment from the French customer at the appointed date.

This process is known as 'discounting foreign receivables', which may be on a recourse or non-recourse basis. If discounting is on a recourse basis, the exporter is obliged to guarantee the importer's payment, leaving the exporter liable should the importer default. Non-recourse discounting of foreign receivables is therefore when the bank agrees to accept the risk with no guarantees required from the exporter. Naturally, the bank's fees will be higher for non-recourse discounting than for recourse discounting.

Discounting on a non-recourse basis has several advantages for the exporter, despite the reduction in revenue due to bank charges. Securing immediate payment in this way means that:

1. The exporter is protected against non-payment.
2. The exporter is protected against fluctuations in foreign exchange rates and interest rates.
3. Payment is received more quickly by simply selling the invoice to a third party than under other established payment methods.
4. Working capital is increased, potentially allowing the company to finance other sales.
5. The need for operating lines of credit is reduced, thereby saving the company money in interest payments.

However, the discounting bank will charge a sizeable fee, which obviously affects the percentage of the invoice value paid to the company. Care must therefore be taken to confirm that the amount receivable after discounting is still enough to deliver a viable return on the contract and that the company will not end up losing on the sale. Banks may also prove reluctant to discount every transaction, preferring to discount the invoices that they are more confident of receiving payment for. This may ultimately mean that the exporter is left with the riskiest receivables and is not able to benefit from this form of financing as much as anticipated.

Medium and long-term finance

Financing for the medium and long term can be achieved in a number of ways and is most likely to be used in conjunction with large-scale projects, such as the import or export of capital equipment. For projects of this nature, short-term finance options are unlikely to be an attractive proposition due to the amount of financing required and medium to long-term finance, which covers substantially longer periods, is more acceptable. Medium-term options generally cover

• Buyer credits	• Supplier credits
• Loans	• Forfaiting
• Factoring	• Leasing

Figure 13.2   Medium and long-term finance options.

finance repayments for up to five years, whilst long-term options may be for as long as 15 years.

Medium and long-term finance will be arranged through banks and other financial institutions that are prepared to take on the risk of not receiving payment from the buyer or the buyer's bank. There are several medium and long-term financing methods available to importers and exporters, and the most common are listed in Figure 13.2.

Buyer credits

One of the common ways of financing a large project is through buyer credits, which may take the form of a line of credit allocation, as described above, or a direct loan (see Figure 13.3). Buyer credits are mechanisms whereby funds are loaned to the buyer to finance the purchase of capital equipment. The lending bank provides funding to the importer on a non-recourse basis to the exporter and only when it has satisfied itself of the buyer's creditworthiness and reliability. The background checks carried out on the buyer will also take into account the economic and political situation in the buyer's country and in many cases the loans will be guaranteed by the buyer's bank or perhaps a government department.

Loans

Direct loans are negotiated by the lending bank and the buyer, with minimal input from the exporter. For example, a British company enters into a contract to design and install a £1.5 million water treatment plant in Romania and, at the request of the buying organisation, approaches its bank to open discussions on establishing finance arrangements on behalf of the Romanian buyer. The bank

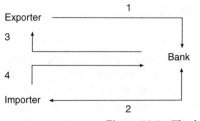

1. Exporter asks bank to open discussions with buyer
2. Bank agrees terms with importer
3. Bank pays exporter
4. Importer repays bank

Figure 13.3   The buyer credit process.

then negotiates directly with the buyer in order to understand the buyer's exact requirements and subsequently makes an offer of a loan.

The agreement will clearly stipulate who the borrower is and will establish that the borrower does in fact have a legal right to enter into the agreement. This is of particular relevance in larger companies where a subsidiary office may wish to enter into such an agreement but may not have the right to do so without the full authority of the parent company. In some cases, borrowing substantial amounts from a foreign bank may also require approval from the buyer's government or central bank.

The agreement will also identify any guarantors of the loan, as well as the guarantor's legal right to borrow.

Secondly, the contract will specify the purpose and value of the loan, the currency in which the loan is to be made and repaid and a detailed schedule of payments. This section will also include details of how the interest rate has been calculated and what fees will be levied by the bank. Additionally, specific conditions may be included; referring to issues that must be addressed before any monies are lent to the buyer. The buyer undertakes in the agreement to repay the sums outlined and may also be requested to agree not to offer its assets as security for other loans and to ensure that its financial ratios (see Chapter 7) do not fall below set levels. If any aspect of these conditions is breached, the buyer will be deemed to have defaulted on the agreement and the lending bank may call the balance of the loan in.

Supplier credits

The opposite of buyer credits is the supplier credit (see Figure 13.4), although both are similar in function. Supplier credits can be arranged through lending banks that agree in advance to purchase the buyer's promissory notes (commitment to pay) from the exporter, thereby effectively financing the transaction for the buyer. In many cases, the promissory note is simply the bill of exchange.

The lending bank negotiates with the exporter, rather than the importer, and establishes a procedure for purchasing the promissory notes so that the exporter receives payment and it falls to the bank to ensure that payment is received from the buyer. Supplier credits are obtained in the form of forfaiting or note purchases.

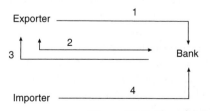

Figure 13.4 The supplier credit process.

Note purchases are the arrangements set up between the exporter and the lending body to outline the terms under which the lender will buy the importer's promissory notes, the interest rate levied by the lender and any other fees charged.

If this method of financing is to be used, the exporter will obtain a quotation for the note purchase from the bank in order to build the additional interest charges and fees into the export quotation. This method is particularly useful when the importer struggles to access credit facilities and, although the buyer does pay more for the purchases, the note purchase arrangement can be a flexible and more attractive finance option than buyer credits.

Forfaiting

Forfaiting is a common form of medium-term financing where a bank might agree to purchase bills of exchange for up to seven years, depending on the circumstances. The bills will normally be 'avalised', meaning that they have also been guaranteed by the importer's bank and therefore provide a greater level of security to the purchasing, or lending, bank. The exporter forfaits the bills by selling them to the bank in exchange for cash.

The entire value of the promissory notes is discounted at a fixed rate at one go, rather than on several occasions as the notes mature. As a result, the exporter receives a cash sum to the value of the notes, less bank charges and interest. These charges can be taken into account when pricing for the transaction and the exporter need not therefore be disadvantaged.

Forfaiting clearly has certain advantages for the exporter. It permits the seller to receive cash for what would normally be a credit agreement and any charges incurred as a result of entering into a forfaiting agreement can be passed on to the importer. The importer, again, pays slightly more for the privilege of having the transaction financed in this way but forfaiting may also be a favourable option if the credit terms offered in the seller's market are more favourable than those offered by the domestic market. It is therefore in the importer's interests to evaluate all the available means of securing finance before agreeing to arrangements drawn up by the exporter and his bank.

Factoring

Factoring occurs when a supplier sells the buyer's debt to a factor in exchange for an agreed percentage of the invoice value, payable either when the credit term has run its course or when the invoice for the transaction is raised. The balance is paid when the factoring house receives payment from the buyer. Factors tend to approve this sort of arrangement only for customers who have been vetted and even then may limit the precise terms of the arrangement, depending on how the factoring house views the risk. A charge will be made for use of this facility, and the exporter will also be liable for any legal costs incurred by the factor in recovering the outstanding debts.

Factors are generally organisations with sizeable international networks of financial and legal experts that are in a good position to maintain regular contact with the companies that owe them money. A buyer who is indebted to a factor will, more than likely, find that there is a local representative in his market keeping a close eye on the company to ensure that payment will be forthcoming.

In the UK, most banks and credit factoring companies are prepared to factor international transactions and organisations such as the Factors and Discounters Association are able to provide information on which organisations specialise in which markets.

Leasing

International leasing is similar to domestic hire purchase and other leasing agreements. The main advantage of leasing is that it does allow companies access to finance even when their credit rating may preclude them from securing other loans. It is also useful when the buyer is subject to import restrictions that prevent purchases of particular foreign goods. By entering into a lease agreement, the buyer is able to benefit from being able to utilise the equipment in question whilst not actually taking ownership of it. The lender (or lessor) retains title to the goods for which the money is borrowed and is therefore in a more secure position than when simply lending money without keeping ownership of the goods in question. Some leasing arrangements cover the short-term supply of machinery or other assets – such as industrial vehicles and machinery – and would be classed as operating leases. An example of this may be a company that leases earth-moving machinery to contractors on a weekly or monthly basis. The lessor charges a fee for the use of the machinery in order to cover running and maintenance costs and will need to lease the equipment regularly to secure a return on the initial investment.

It is also possible to enter into financial leasing agreements whereby the lessor provides the cash to enable a buyer to purchase goods or assets. The buyer agrees to repay the money, as would be the case for a direct loan, but the goods remain the property of the lessor until the debt has been repaid.

International trade risks

The risk of not receiving payment for goods sold is perhaps more pronounced with international trade due to the number of different processes and procedures that importing and exporting entail. Companies that have substantial experience of domestic trade may not fully appreciate the new risks associated with buying and selling overseas. Country risks, such as war, strikes, import/export restrictions, sanctions and the like will impact on transactions in the market and may result in the foreign supplier not receiving payment or the buyer not receiving the goods purchased. Of all the risks associated with international trade, it is the risk that the foreign buyer fails to meet its financial obligations, either deliberately or through insolvency, that most regularly affects exporters.

There are steps that companies can take to minimise their exposure to credit risk and these should be identified and included as part of the company's overall international marketing plan. It is also prudent for the company to identify the precise nature of the risks to which it is likely to be exposed.

Customer risk

One of the most important issues to address before entering into a contract with a foreign buyer or supplier is to assess their creditworthiness and ability to fulfil the terms of the contract. The risk assessment takes into account a wide range of considerations, from financial position and trading history to the political and economic climate of the country in which they operate. Many companies also take account of the buyer's commercial reputation, standing and how existing suppliers are treated, although even the most glowing of reputations will not disguise financial difficulties.

Several of the ratios explained in Chapter 7 are instrumental in gauging the relative financial strength and position of a buyer or supplier and should certainly be employed as part of a full credit assessment. The financial strength of a company is its ability to meet its financial obligations and up-to-date information on the company's finances should be readily available through reports compiled by banks and credit reference agencies. It should also be possible to obtain a current balance sheet and P&L account from the company.

From this information, the exporter is able to develop a picture of the buyer's liquidity and overall ability to meet short-term debts, whilst the acid test, debtors and creditors ratios will also provide background data on the company's position.

Another useful tool that can give an insight into a company is 'gearing', which is a measure of how much the company is using debt to finance its operations. Gearing, or leverage, is the amount of debt expressed as a percentage of the company's assets. For example, a company with assets of US$24 million and liabilities of US$4 million has a gearing of approximately 16 per cent. The danger signs to watch out for are in companies that have a very high proportion of liabilities and that consequently may not be able to meet their repayment obligations, let alone any new liabilities.

Country risk

Country risk is the risk associated with doing business with a specified geographic territory. Many of the issues covered in the chapter on market research also have a bearing in this respect, although from the credit risk perspective the main considerations are the likelihood of non-payment through civil action, war, revolution and so on, as well as some of the macro factors such as import and export restrictions. Professional credit management agencies spend a great deal of time researching and reviewing countries and allocating them a risk rating on the basis of their stability (politically and socially), international policies and domestic economic policies. Factors such as interest rates, inflation, GDP, GNP and unemployment also influence the credit rating awarded to a country. The overall economic position of the country in question and its balance of trade also affects the perceived risk of doing business in the market. This is particularly true of countries that rely primarily on the trade of commodities susceptible to price variations on the international market. Countries dependent on securing a good price for their produce, be it coffee, sugar, cocoa or any other item traded as an international commodity, may suffer economically as a result of a market downturn. This in turn affects sovereign risk, which is effectively a measure of the country's ability to meet the interest payments on its international debts as well as the debts themselves.

> **Activity**: Compile a list of five nations whose economies are dependent on the production and trading of commodities. Find out just how reliant the countries are on the commodities and examine the ramifications of a sudden decline in demand or reduction in the international price of the goods on the market.

This is of particular relevance in some African states where the whole issue of third-world debt is the subject of international debate. Russia, too, has struggled to meet its repayment obligations and, like the African states, has renegotiated the schedule of payments with the World Bank and its other international creditors.

Sovereign and country risk are often encompassed under the term political risk. Although exporters and importers can usually judge the relative stability of the countries with which they are dealing, it is advisable to seek professional advice and to make use of credit insurance agencies to ensure that the risk of trading with a particular company or market is insured. In addition, organisations such as Dun & Bradstreet regularly publish reports on individual markets, which can be a useful source of background information.

How credit risk insurance works

Export credit insurers are organisations that undertake to cover aspects of international trade risk such as ensuring that a company will be paid the value of its foreign receivables in the event that a client defaults on payment and is unlikely to be able to meet its obligations. Credit insurance policies are tailored to meet each company's needs and will be based on:

1. the nature of the company's international activities
2. the number and type of markets the company is active in
3. the nature of the goods sold overseas

4. the company's preferred trading terms
5. how the company currently manages its credit control procedures

although the individual requirements of each company will also be taken into account.

The most common type of policy is the comprehensive annual policy, which is designed to ensure that the exporter is insured against all credit risks for international transactions that have a credit period of no longer than six months. The cost of taking out such a policy is a fee payable to the insurer, normally in the region of between 0.5 and 1.5 per cent of the company's anticipated export sales.

The comprehensive policy protects the company against buyer insolvency, defaulted payments and additional costs incurred as a result of having to change the route of the shipped goods, assuming that the buyer will not cover these costs. The policy will also cover the exporter in situations where the buyer refuses to accept goods that have already been shipped, but only in cases where the exporter is not at fault.

Companies are not insured for the full contract value but must bear a minimum of 10 per cent of the losses incurred through 'commercial' risks (buyer insolvency, and so on) and 15 per cent of the losses incurred as a result of political issues.

Claims made against the insurer will normally be paid out on evidence of the foreign buyer's insolvency, or six months after a defaulted payment. If the goods have been sold at a loss to a third party due to the buyer's refusal to accept them, the insurer will pay out the difference one month after the resale has taken place (subject to the provisos mentioned above). Where the loss is attributable to any other reason, the insurer will pay out approximately four months after the date of the loss.

In the event that a company contracts to supply capital equipment on long-term credit, the exporter may opt to take out a 'specific cover' policy to provide protection solely for the project in question. A specific cover policy is more expensive to take out, due to the nature of the cover required and the risks associated with the project, but it does offer peace of mind to exporters engaged in large-scale transactions that could cripple the company if payment is not received on time. In the UK, the government's Export Credit Guarantee Department (ECGD) is a facility that offers longer term insurance to support the sale of capital goods overseas. ECGD insures loans issued by UK banks and thereby allows buyers to obtain credit as well as ensuring that the seller receives payment for the goods sold quickly and securely.

Conclusions

This chapter has demonstrated that there are many ways for exporters and importers to finance international trade. Conventional payment methods and tailored finance solutions each have a role in facilitating import/export transactions for short, medium or long-term situations. Financing arrangements are not just a means of quickly realising hard cash from a credit contract but can also be a useful bargaining tool in terms of being able to offer a client a finance package tailored to meet the specific needs of the transaction.

However, as the chapter and other sections of the book have shown, international trade does present numerous risks that can potentially expose companies to financial difficulties. The most common approach to avoiding such risks is through credit risk insurance, which readers should also be able appreciate and understand the principles of.

Sources of information

Harvard Business School Project Finance Portal – www.hbs.edu/projfinportal/
Association of Forfaiters in the Americas – www.afia-forfaiting.org
Factors and Discounters Association – www.factors.org.uk
UK official export credit agency – www.ecgd.gov.uk
Malaysian export credit agency – www.mecib.com.my
NCM Credit Management Worldwide – www.ncmamericas.com
Dun & Bradstreet – www.dnb.com

Further reading

Briggs P, *Principles of International Trade and Payments* (Blackwell, 1994).
Gianturco D E, *Export Credit Agencies* (Quorum, 2001).
Guild I, *Forfaiting: An Alternative Approach to Export Trade Finance* (Universe, 1986).
Stephens M, *The Changing Role of Export Credit Agencies* (International Monetary Fund, 1999).
Venedikian H M and Warfield G A, *Global Trade Financing* (Wiley, 2000).
Weiss K D, *Building an Import/Export Business* (2nd ed) (Wiley, 1997).

QUESTIONS FOR CONSIDERATION

1 Why might importers and exporters need support in financing their international transactions?
2 How can international payment methods become sources of finance?
3 What are the main instruments for medium and long-term finance options and what are the limitations and benefits of each?
4 How might an exporter use the financial ratios explained in Chapter 7 to gauge client risk and creditworthiness?
5 What are the key issues to take into account when taking out export credit risk insurance?

Case study: Locum Destination Consulting

Locum Destination Consulting is a UK-based business specialising in advising public and private sector organisations involved in culture, tourism, leisure and property. The company is primarily involved in the creation, management and regeneration of destinations and locations. The company brings together a team of specialist destination consultants with a variety of expertise to give Locum an extremely skilled pool of experts to work with on projects that range from improving the daily operations of a local museum to enhancing the market position of an entire country.

Certosa Reale di Collegno and Forte di Exilles

In 1999, the company undertook two strategic studies for the Region of Piedmont in partnership with Ecosfera, a Rome-based economic and architectural practice. The Culture Department of Piedmont's Regional Government wanted to investigate re-use options and strategies for two sites of considerable heritage and value: Forte di Exilles, a seventeenth-century fortress in the Valle di Susa and the Certosa Reale di Collegno, a sixteenth-century monastic complex later developed as a major mental health hospital on the outskirts of Turin. Although commissioned in tandem by the same client, the two projects presented many differing issues requiring different solutions. For the former, which was already advanced in terms of redevelopment as a visitor attraction, Locum was able to provide clear ideas for the ultimate vision and mission for the site (for example, retail, catering, premium hotel and conferencing facilities). By contrast, for the Certosa Reale di Collegno, a much larger and more complex site, Locum explored various propositions including Lifelong Learning, Health and Well-being, that could help catalyse a mixed-use culture, leisure, housing and commercial destination development.

Origin of the project

Locum was not particularly well known in Italy and the company was fortunate to come across Ecosfera through personal networks (one of Locum's consultants had previously worked with one of Ecosfera's partners for another Italian company). Having seen Locum's promotional literature, Ecosfera recognised that there was considerable scope to work with the company on a number of different projects in Italy.

Ecosfera asked Locum to subcontract as specialist destination advisers in a larger project that sought to identify a re-use strategy for the two key heritage sites. The contract was won through a competitive tendering process, with Ecosfera undertaking practically all of the pre-tender sales work (contacting the client, researching the brief, drafting the proposal and so on). Locum was asked to provide background material on the practice and CVs for the personnel who would be involved.

The timescale from the initial invitation to tender to the actual contract signing was considerably longer in Italy than the company was used to in the UK and took almost four months. Ecosfera undertook to set up the joint venture agreement necessary to bring together the specialist expertise required to deliver the project. Locum was therefore subcontracting directly to a trusted local partner rather than contracting with the Italian client, and it was consequently easier to agree mutually acceptable terms. Ecosfera accepted and paid a commissioning invoice from Locum in advance of payment from the client, whilst Locum accepted Ecosfera's condition of payment within 60 days of invoice as opposed to their standard 30 days. Payment insurance was not considered necessary as Locum was working with a trusted partner.

Key issues

By far the most difficult obstacle was the perceived expense to the client of commissioning consultancy from abroad. Locum's daily rates are competitive in their primary market of the UK, and the company prefers to compete on value not price. At the same time, the consultancy market in Italy is hugely competitive and daily rates tend to be lower. This was exacerbated by the high value of sterling against the lira and the fact that an overseas consultancy such as Locum would need to charge expenses for travel, accommodation and so on, whereas a local consultant would not.

However, by restructuring the work programme, the company was able to reduce its overall fees by concentrating effort in the areas where most value could be added: Ecosfera retained responsibility for market research, analysis, planning and so on, whilst Locum addressed the high level strategic issues. Consequently, the company made a demonstrable contribution to the study in a minimum number of days. Again, this was largely due to the effective working relationship with Ecosfera.

On the administrative side, chasing invoices, ensuring payment and meeting the contractual criteria of complex briefs would have become a burden were it not for the fact that Locum remained virtually insulated from these details precisely because Ecosfera dealt with them on their behalf. Timescales for all aspects of the project were all extended in comparison to the company's experience of working in the UK. Even Ecosfera's standard terms and conditions regarding invoicing and payment were different from Locum's.

Summary

Locum's key to securing consultancy work in Italy was in working with a local partner. Unlike most UK consultancies, Italian companies are likely to have a bespoke sales department devoted to researching and responding to public and private tender opportunities. Having a local partner to take a lead in the sales process was invaluable, particularly as there is often a risk that an invitation to tender is issued by statutory requirement even though the preferred consultancy has already been identified or even appointed to deliver the contract. A local company with extensive client and corporate networks is more likely to be able to anticipate these eventualities. Building strong partnerships of this type is critical for success in working overseas.

Since the original assignment, Locum has won two further contracts and is in consideration for several more. Directors from both organisations have met in Rome specifically to help gel the relationship between the two companies. This is a model that will be replicated in Locum's future international expansion and the company has already appointed a senior Spanish consultant to lead on the sales effort into Spain.

☒ 14 Suppliers and support organisations

Introduction

For companies that rely on external suppliers to provide components or services, effective supply chain management is essential to the smooth running of the operation. This chapter highlights the importance of maintaining good relationships with suppliers, and demonstrates that companies who view suppliers more as partners will gain further advantages.

Examples of the different types of suppliers are discussed, and the chapter concludes by introducing some of the key organisations that provide international trade support and advice to internationally active companies.

Suppliers and partners

Companies involved with international trade are as reliant on their suppliers as those that are not. It is not just the suppliers of raw materials or components for the finished product that are important, but also the organisations that provide valuable services for exporters and importers. These will include freight forwarders, export management companies and customs brokers as well as advisers and consultants. Banks can also be classed as suppliers as they provide essential financial services for international trade, as has been demonstrated in Chapter 11.

Generally these services are bought from the suppliers on a casual basis as required. Whilst there is nothing wrong with this approach, companies do stand to gain more from developing these irregular relationships into more effective working partnerships, which deliver additional benefits:

- As suppliers become increasingly familiar with the company they can often adopt an approach that precisely meets the client's needs.
- The company may be able to secure discounts or preferential trading terms from a trusted and regularly used supplier.
- Suppliers that know their clients well may be able to offer advice or recommend improvements to systems and procedures.
- Suppliers who are also trading in the companies' target markets are likely to identify other complementary opportunities for their clients to explore.

Effective partnerships will also benefit the supplier. After all, if the exporting company is doing well, the chances are that the supplier's services will be increasingly in demand and it is therefore in the supplier's interest to assist the client in whatever ways are appropriate.

Suppliers of components

Companies that purchase components or raw materials for their products from third parties are dependent on being able receive the goods on time and at an affordable price. The process of appointing these suppliers will take into account the quality of service likely to be provided as well as the quality of goods. It is essential for the company to work with suppliers it can trust and who are able to fulfil its needs efficiently.

Increasingly, as the potential for more effective partnering is realised, companies are looking to their suppliers to provide more support and assistance with domestic and international trade.

For instance, some companies use their suppliers to facilitate the financing of a particular order by paying for the components only when the finished product has been sold. Providing that the supplier is able to support the cost of the goods and is prepared to wait for payment, this relationship can assist the company in managing cash flow. As the supplier would normally be able to charge an interest premium on the goods delivered in advance of payment, all parties can benefit.

Suppliers may also be willing to manufacture on a 'just in time' basis or store larger quantities of components and raw materials on behalf of their clients if the companies have limited warehousing space. Much will depend on the value that the supplier places on the business it is getting from the client and relationships that deliver little in the way of benefits for the supplier will ultimately not be of benefit to the company. An effective, mutually satisfying relationship will bring the company greater competitiveness and the supplier an increase in business.

Freight forwarders

As this book has already demonstrated, freight forwarders play an important role in the shipping of goods overseas. They will normally be responsible for every aspect of the logistics function, including documentation and insurance. It is therefore in the exporter's interests to ensure that the freight forwarder used by the company is fully briefed on its products and requirements, and has almost as much knowledge of the goods as the company itself. The freight forwarder is consequently in a good position to understand precisely what steps need to be taken to ensure the safe transit of the goods from the exporter to the intended recipient.

Wherever possible, exporting companies are advised to try and develop lasting relationships with their freight forwarder, once they have found an organisation capable of meeting their needs. The preferred forwarder should ideally become an extension of the company itself, effectively as a 'bolt on' shipping department. This can be achieved by encouraging regular contact with the forwarder and integrating many of the company's own procedures with those of the freight forwarder. Where the relationship is particularly successful the transfer of information between the two parties is seamless and the shipping process runs smoothly. It is also likely that the freight forwarder, through its international network of correspondent firms, will be able to pass on market information and even leads to the client. Again, this is in the forwarder's interests as the client could increase the volume of goods sold overseas and requiring shipping.

A business that does not take steps to work as closely as possible with its freight forwarder and treats them simply as a service provider are likely to find their distribution procedures slower. Under these circumstances the forwarding company will not possess enough knowledge of the clients' goods, which in turn may lead to an inappropriate level of service being offered.

Freight forwarders do carry a lot of responsibility on behalf of their clients, but the onus is very much on the exporter to ensure that the goods are shipped in an appropriate manner. It therefore pays to invest time and effort in fostering sound relationships with freight forwarders.

Export management companies

In some cases, companies are more inclined to let other organisations take on the export function on their behalf. The services offered by export management companies can allow firms to export goods without having to worry about the logistical, financial and documentary requirements that normally accompany international trade. Export management organisations differ from trading houses, as they do not take ownership of the goods to be exported. Instead they act in a similar capacity to an agent, carrying out many of the agent's duties from marketing of the products to the shipping of the goods to the buyer. As a result, export management firms work very closely with their clients to ensure that as much knowledge as possible is gained of the companies' products, processes and business strategies.

A trading house, by contrast, purchases goods from the client company and takes ownership of the products. The trading house then aims to sell the goods at a profit in markets overseas. Whilst companies have less control over trading houses than they do over export management companies, it is possible for effective relationships to be developed, permitting the company to influence how and where the trading houses promote the goods.

Customs brokers

Customs brokers are organisations that are completely familiar with the Customs procedures and requirements of the country in which they are active. They are able to handle all the relevant documentation needed to clear goods through Customs and will be engaged by exporters and importers who pay to have their goods cleared as quickly (and as cost effectively) as possible.

Exporters who trade under EXW, FOB and other terms will not require the services of a Customs broker as the Incoterms specify that it is the buyer's responsibility to clear the goods through Customs. Companies exporting under other Incoterms and importers bringing foreign goods into the country will make more use of brokers as the trading terms are likely to be against them.

As the company pays a fee to facilitate Customs clearance, the appointment of a Customs broker should be made in the same way that any other supplier would be approved. Having found a broker who can meet the business' needs in terms of cost and quality of service, it makes good sense to build up an amicable relationship as the broker may be able to offer discounts on larger volumes of goods to be cleared and can effect clearance quickly.

As a result, businesses, which have regular need of Customs brokers, are likely to build up strong relationships with a particular broker with a view to securing long-term benefits in terms of the cost and speed of clearance.

Note: Bribery of officials to 'encourage' speedier clearance through Customs is not unheard of. Many companies involved in importing and exporting will, sooner or later, find themselves in a position where a decision is potentially influenced by incentives such as backhanders and gifts. It is good practice to steer clear of such activities, as well as the company or individual offering the incentive, as a business built on corruption is unlikely to prosper long. In February 2002, a new law came into force to dissuade UK companies from bribery overseas – individuals or business found guilty of the offence are liable to prosecution in the UK.

Investors

Companies that have received substantial financial backing from external investors should not ignore the other, non-financial advantages they can bring. In many cases, the suppliers of capital will possess strengths and expertise that the company does not yet have. As investors are keen to see a return on their capital they should be approachable and willing to provide advice and assistance to ensure the continued development of the company. Businesses should therefore be encouraged to make every effort to employ the different skills and experiences of their investors to mutual advantage.

Sources of support

Exporters and importers in the twenty-first Century are able to access unparalleled levels of international trade advice and information due to the growing number of business support organisations and the rise in Internet usage. With this wealth of knowledge, experience and expertise so readily available, there is no reason why businesses cannot receive guidance and advice at every stage of their international development. Some of the organisations that companies can look to for support in their bid for overseas success are described

Local	National	International
• Chamber of Commerce	• Trade Partners UK	• ICC
• Business Link	• Institute of Export	• FIATA
• Euro Info Centre	• Customs & Excise	• World Trade Organisation
	• CBI	• European Union
	• Sitpro	
	• Pira	
	• Bifa	
	• RHA	
	• Technical Help for Exporters	
	• BexA	
	• Trade associations	

Figure 14.1   Sources of international trade support.

below (and listed in Figure 14.1), although readers should bear in mind that most trade associations will also provide advice for companies within their industry sector looking to expand internationally. For example, the British Wool Textile Export Corporation (BWTEC) assists textile companies in the UK to identify and exploit export opportunities; the Motorsport Industries Association (MIA) undertakes similar activities for the automotive sector, and so on.

British Chambers of Commerce
(www.britishchambers.org.uk/exportzone)

Chambers of Commerce are independent providers of business support services. Chambers operate in business communities across the UK and their core membership of local companies ensures that they are run by, as well as on behalf of, businesses. Chambers also represent the interests of their members at local, regional and national level, produce regular surveys of local opinion and lobby MPs and government officials on a wide range of issues. The portfolio of international trade services available to businesses varies from Chamber to Chamber, but will generally include the legalisation and certification of export documentation, translation services, market research, trade missions, training and consultancy.

The British Chambers of Commerce (BCC) is the umbrella organisation for the national network of accredited Chambers of Commerce in the UK, and is part of the global network of Chambers. The services provided by the BCC are designed to assist exporters at every stage of their international development and should ideally be used in conjunction with the support available through Trade Partners UK (see below).

International Chamber of Commerce
(www.iccwbo.org)

The ICC is a global organisation that promotes international trade and investment. Incoterms, the definitions of export delivery terms used in international trade (covered in Chapter 8), are published by the ICC, as are many other guidelines and rules that facilitate cross-border trade. In addition, the ICC provides a number of other services to exporters, including the ICC International Court of Arbitration, which is one of the world's foremost arbitration institutions.

The ICC has over 80 years' experience in the promotion of international trade and the procedures it has developed and implemented in that time are the bedrock on which the foundations of exporting and importing are laid.

Trade Partners UK (www.tradepartners.gov.uk)

Trade Partners UK (TPUK) is the British government department that provides support for businesses overseas, and it also represents the interests of UK exporters at government level.

TPUK is part of British Trade International, which encompasses the overseas trade services of the Department of Trade and Industry (DTI) and the Foreign and Commonwealth Office (FCO). The department offers a wide range of generic and market specific support and information through its network of country desks (based in London) and the commercial sections in over 200 diplomatic posts around the world. Through these overseas posts (High Commissions, Embassies, and so on) exporters can obtain up-to-date market knowledge through tailored market reports (TMR), which often include lists of potential agents and distributors as well as advice on how best to approach the market. These reports can form a valuable part of the company's overall market research activity. TPUK is now offering the TMR service online through several of its overseas posts, for example Poland and Singapore.

In addition to the TMR facility, TPUK also operates the Support for Export Marketing Research scheme in conjunction with the British Chambers of Commerce. The scheme subsidises market research for eligible companies, subject to various criteria, and has proven invaluable in helping countless businesses to develop effective export strategies.

Trade Partners UK has also developed TradeUK, an online export sales leads service that makes details of British companies available to international buyers as well as emailing relevant export enquiries to the UK exporter. TradeUK is a useful tool for exporters trying to identify global opportunities and will certainly complement other promotional and research activities.

The range of services provided by Trade Partners UK has one aim, namely to help British exporters become even more successful globally. To this end, TPUK provides financial support in the form of grant subventions to offset some of the travel and accommodation costs incurred by companies visiting foreign markets as part of sponsored 'trade missions' (group visits organised by Chambers of Commerce, trade associations and so on to particular markets).

Through its international network of offices, TPUK is able to quickly access information and advice from around the world. All companies involved with international trade, regardless of industry sector, should make a point of maintaining regular contact with the organisation in order to benefit from its ongoing support and advice.

Small Business Service (www.businesslink.org)

The Small Business Service is a government department that seeks to improve the provision of support to small businesses in the UK as well as representing their interests. Through its network of 'Business Link' offices across the UK, companies can access experienced business advisers whose aim is to ensure that their clients receive affordable and appropriate guidance and support. Business Link's international trade teams provide Trade Partners UK services on a regional level with the aim of improving the international competitiveness of local industry.

Euro Info Centres (EICs) (www.euro-info.org.uk)

The European-wide network of nearly 300 EICs is another valuable resource for exporters. In the UK, 24 EICs offer local support to companies through the provision of specialist information and advice relating to business in Europe. This includes market information and promotion of business opportunities across Europe as well as more technical information such as details of EU legislation, standards and tendering opportunities issued by the European public sector. EICs are staffed by teams who are familiar with the needs of local, regional and European businesses and run regular briefing events on a wide range of relevant topics. For example, during 2001 the EIC network in the UK organised the 'Three Es' initiative, which raised companies' awareness of e-business, exports and the euro.

The Euro Info Centre network is expanding into the emerging markets of Central and Eastern Europe and is therefore also able to offer advice and information on business opportunities outside Western Europe.

Customs and Excise (www.hmce.gov.uk)

UK Customs and Excise is the government department responsible for collecting revenue from value added tax, customs duties and other taxes. The department can provide technical advice on all import and export procedures and requirements as well as information on VAT, excise and customs duties. Customs and Excise are also able to advise businesses on the most appropriate methods and procedures for transporting goods across customs frontiers both in the UK and overseas.

As mentioned in Chapter 9, it is important for exporters and importers to be fully aware of their customs obligations as incorrect customs declarations can be costly and, in some cases, may lead to prosecution.

CBI (www.cbi.org.uk)

The Confederation of British industry (CBI) is an independent, membership organisation that carries out surveys of business trends and issues economic forecasts. For the exporter, the information and statistics available through the CBI may be useful in the collection of data for market research purposes.

The CBI also provides information on a range of policy issues that can affect UK business, as well as acting as the voice of British industry on the needs of businesses and commenting on European and international policies.

SITPRO (www.sitpro.org.uk)

The Simpler Trade Procedures Board, SITPRO, is the UK agency that encourages international trade by simplifying many of the bureaucratic import/export procedures. SITPRO's Board and Policy Groups are comprised of representatives from the commercial, transport and financial sectors who give their time voluntarily to provide advice and guidance on international trade practice. The Board manages the 'UK aligned' system of export documentation used by British companies and publishes a range of advisory briefings and checklists to assist with many elements of the international trade process.

Pira (www.pira.co.uk)

Pira is a specialist organisation providing consultancy services to the printing, paper, publishing and packaging industries. The knowledge that Pira has in the packaging field is of particular use to exporters and importers who need to ensure that their goods are appropriately packaged for distribution and so on. Whilst the BSI can offer advice on any climatic considerations likely to affect packaging in the target market, Pira can advise on the range of packaging issues covered in Chapter 5, especially with regard to content and safety of packaging materials and whether or not this meets the local requirements. This is particularly relevant to companies shipping dangerous goods, as Pira is the only UK organisation that can approve and certify packaging for this usage.

BIFA (www.bifa.org)

The British International Freight Association, BIFA, is the leading trade association that covers freight, distribution and allied services. The association is committed to ensuring that high standards of quality and professionalism are demonstrated by its core membership of companies involved with all aspects of the distribution function. BIFA is primarily involved with six areas of activity, covering forwarding by air, packers, distribution within Europe, deep sea and multimodal transport, air cargo and customs issues.

Businesses that require the services of a freight forwarder or a customs agent are advised to make contact with BIFA to ensure that their chosen supplier is both reputable and appropriate to their needs.

FIATA (www.fiata.com)

The International Federation of Freight Forwarders Associations (FIATA) has been in existence since 1926. It is an independent body that now represents the interests of some 40 000 freight forwarding companies in 150 countries. FIATA is recognised by the major transport bodies as the largest non-governmental organisation in the field of distribution, and as a result several United Nations departments (including ECOSOC, UN/ESCAP, UN/ECE and UNCTAD) seek its opinions.

FIATA comprises the Airfreight Institute (AFI), Customs Affairs Institute (CAI) and the Multimodal Transport Institute (MTI), as well as a series of advisory groups covering areas such as dangerous goods, information technology and legal issues. As well as promoting the industry worldwide, FIATA encourages the use of e-commerce tools for freight forwarding, including EDI, and has developed a uniform system of documentation and standard trading conditions used internationally.

RHA (www.rha.net)

The Road Haulage Association (RHA) provides information and advice for the haulage industry, and is the trade association for UK companies involved with the transport of goods by road. As it is impractical for the majority of exporters to operate their own trucks for international distribution, the transport of goods is likely to be subcontracted out to a third party, the haulier. Exporters considering employing the services of a haulage company can obtain advice from the RHA to ensure that their choice of haulier will meet their distribution needs.

Technical Help for Exporters (www.bsi-global.com)

The British Standards Institution's Technical Help for Exporters (THE) service exists to help companies surmount some of the technical difficulties and obstacles that hinder successful international trade. Technical Help for Exporters provides companies with technical information to ensure that products to be exported do meet the technical requirements and standards of overseas markets. The service also takes into account packaging and labelling restrictions, requirements for product inspections, testing and the like.

THE offers a comprehensive reference library and contacts with international standards agencies, as well as regulatory and testing bodies around the world. The service is run by a team of technical experts and researchers who are well placed to advise exporters on the specific technical and regulatory requirements laid down by markets around the world.

BExA (www.bexa.co.uk)

The British Exporters Association (BExA) is the trade association that represents exporters. It is an independent organisation that encompasses manufacturers, export houses and other organisations including banks and credit insurance agencies. BExA's core objective is to lobby on behalf of exporters at national government and European Parliament level, and members of the association can also make use of an information forum which has been designed to meet the needs of British exporters from all industry sectors.

Institute of Export (www.export.org.uk)

The Institute of Export (IOE) is the only professional body in the UK to offer qualifications in international trade. The Institute exists to raise the standard and competence of personnel involved in all aspects of international trade and students who pass the Advanced Certificate in International Trade and Diploma in International Trade examinations are eligible for graduate membership of the Institute of Export. Aside from the training and development work undertaken by the Institute, it remains a strong voice that represents the interests and views of the international trade community. The IOE also operates a help desk, which provides practical advice for members on key international trade disciplines and procedures.

Conclusions

The ability to make optimum use of different suppliers is a useful means of improving efficiency and controlling costs. Effective partnerships can yield many benefits for companies and suppliers prepared to work closely together. Given the more demanding nature of international trade, exporters and importers in particular should consider how best to build on their suppliers' strengths and experiences in order to increase the chances of success overseas.

This chapter has also shown that, although there is no reason why companies cannot succeed in international trade without the aid of external organisations, there are many bodies that exist solely to improve the import/export performance in firms of all sizes. Businesses that resolutely ignore the services available to them do themselves no favours and are ultimately missing out on sound advice and numerous international opportunities.

Sources of information

British Wool Textile Export Corporation – www.bwtec.co.uk
Croner's handbooks for exporters and importers –
    www.tradeinternational-centre.net
Independent Customs & Excise advice and consultancy –
    www.portcullis-isc.co.uk

Institute of Linguists – www.iol.org.uk
Institute of Practitioners in Advertising – www.ipa.co.uk
International Air Transport Association (IATA) – www.iata.com
Motorsport Industries Association – www.mia.co.uk
For a better understanding of how Chambers of Commerce and Business Link can offer complementary support to local companies, visit the Mid Yorkshire Chamber of Commerce website at www.mycci.co.uk and Business Link for West Yorkshire on www.blwy.co.uk

Further reading

Bennett R, *Getting Started in Export* (2nd ed) (Kogan Page, 1998).
British Chambers of Commerce, *International Trade Manual* (Butterworth-Heinemann, 1997).
Chopra S and Meindl P, *Supply Chain Management* (Prentice Hall, 2000).
Van Weele A, *Purchasing and Supply Chain Management* (3rd ed) (Thomson Learning, 2001).

QUESTIONS FOR CONSIDERATION

1　What are the benefits of maintaining good working relationships with suppliers and what steps might a company take to increase the effectiveness of the relationships?

2　Explain the role of customs brokers and trading houses and discuss the benefits and drawbacks of using each.

3　How do the following organisations differ from one another and what sort of support could a company expect to receive from them?
BIFA
Business Link
Chamber of Commerce
FIATA
ICC
Trade Associations
Trade Partners UK

▪ ▼ **15** Summary

Introduction

The core elements of a successful international trade strategy have now been covered in detail. Readers have been given a thorough grounding in the main procedures and considerations that should be addressed in the preparation of an import/export plan and will appreciate the amount of care and thought required to bring the plan to fruition. This book has hopefully demonstrated that international trade relies on information, communication and accuracy at every stage of the process and that sustained overseas success cannot be achieved without commitment and tenacity.

This chapter draws together the individual threads of the international trade strategy, highlighting the key issues of each element and building a model export marketing plan. The honeycomb approach to exporting is then explained and the importance of communication is reiterated. On completion of the chapter, the reader will be able to put all the topics covered in this book into the context of an export plan and will understand how the strategic importance of individual disciplines combine to form a comprehensive strategy.

The need for a defined export marketing plan

International trade, as we have seen, is not a 'quick fix' to boost turnover or clear surplus stock. It requires patience, time and resources to achieve overseas success and in some cases it can take several years before an exporting company sees a return on its investment. Effective business planning is therefore the key to successful international ventures and the results will be proportionate to the amount of work that goes into the preparation of the export marketing plan. A clearly defined plan sets out the requirements and responsibilities that the company must meet if the objectives of the strategy are to be fulfilled and as such the plan provides management with a list of considerations to research and address.

The export plan should retain the flexibility to accommodate any modifications that become necessary as a result of information gained through experience, ongoing research and improved market knowledge. Some of the key issues to include in the plan are summarised in Figure 15.1.

Internal review	• Company experience, skills and resources • Strength and weaknesses • Opportunities and threats • Analysis of competitors and customers
Marketing issues	• Product issues • Pricing • Promotional methods • Place/channels of distribution • Business planning
Market selection	• Primary and secondary research • Identification of competition • Country risk and product fit • Tariff and non-tariff barriers • Market segmentation and structure • Potential client base • Packaging and labelling • Transport restrictions
Visiting the market	• Cultural considerations and language barriers • Efficient preparation in advance of visits • Use of trade fairs and exhibitions • Supporting partners and representatives
Appointing partners	• Type of partner (joint venture, agent, distributor and so on) • Geographical coverage • Reputation, contacts, resources • Technical experience and product portfolio • Quality control and after-sales support • Warehousing capacity
Managing costs	• Fixed and variable costs • Other production cost (for example modifications) • Regulatory compliance costs (standards, packaging, registration, and so on) • Tariffs and duties • Cost of sales and marketing • Insurance and finance premiums • Foreign exchange costs
Transportation issues	• Selecting a transport intermediary • Method of distribution • Documentary requirements • Delivery terms • Insurance • Warehousing and storage
Securing payment	• Choosing an appropriate method of payment • Customer risk • Bills of exchange • Finance issues (forfaiting, factoring and so on)
External support	• Identification of organisations that can provide additional support and advice (trade associations, embassies, chambers of commerce, banks and so on)

Figure 15.1   Key issues in the export marketing plan.

Model export marketing plan

The export marketing plan is a written document that secures the commitment of all levels of the company to pursue international opportunities and to maximise their potential. It covers every function of the company that can conceivably have a bearing on overseas trade, from purchasing and production to sales and administration. Every component of the strategy can affect the other elements. For example, market research affects the route to market, promotional strategy, sales, finance and distribution of goods, whilst the choice of partner or representative can influence payment and delivery terms, marketing, pricing and so on.

It is useful to think of the export process as a honeycomb (see Figure 15.2), with the company's own internal review at the heart of the strategy, surrounded by the main international trade considerations and disciplines. The outer rim of the honeycomb is made up of the organisations that lock in to the company to provide support at every stage of the strategy's development and implementation. The most important aspect of the process is the constant review of how individual components of the strategy impact on the company. The review acts as a line of defence against inappropriate courses of action and the company should be prepared to regularly examine the potential repercussions of its actions. It is feedback from the various departments involved with the strategy that will ultimately determine whether or not the export marketing plan should be modified or adapted to meet emerging needs and requirements.

Figure 15.2 The export plan honeycomb.

Content of the export marketing plan

A comprehensive export marketing plan covers every aspect of the international trade process and identifies how each will affect the normal running of the company as well as what the company must do to meet the requirements of exporting or importing. The document must be laid out clearly and in a logical order so as to facilitate flexibility and ease of understanding. A standard export plan may be structured in the following way:

1. **Summary** – the document should open with a concise summary of the plan that takes no more than one or two pages to describe. The summary is a brief explanation of the company's international trade objectives, the key issues to consider and an overview of the recommended course of action to be taken.
2. **Introduction and background** – the export plan must be put in the context of the company's current position and should explain why the decision to export has been taken. This section may also include basic information about the company's products, existing markets and business plans to provide a point of reference in comparing the export marketing strategy with current practice.
3. **Objectives** – the core objectives of the plan should be listed concisely to identify the company's aims. By doing so, the company is not just listing what it hopes to achieve, but is also setting out the criteria by which the success of the plan will be measured. The company may highlight its objectives as:
   (a) to research the Bulgarian and Romanian markets for reconditioned printing machinery;
   (b) to appoint distributors for the markets;
   (c) to achieve sales of at least £800 000 in the markets over a 12-month period, maintaining current gross contribution levels;
   (d) to be mindful of opportunities arising in other overseas markets and be prepared to develop a strategy to maximise their potential.

   Objective (d) is not used as a measure of the strategy's success, but serves to remind all those involved in the delivery of the strategy of the company's commitment to pursuing international trade opportunities as and when they arise.
4. **Internal analysis** – the export marketing plan must be built around the company's capabilities and strengths. For this reason, the plan must include an indepth analysis of all the internal factors that affect the operation and management of the company, including production, resources, skills and experience. The internal review should include a full and honest SWOT analysis showing that the company has recognised and understood its strengths and limitations, allowing a realistic and achievable export plan to be developed.
5. **Market research** – this section summarises the market research that has been undertaken in the preparation of the export plan and is the rationale

behind the strategy. The market research justifies the company's decision to export to the target market as the research report has highlighted the market potential, competition and other relevant issues. This section should therefore contain a full summary of the research findings, which will act as a foundation for the rest of the strategy.

6. **Marketing activities** – again, the plan should include detailed information relating to the company's existing marketing practices. This section should break down the marketing mix to show how the organisation has established its marketing and promotion strategy and should then show how the marketing mix will be adapted to meet the needs of the new export markets. For example, the section will show how the product will be priced for export and what added value the customer will get for that price. It will also explain what modifications need to be made to the products to make them acceptable to the target market, the channels of distribution to be used and what promotional methods will be employed.

7. **Market entry** – the company's choice of entry strategy should be outlined with an explanation of how the route to market was identified. This should include relevant information on partners, representatives, franchisees and licensees (using the PARTNERS tool) and should provide an indication of what controls will be put in place to ensure the effective management of the entry strategy.

8. **Distribution** – the physical distribution of goods overseas is an essential component of the export strategy and the plan consequently needs to demonstrate that research into the most appropriate and cost-effective form of transport has been undertaken. Packaging, marking and labelling issues should be highlighted, as should the insurance considerations, delivery terms and documentary requirements necessary to facilitate transport to the destination.

9. **Financial issues** – the company must include as much financial information as possible in the export plan. Ideally, this should demonstrate how the product's cost structure, profit margins and net contribution have been calculated, both for domestic and international sales. A cash flow forecast showing income generated and expenditure incurred in the target markets ought to be included within the framework of the company's overall forecasting. It is also recommended that a budget be drawn up for the implementation of the export plan, taking into account additional production costs, sales, marketing and travel costs, commissions, premiums, shipping costs and so on.

   If additional financing is required before the company can put the export plan into practice, this section should also show how the venture is to be financed and what the cost implications are.

10. **Additional support** – given that there are numerous sources of support available to companies to assist in their international development, the export plan should list all the organisations that the company may turn to for advice, with a brief explanation of the services offered and the circumstances in which the company may need them.

11. **Implementation and monitoring** – this section of the export plan examines how the strategy is to be rolled out and who will take responsibility for it. It will incorporate a timescale for its implementation, setting out dates by which elements of the plan will be achieved, as well as systems for monitoring progress, reporting and measuring success.

12. **Conclusions** – the final part of the document pulls together the main elements of the strategy to summarise the activities that need to be undertaken by each department to meet the objectives of the export plan.

13. **Appendices** – the final plan should include information in the appendices to support the recommendations and actions contained in the main document. This may include:

 – technical drawings and data pertinent to the products to be sold overseas, together with details of the modification requirements;
 – a copy of the company's SWOT analysis, current marketing strategy and business plan;
 – a copy of the full market research report;
 – a list of potential partners in the target market;
 – Financial information, including a profit and loss account, balance sheet and cash flow forecast;
 – an organisational chart identifying key personnel involved in the delivery of the project;
 – any other additional background information that the company feels ought to be included as supporting material.

The importance of communication

The export strategy is a working document. Whilst it demonstrates how a company aims to develop internationally, setting out a defined course of action, it is by no means set in stone. Elements of the strategy may be improved or modified as the company gains experience and knowledge in its overseas markets, carries out further market research to identify opportunities and clients or introduces a new product to its range. Consequently, it is unlikely that an export plan will be implemented successfully without effective communication within the company or between the company and its customers, intermediaries and advisers. International trade relies on the swift and accurate processing and management of information to ensure that every component of the strategy is kept up to date and is appropriate to the company's needs.

International trade also requires accurate information in the preparation of appropriate documentation, sales contracts, transportation, Customs, payment and so on. There is little point in an export sales manager entering into a contract to supply goods within four weeks if the production department has failed to inform the sales team that it requires a six-week lead-time. Equally, an exporting company cannot expect its freight forwarder to negotiate cost-effective shipping at short notice and without all the necessary paperwork. In situations where communication is hampered by language or culture, additional effort must be made in order to prevent misunderstandings and to ensure that all parties are fully aware of their responsibilities and receive accurate information throughout the export process. The effective communication of information is therefore instrumental in the implementation and delivery of the export plan.

Conclusions

The introduction to this book stated that international trade is logical and systematic, even if it does demand more from companies in several areas. It should now be apparent that there is no mystery behind exporting and importing and that careful preparation and research will provide most of the information required to successfully develop business overseas. The preceding chapters have covered individual aspects of the international trade process and the reader should now be able to understand the purpose and requirements of each. By following the advice and guidelines laid down in each chapter, readers will be in a position to develop a comprehensive export marketing plan that contributes to the company's international development and growth as well as delivering a financial return on investment.

Even so, this book has provided only the foundations on which to build a successful international trade strategy. Further advice can be sought from some of the business support organisations introduced during the course of the book, but there is really no substitute for the experience gained in putting the principles of export marketing and importing into practice.

⩔ Glossary of terms

Acceptance – (1) where an offer has been made to supply goods or services to a client, the contract will only be formed when the client has formally accepted the offer. Acceptance is therefore the process in which the client agrees to enter into contractual agreement with the seller. (2) When a buyer agrees to accept the bill of exchange presented by a collecting bank, thereby agreeing to honour its terms and make payment to the exporter.

Acid test – also known as the 'quick ratio', the acid test is a measure of a company's liquidity in the event that creditors were to demand immediate payment for outstanding debts.

Acquisition – the process by which a company increases its assets by buying those of another business. Companies may buy out competitors, suppliers or firms offering complementary goods in order to improve market share and presence.

Advice of fate – in documentary collections, the advice of fate is the communication between the collecting bank and remitting bank advising whether or not the documents presented have been rejected or accepted.

Advising bank – in a letter of credit transaction, the buyer's bank opens dialogue with a correspondent bank in the exporter's country in order to facilitate the transfer of documentation and payment. The advising bank passes all information and shipping documentation received to the exporter.

Agent – agents are individuals or organisations that undertake to represent a 'principal', in this case, the exporter, in a designated market. Agents do not take title to the exporter's goods but are paid a commission on sales generated as a result of their promotional work.

Air Waybill – in situations where goods are transported by air, the Air Waybill acts in similar fashion to the bill of lading by providing the exporter or agent with a receipt for cargo and confirmation of the contract of carriage. It is not a document of title.

Anti-dumping law – dumping occurs when goods are exported at much cheaper prices than they are sold at in the exporter's country. As cheap imports impact on productivity, dumping is not encouraged by governments, who may impose anti-dumping laws as a protective measure.

Assets – the physical infrastructure of a company, its buildings, machinery, fixtures, fittings, outstanding monies owed by clients, cash reserves and stocks held are all classed as long-term or short-term assets.

ATA Carnet – a form of documentation used by companies to cover temporary imports (for instance, exhibition materials and samples). Carnets can only be issued to companies that have the express intention of bringing the goods back into the domestic market. The carnet is therefore instrumental in preventing unnecessary import and export duties.

Autonomy principle – all banks involved in letter of credit transactions work under the autonomy principle, meaning that they will honour all letters of credit if the terms of the credit are fully met, regardless of whether the beneficiary is in breach of contract. The bank's primary objective is to ensure that the specific conditions set out in the L/C raised by the buyer are met by the exporter.

Avalised bill of exchange – a bill of exchange that carries an additional 'aval' from the buyer's bank guaranteeing that payment will be made to the exporter in the event that the buyer is reluctant or unable to accept the bill and make payment.

Back-to-back letter of credit – *see* transferable letter of credit.

Balance of payments – a table demonstrating a nation's overall financial position against other countries. The BOP shows the credits and debits incurred as a result of the international trade of goods and services. The balance of payments is the net result of all income received from overseas less all expenditure accruing to foreign markets.

Balance sheet – one of the main financial reporting mechanisms, providing a snapshot of the company's current financial position. The balance sheet is a summary of the company's assets and liabilities at a specific moment in time and shows what the company has bought and how it has paid for its purchases.

Bank operating line of credit – a short-term finance option, effectively a loan to cover the cost of a specific transaction pending receipt of payment from overseas.

Battle of the forms – as sales contracts are negotiated, each party will attempt to impose their terms and conditions. The seller's original offer may be accepted by the buyer but changed to include the importer's terms. The contract will pass back and forth between the two until agreement has been reached.

Bill of exchange – one of the most important documents in the international trade process, evidencing proof of a buyer's obligation to pay. The bill of exchange is an unconditional order addressed by the drawer to the drawee, requiring the drawee to pay a specific amount to the named person or bearer of the bill.

Bill of Lading – a form of transport documentation that acts as a receipt from the carrier to the exporter confirming that the consignment has been received in apparent good order and condition. The B/L also sets out the contract of carriage between the exporter (or shipping agent) and carrier.

Bonded warehouse – *see* Customs warehousing.

Breach of contract – where a contract of sale is unfulfilled as a result of non-performance, such as the exporter's failure to supply the specified goods or the buyer's failure to pay.

Break-even – the point at which a company has covered all its costs through product sales.

Business plan – a strategy document that comprehensively details the company's plans for business development.

Buyer credit – a method of financing international transactions by loaning funds to a buyer to finance the purchase of capital equipment over a specified period of time.

Carrier – (1) a firm commissioned by the exporter or shipping agent to undertake the transport of the export consignment. (2) In piggy-backing co-operation agreements, the company that promotes the exporter's (rider's) goods in the target market.

Cash flow – cash flows are projections of income and expenditure over a given period and are instrumental in the business planning process as they permit management to evaluate the short, medium and long-term impact of their strategies on the financial position of the company.

Certificate of shipment – a Customs-endorsed copy of the exporter's commercial invoice, held by the exporter as part of VAT record-keeping procedures.

Claused bill of lading – if the carrier believes that the goods shipped are not in apparent good order and condition, the bill of lading may be claused to reduce the carrier's liability in the event of a claim for recompense.

Clean collection – a form of documentary collection that requires only the financial documents such as invoices to accompany the bill of exchange.

Collecting bank – in documentary collections, the collecting bank is the bank in the importer's country that receives the documents from the remitting bank in the exporter's country and presents them to the buyer for acceptance.

Co-marketing – a method of reducing the cost of market entry by co-operating with one or more other companies to jointly promote complementary goods in an export market.

Combined transport bill of lading – transport document used to cover the movement of goods under a single carriage contract but with different methods of transport.

Commissionaire – similar to agents, commissionaires act on their own behalf in return for a commission on sales and are intermediaries between exporters and their customers.

Common bill of lading – a standard form produced by SITPRO, the common B/L can be tailored to meet the needs of individual carriers and is not a pre-printed document produced by transport companies.

Confirming bank – in letter of credit transactions, a bank may be approached to add its own guarantee that the exporter will receive payment in the event that both the buyer and the buyer's bank are unable to make payment. The confirming bank may be the exporter's own bank or another in the same market.

Confirming houses – provide a service to foreign buyers by acting as guarantors of payment to the exporter.

Containerisation – the use of ISO containers to transport freight.

Correspondent bank – banks in one particular country will have their own global networks of other banks that they can work with in letter of credit transactions and so on. Good relationships will be established within this network of correspondent banks to improve the effectiveness and speed of international co-operation and transactions.

Counteroffer – clients who respond to a supplier's offer to supply goods or services by making subtle changes to the offer, for instance by altering payment terms, delivery dates or other terms and conditions, are effectively making a counteroffer. The supplier must therefore check to ensure that the terms of the counteroffer are still acceptable. Counteroffers form part of the overall negotiation process.

Credit risk insurance – an insurance policy taken out by exporters selling on credit terms to guard against the risk of non-payment by the buyer.

Creditors ratio – expressed as creditor days, the creditors ratio is a measure of the length of time it is likely to take the company to repay its debts.

Currency account – a bank account set up to operate in a specific currency in order to assist the company to more effectively control its currency management and costs.

Currency option – a currency management tool. Option contracts permit companies to exchange currencies either at the spot rate when the contract reaches term, or at the agreed rate specified in the contract.

Current ratio – the current ratio is a measure of a company's liquidity. It is also known as the working capital ratio and shows how easily companies can meet their financial liabilities.

Customs broker – an organisation that assists exporters to clear goods through Customs in return for a fee.

Customs warehousing – a facility used by companies to manage import/export duty payments when bringing goods into a country for immediate re-export, or for re-export after assembly, re-packaging/labelling, and so on.

Dangerous Goods Note – document that accompanies a consignment of dangerous goods transported by road, rail or sea. The document contains details of the buyer and seller as well as a full description of the class of dangerous goods being shipped.

Debtors ratio – the average length of time it takes for a company to receive payment from its customers.

Del credere agent – an agent that undertakes to reimburse the principal in the event that the buyer fails to pay for the goods sold in an agreement brokered by the agent.

Demurrage – where it is necessary to place consignments in storage at docks or airports. Well-managed transport strategies will avoid incurring demurrage charges.

Direct exporting – where the company has direct responsibility for the promotion and distribution of its goods overseas through agents, distributors, retail outlets or direct to the end user.

Dirty float – *see* managed float.

Discounted rate – a term used to denote that a currency exchange rate has been reduced to reflect the anticipated growth of the domestic currency during the period covered by a currency contract.

Distributor – an individual or organisation that represents the exporter in the target market. Distributors purchase goods from the exporter at favourable rates for resale in the target market at a profit.

Diversification – the process of altering components of the marketing mix in order to open up new opportunities or meet the demands of new markets.

Doctrine of strict compliance – banks involved in letter of credit transactions work under the doctrine, which demands that all the documentation presented with the L/C wholly complies with the terms of the credit.

Documentary collection – a method of payment that requires the exporter to send all shipping documents and documents of title to a collecting bank for presentation to the buyer. Once the buyer has accepted the documents, title is transferred and the exporter will receive payment as agreed.

Documentary letter of credit – the most common form of payment used in international trade, offering different levels of security to the exporter, depending on the nature of the letter of credit specified. L/Cs are raised by the buyer and, as a minimum, guarantee acceptance of the shipping documents. The most secure form of L/C is the confirmed irrevocable L/C which, as well as carrying the guarantee of another bank, cannot be amended without prior agreement.

Drawer – the person who presents a bill of exchange for payment.

Drawee – the person who receives a bill of exchange presented for payment.

EC sales list – a Customs document listing the VAT numbers of companies in the EU that the exporter has sold to over a given period of time. The purpose of the EC sales list is to provide evidence for transactions that qualify for duty-free status.

Economic exposure – the effect that changes in exchange rates may have on a company's cash flow forecasting and future growth.

Economies of scale – being able to reduce production costs by manufacturing greater numbers of the product, thereby reducing the amount of fixed cost allocated per unit.

End-to-end transport – *see* integrated transport.

Entry strategy – the approach adopted by companies to penetrate a target market, for instance by using agents, distributors, joint ventures and so on.

Euro – the single European currency that came into effect on 1 January 2002.

European Central Bank – established in 1998 to monitor and control monetary policy in the euro-zone.

European Currency Unit – part of the European Monetary System created in 1979 to revive the objective of introducing a single European currency.

Euro-zone – the geographic territory in which the euro is legal tender. At the time of writing, this includes Austria, Belgium, Denmark, Finland, France, Germany, Greece, Ireland, Italy, Luxembourg, Portugal and Spain.

Exchange controls – protectionist regulations imposed by national governments to limit the inward and outward flow of foreign and domestic currencies.

Exchange rate – the value of one currency expressed in another.

Export licence – normally used to restrict the international sale of goods that may subsequently prove to be a security threat.

Export management company – similar to agents in that export management companies undertake to represent the exporter overseas as well as taking on responsibility for shipping, finance and documentation. Export management companies do not take ownership of the goods they represent.

Exporter – an individual or organisation that sells goods outside the domestic market.

Factoring – occurs when an exporter sells the importer's debt to a financial organisation (factor) in exchange for an agreed percentage of the invoice value. Factoring is a common form of financing international trade.

Facultative policy – *see* specific policy.

Financing – the method by which companies are able to meet their cash needs when there are insufficient funds to cover day-to-day expenditure. Financing may be through loans, discounting, lines of credit and so on.

Floating rate of exchange – where international exchange rates are governed by open market currency trading.

Foreign receivable – payment due from export sales, probably in the form of a bill of exchange.

Forfaiting – a common form of medium-term financing where a bank agrees to purchase bills of exchange from the exporter. The total value of the bills is discounted at the outset, meaning that the exporter receives payment less a fee claimed by the bank.

Forward contract – currency contracts that are arranged at either fixed or option rates, specifying the date on which the exchange will take place.

Franchising – a market entry method, whereby the exporting company licenses a company in the target market to sell its products.

Free circulation – a term to describe intra-European trading, especially in Customs documentation.

Freight forwarder – a transport intermediary that is contracted to undertake part or all of the distribution function on behalf of the exporter or importer.

General average – loss of goods as a result of a voluntary decision to sacrifice the cargo in question in the interest of the remaining cargo. Under general average terms, the cost of the lost goods is recouped on a pro rata basis from the owners of the cargoes that were saved as a result of the sacrifice.

Green clause letter of credit – a letter of credit that grants the importer the facility to withhold a percentage of the payment after the shipping documentation has been presented in case the goods fail to meet the terms of the contract.

Greenfield site – in the context of market entry strategies, a greenfield site is a piece of land on which the exporter constructs a purpose-built facility to serve the target market.

Groupage – the consolidation of several different export shipments into one larger consignment for easier handling and more cost-effective use of cargo space.

Groupage bill of lading – used by freight forwarders to cover a load consisting of several different consignments.

Hague–Visby Rules – convention governing the carriage of goods by sea. Originally called the Hague Rules (1921) and subsequently amended in the 1968 Brussels Protocol to become Hague–Visby Rules.

Hostile take-over – a form of acquisition in which one company forcibly acquires another to gain market share, reduce competition or to preserve an exclusive supply of components.

Igloo – nickname for a form of container used in airfreight, derived as a result of its shape. Properly called a unit load device, or ULD.

Import licence – generally demanded by governments trying to protect their native industries. Importers may require a licence to import certain goods into developing or emerging economies.

Importer – an individual or company that purchases finished products, components or raw materials from overseas.

Incoterms – International Commercial Terms used to identify the responsibilities and obligations of both the buyer and the seller in international trade transactions.

Indirect exporting – exporting via intermediaries such as buying agents, trading houses or export management companies.

Individual policy – *see* specific policy.

Insurable interest – marine insurance can only be obtained on the strength of an identified insurable interest, namely that the assured client will benefit from the safe arrival of the goods at their destination and will lose financially if they are lost or damaged. The insurable interest is therefore the vested interest that the owner of the goods has is in the consignment.

Insurance broker – intermediary or organisation that 'shops around' on behalf of importers and exporters for the best insurance quotations and premiums.

Insurance underwriter – intermediaries with expertise in risk assessments and managing funds from which insurance claims are paid. Underwriters take on the financial risk of goods being lost or damaged in transit.

Integrated transport – where a freight forwarder arranges every aspect of the transport process, from collection at the seller's premises to delivery at the buyer's, including all the different modes of transport utilised in between.

Intellectual property – the original idea, concept or design behind a product. Also the trademark, copyright or patent taken out to protect the intellectual property.

Irrevocable letter of credit – a letter of credit whose terms cannot be amended without the consent of all parties to the credit.

Issuing bank – the bank instructed by the buyer to raise a letter of credit and to notify a correspondent bank in the exporter's country that the L/C exists. The issuing bank also passes all relevant shipping documentation to the importer when payment is agreed or made.

Kyoto Agreement – a commitment to reducing greenhouse gas emissions signed in 1997 by most of the world's industrialised nations.

Leasing – a hire purchase facility that allows the importer to utilise equipment or machinery purchased without taking title. The lender retains ownership until the goods have been fully paid for.

Letter of credit – *see* documentary letter of credit.

Liabilities – whereas assets represent what the company owns, liabilities are what it owes. They include sources of finance such as loans and other investments made in the company, short-term debts, overdrafts and any monies owed by the company to suppliers and so on.

Licensing – a method of indirect exporting whereby the exporter agrees to sell the intellectual property rights to its products to an overseas manufacturer. The licensee agrees to make regular payments to the exporter, who may also supply the manufacturer with components or raw materials.

Liquidity – cash readily available as money in the bank or as assets that can be quickly sold to raise money. Also known as solvency, liquidity is a measure of how well a company is performing and how likely it is to be able to meet its debts.

Local company – often opened due to a need to increase the company's presence in a particular market, local companies or branches set up in the target market are likely to be in the form of manufacturing units, sales offices or distribution centres.

Maghreb – covering Algeria, Morocco and Tunisia. The EU has a preferential trading agreement in place with these countries.

Managed float – the most common form of international exchange rate policy, which is monitored and influenced by the role of the central banks in maintaining stable currencies.

Margin of safety – the difference between the break-even point and the total volume of additional sales is the margin of safety, where the sales strategy has covered all production and other costs and is actually delivering a positive return.

Market research – the process of collecting and interpreting meaningful information to enable the company to formulate a sound strategy for penetrating foreign markets.

Market segmentation – division of a market by sector, sub-sector, customer types and so on. Exporters should segment their markets to better understand how they are composed and to provide a clear picture of how each sub-sector contributes to the whole market.

Marketing mix – a business tool comprising product, place, price and promotion (the 4 Ps), which is used by companies to evaluate and develop their marketing strategy. Each element of the mix can be altered to achieve a different effect, but as the elements are interrelated, changing one aspect of the mix impacts on the whole marketing plan. The marketing mix should be central to a company's marketing plan.

Marketing plan – a working document prepared by the company in order to meet specified marketing and business development objectives.

Marketing research – as opposed to market research, marketing research examines the company's current marketing strategy, including an internal review and analysis of the core components of the marketing mix. The research should show the areas in which the company is successful and those that need to be addressed.

Mashraq – covering Egypt, Jordan, Lebanon and Syria. The EU has a preferential trading agreement in place with these countries.

Merger – where one company joins forces, either by agreement or by hostile take-over, with another in order to consolidate its position or improve market share. Mergers may be vertical, where a company merges with a supplier, horizontal, if merging with a related business to build a monopoly, or extensional, to allow two or more businesses to reduce their costs in entering the same market.

Non-tariff barrier – regulatory controls that affect the import and export of goods, often imposed by governments seeking to protect their home market from foreign imports. For example: import quotas, standards, voluntary export restraints, subsidies and so on.

Offer – every sales contract contains an offer setting out the nature of the goods or services to be sold, their monetary value, quantity, quality and so on, as well as delivery and payment terms. These details will form the basis of the contract.

One-off policy – *see* specific policy.

Open account – the most favourable payment option from the buyer's perspective. Trading on open account terms grants the buyer the facility to pay for goods purchased after taking receipt of them. Payment may be made after an agreed length of time. This is the riskiest form of payment term for the exporter.

Open policy – a longer term insurance contract that covers all of a company's shipments within the period of the contract, subject to the company declaring all the shipments made under the cover offered by the policy.

Orange Book – the United Nations' publication governing the carriage of dangerous goods entitled 'Recommendations on the Transport of Dangerous Goods (Model Regulations)'.

Overheads – also known as indirect costs. Overheads are the essential expenses, which a company incurs in the day-to-day running of the business, including heating, lighting, rent, rates and the cost of maintaining the non-income generating functions of the company.

Particular average – unintentional loss of, or damage to, part of a consignment.

Patent – official recognition of an inventor's sole right to produce and use an original idea or concept.

Piggy-backing – a form of co-marketing where one company makes use of the services of another to enter an export market. The carrier company will normally undertake to promote the rider's products in the target market in return for a commission or by purchasing the goods for resale at a profit.

Premium rate – a term used to denote that a currency exchange rate has been increased to reflect the anticipated decline of the domestic currency during the period covered by a currency contract.

Prepayment – the most favourable payment term from the exporter's perspective as payment for the order is received either in advance or when the goods are shipped, and therefore before the buyer has taken title to them.

Primary data – information collected by the company as part of a current market research project, generally obtained through personal contact with the information source (interview, questionnaire and so on).

Principal – the company or exporter that agents and distributors undertake to represent.

Profit – the amount of money made on a sale once the costs have been taken into account. Profit can be described as gross, net, after interest, before tax, net after tax, operating or retained.

Profit and Loss account – *see* Trading and Profit and Loss account.

Protest – public legal action to re-present an unaccepted bill of exchange, but not a guarantee that the exporter will receive payment.

Quick ratio – *see* Acid test.

Quotas – a form of non-tariff barrier that imposes restrictions on the amount of product that can be imported to or exported from a country.

Received bill of lading – confirmation that the carrier has received the goods, but that the goods are still waiting to be loaded for shipping.

Red clause letter of credit – an L/C that permits a proportion of the payment to be paid up front to cover production costs, purchase of raw materials and so on.

Revocable letter of credit – an L/C that can be cancelled or altered by the issuing bank.

Revolving letter of credit – an L/C set up to cover payments for several similar shipments over a specified period of time.

Rider – an exporting company that sells its goods overseas by piggy-backing on a 'carrier' company. *See* piggy-backing.

Route to market – the market entry strategy chosen by the exporting company.

Secondary data – information collated by the company from a range of information sources, such as previously published research, libraries and so on. Generally referred to as desk research.

Shipped bill of lading – a received bill of lading that has been date stamped to show when the consignment was loaded onto the vessel.

Shippers Declaration for Dangerous Goods – document that accompanies a consignment of dangerous goods transported by air. The document contains details of the buyer and seller as well as a full description of the class of dangerous goods being shipped.

Short form bill of lading – a standard bill of lading, but with the clauses, terms and conditions normally printed on the reverse of the document replaced with a short reference to the carrier's standard terms.

Sight draft – a bill of exchange instructing the importer's bank to make payment on receipt of the document.

Sovereign risk – a measure of a country's credit-worthiness, particularly whether it is capable of meeting its financial obligations in terms of repaying interest and capital on international loans.

Specific policy – an insurance policy that covers a specific, one-off shipment of goods on a specified voyage.

Spot rate – the market rate of exchange between two currencies at a given point in time.

Stability and Growth Pact – agreement signed following the European Council meeting in Amsterdam (1997), which met to discuss long-term economic convergence in the Economic and Monetary Union member states.

Stale bill of lading – arises as a result of a bill of lading not being available for presentation, thereby preventing the goods from being cleared until an original copy is presented.

Standby letter of credit – an undertaking from the importer's bank to pay the exporter in the event that the buyer fails to make payment.

Supplier credit – a method of financing transactions by securing a bank's agreement in advance to purchase the buyer's bill of exchange from the exporter.

Target market – the country identified as a potential export market, and therefore a focus for the marketing strategy.

Tariff barrier – where the export of goods to a country is subject to Customs duties set by the target market's government as a protective measure.

Term draft – a bill of exchange instructing the importer's bank to make payment at a specified future date.

Title – ownership.

Trading and Profit and Loss account – usually abbreviated to the P&L account; this is one of the main financial reporting mechanisms. The Trading and Profit and Loss account summarises the financial changes that the company has undergone over a period of time and is a useful means of demonstrating annual performance.

Trading house – an organisation that purchases goods from a company, takes title to the products and then sells the goods on at a profit overseas.

Transaction exposure – the potential risk of a company receiving less money for a currency transaction than expected due to unfavourable currency fluctuations.

Transferable letter of credit – also called a back-to-back letter of credit. Used by the exporter to finance the production of goods to meet an international order, by using the buyer's L/C as surety for a second L/C raised to cover production costs.

Transhipment bill of lading – shipment of a consignment may require the goods to be unloaded from one vessel and reloaded onto another for the onward journey. The transhipment B/L identifies where this will take place.

Translation exposure – the potential impact of exchange rate fluctuations on the company's balance sheet.

Uberimae Fidaes – Latin term meaning 'utmost good faith', referring to the issuing of insurance policies on the strength of the insurance company's 'good faith' that the client has reported all pertinent information that could affect the policy.

Unit load – a single item of freight, normally palletised for easy handling.

Voluntary export restraints – a form of non-tariff barrier imposed by a government to prevent companies in specified markets from exporting products to its home market.

Voyage policy – *see* specific policy.

Warsaw Convention – 1929 agreement governing the carriage of goods by air.

Working capital – the net current assets of a company that can be used to finance the day-to-day running of the business. Also a measure of the company's liquidity.

▮ ⩔ Index

4ps, *see* marketing mix

acceptance, 120
  electronic, 122
acceptance credit, 172–3
accession countries, 45
Accord Dangereux Routiers, 66
acid test, *see* ratios
  customer risk, 206
acquisitions, 11–12, 79
  legal and financial implications
      of, 80
act of God, carrier liability, 130
added value services, 47
admission temporaire, *see* carnet, ATA
advance payment guarantee, 170
advertising, *see* promotion
advice of fate, 180
advising bank, 174
agency agreement, 83
agent, 82–4
  buying, 73, 75
  commission rates, 83
  comparison with distributor, 86
  customs clearance, 134
  del credere, 83
  selection of, 86–8
  working with, 87–8
air waybill, 144–5
Airfreight Institute, 221
aligned system of export documentation,
    see SITPRO
APG, 170
apparent good order and condition, 143
ASEAN, 45
assets, 95, 101
  currency risk, 190
ATR1, 148
autonomy principle, 174
avalised bill of exchange, 172, 204
average, general and particular, 133

b/l, *see* bill of lading
balance of payments, 185

balance sheet, 95–6
  customer risk, 206
bankers draft, 181
banks, advising, 174
  central, *see* central banks
  collecting, 179
  confirming, 174
  documentation, 178
  electronic data interchange, 136
  influence on exchange rates, 185–6
  issuing, 174
  operating line of credit, 200
  remitting, 180
  role in letter of credit transactions,
      174–6, 178
  suppliers, 213
battle of the forms, 119
BExA, 74, 222
BIFA, 220–1
bill of exchange, 167, 171–3
  avalised, 204
  documentary collections, 179
  financing agreements, 200
  forfaiting, 204
  unaccompanied, 200
bill of lading, 142–5
  carrier liability, 130
  documentary collections, 179
Biological Weapons Convention, 62
branch office, *see* local company
breach of contract, 120, 174
break-even, 99–100
British Chambers of Commerce, 217
British Exporters Association, 74, 222
British International Freight Association,
    220–1
British Standard Institution, *see* BSI
BSI, 63
  advice on labelling, 65
budgets, 32, 101–3
bulk shipment, 126–7
  bonded warehousing, 152
Business Link, 17, 219
business planning, 29–32

electronic commerce, contract
    acceptance, 122
  payment, 181
  signatures, 121
  United Nations law, 121
electronic data interchange, *see* EDI
embargo, 62–3
EMU, 191–2
end-to-end transport, *see* transport
enemies of the state, carrier
    liability, 130
environmental issues, 2
  as opportunity or threat, 32
  packaging, 64–5
EUR1, 148
euro, 2
  arguments for and against, 193–5
  British, Danish and Swedish
    positions, 192–3
  Central Europe, 194
  history of, 191–2
Euro Info Centre, 219
European Central Bank, 192
European Common Market, 191
European Community, 44, 147
  sales list, 147
European Currency Unit, 191
European Economic Area, 44
European Economic and Monetary
    Union, 191–2
European Monetary System, 192
European quality standard, 45
European Union, 15, 17
  agency legislation, 84
  Community Trade Mark, 58
  contract law, 118
  Council meetings in Dublin
    and Amsterdam, 192
  Council of Hanover, 191
  documentation, 147–8
  expansion of, 45
  Hague conference, 191
  legislation on quality standards, 63
  member states, 44
  origin regulations, 149
  open account trading, 171
  primary UK export market, 17–18
  protection of intellectual property
    rights, 58
  stability and growth pact, 192
  support with legislation, 219
  tenders, 219
Eurosystem, 192
eurozone, 194
ex works, 108
exchange controls, 60

exchange rates, 184–6
  calculation, 186
  fluctuations, 185
exhibition, 28, 51
explosion hazard, *see* dangerous goods
export cargo shipping instructions,
    see ECSI
export clearance, under incoterms, 111
Export Control Organisation, 63
export costing, 106–18
  calculation, 114–15
Export Credit Guarantee Department, 208
export development advisers, 17
export licence, 61–3
  under incoterms, 109
export management company, 74, 213, 215
export marketing plan, 224–9
  honeycomb, 224, 226
  internal analysis, 227
  market research, 227–8
export order process, 121
export restrictions, risks, 205, 207
export trading company, 73, 215
exporter, types of, 9
exporting, 1, 5–9
  production-led, 7
  to improve image, 8
  to increase sales, 6
  to spread risk, 6–7
exposure, 190
  see also currency risk
EXW, 108

factoring, 204–5
Factors and Discounters Association, 205
FAK, 125
FAS, 109–10
FCA, 108–9
FCL, 127
FIATA, 221
finance, for international trade, 197–205
  general business, 93–104
  medium and long-term, 201–4
  short-term, 199–201
financial issues, in export marketing
    plan, 228
fixed costs, *see* costs
fixed rate, 89
float, managed (or dirty), 186
FOB, 109–10
Foreign and Commonwealth Office, 218
foreign receivables, 200
forfaiting, 203–4
forgery, 179
forward rate, 187–8
franchisee, 87

franchising, 71, 80
fraud, 174, 179
free alongside ship, 109–10
free carrier, 108–9
free circulation, 152–3
free on board, 109–10
free ports, 152
free trade agreements, *see* preferential
    trade agreements
free trade area, 150
free zones, 152
freight all kinds, 125
freight forwarder, 213
    electronic data interchange, 136
    FIATA, 221
    groupage operation, 127–8
    relationship with, 214–15
    role of, 125–6
    shipping without, 129
freight, palletised, 126
Friends of the Earth, 14

G8, summits and demonstrations, 14
    relationship with central banks, 186
GDP, 42, 207
gearing, 206
Generalised System of Preferences,
    44, 148
    customs tariffs, 150
globalisation, 2, 14–15
GNP, 40, 42, 207
good faith, 132
green clause letter of credit, 176
greenfield site, 73, 76, 78–9
Greenpeace, 14
Gross Domestic Product, 42, 207
Gross National Product, 40, 42, 207
gross profit, 96
groupage, 127
    bill of lading, 143
guarantee, 65

Hague–Visby Rules, 130, 133, 145
harmonised system, 150
holder in due course, 172–3

ICC, *see* International Chamber of
    Commerce
igloo, 128
IMF, 185
import clearance, under incoterms, 111
import duties, 11
import licence, 61–2, 134
    under incoterms, 108–9
import quotas, 46
import restrictions, risks, 205, 207

importing, 9, 10
    for resale, 9–10
    see also distributor
imports, high or low level of, 40
incoterms, 106–13, 117, 124, 130
    classes, 107
    from the importer's perspective, 112
    maritime, 109
    multimodal, 109
    use with customs brokers, 215, 216
indirect exporting, 73
industrialised nations, 13
inflation, 185, 207
inherent vice, carrier liability, 130
inland clearance depot, 128
Institute Cargo Clauses, 132
Institute of Export, 222
Institute of London Underwriters, 132
Institute Strike Clauses, 132
Institute War Clauses, 132
insurance, 11, 130–3
    credit, *see* credit insurance
    in documentary collections, 179
    marine, 130
    under incoterms, 110
    underwriter, 131
insurance claim, 133–4
insurance policy, certificate, 132
    open, 132
    specific (or voyage), 131
intellectual property rights, 57–9
interest rates, 185, 207
intermediaries, 87–8
    indirect exporting, 73
    local, 71
    transport, 124
internal audit, 22–3
international business, 1, 2, 5, 15
International Chamber of Commerce, 180,
    217–18
    globalisation, 15
    incoterms, 106
international companies, 15
International Federation of Freight
    Forwarders Associations, 221
International Maritime Dangerous Goods
    Code, 66
International Monetary Fund, 185
    globalisation, 14–15
International Standards Organisation, 126
international trade risks, 205–7
internet
    as promotional tool, 26–8
    as research tool, 40
    contracts and acceptance, 122
    documentation, 154–5

revolving letter of credit, 177
RHA, 221
rider, 75
risk, country, 206–7
risk, customer, 206
risk, import and export restrictions, 205, 207
risk, insurance, *see* credit insurance
Road Haulage Association, 221
road waybill, 145
ROCE, *see* ratios
ROS, *see* ratios
rules of origin, 149–50

SAD, 148, 166
  customs warehousing, 152
  electronic reporting, 155
  for CFSP, 154
safety standards, 63
sale of goods, 106, 118
sanctions, 62, 205
Schengen Agreement, 147
secondary data, 50
segmentation, 23–4
service sector, 3
  entry strategies, 72
SESA, *see* Trade Partners UK
shipped bill of lading, 143
shipping instructions, *see* ECSI
short form bill of lading, 144
short-term finance, 199–201
short-term loan, 200
sight draft, 180
  as finance method, 199
signature, digital, 155
Simplified Trade Procedures, 144, 220
Single Administrative Document, *see* SAD
Single European Act, 44, 147
  economic and monetary union, 191
SITPRO, 144, 220
small and medium sized enterprises, 16
Small Business Service, 219
SMART analysis, 29–30
SME, 16
Society for Worldwide Interbank Financial
  Transmissions, 181
sources of support, 216–22
special security label, 62
spot rate, 187
spread, 187
stability and growth pact, 192
stale bill of lading, 143
standard shipping note, 145, 164
standards, of goods, 63
standby letter of credit, 178
stereotypes, 56
strengths, *see* SWOT

subsidies, 46
supplier credit, 202–3
suppliers, 213–14
Support for Export Marketing Research, 218
suspension, *see* inward processing relief
SWIFT, 181
SWOT analysis, 30

Tailored market report, 218
tariff barriers, 15
  market research into, 39
tariff, codes and classification, 151
Technical Help for Exporters, 64, 221
  see also BSI
technical standards, European Union
  harmonisation of, 44
temporary exports, *see* carnet, ATA
temporary imports under NES, 155
term draft, 180
  as finance method, 199
terms and conditions, 25, 118
test marketing, 51
through bill of lading, 144
TIR, 128
title, of goods, 83
  under documentary collection, 179
  under letter of credit, 174
  under open account, 171
TMR, 218
trade association, 49
trade fairs, 28, 51
Trade Partners UK, 218
  service sector statistics, 3
  support for exhibitions abroad (SESA), 28
Trade-Related Aspects of Intellectual
  Property Rights, 58, 60
trade secrets, 58
Trade UK, 218
trading and profit and loss account,
  see profit and loss account
trading houses, 73–4
transaction exposure, 190
transferable letter of credit, 178
transhipment bill of lading, 144
translation exposure, 190
translations, 57
Transport Internationaux Routiers, 128
transport, 124–5
  integrated, 125
  intermodal, 126
  liquid natural gas, 127
  ore and oil, 127
  ore, bulk and oil, 127
Treaty of Maastricht, 192–3
Treaty of Rome, 191
TRIPS, 58, 60